CHILDREN'S RIGHTS

LAWS AND PRACTICES IN SIXTEEN NATIONS

CHILDREN'S ISSUES, LAWS AND PROGRAMS

Additional books in this series can be found on Nova's website
under the Series tab.

Additional E-books in this series can be found on Nova's website
under the E-book tab.

HUMAN RIGHTS: BACKGROUND AND ISSUES

Additional books in this series can be found on Nova's website
under the Series tab.

Additional E-books in this series can be found on Nova's website
under the E-book tab.

CHILDREN'S ISSUES, LAWS AND PROGRAMS

CHILDREN'S RIGHTS

LAWS AND PRACTICES IN SIXTEEN NATIONS

BROOKE DABNEY

AND

MICHAEL ELDRIDGE

EDITORS

nova
publishers

New York

For permission to use material from this book please contact us:
Telephone 631-231-7269; Fax 631-231-8175
Web Site: http://www.novapublishers.com

NOTICE TO THE READER

Additional color graphics may be available in the e-book version of this book.

Library of Congress Cataloging-in-Publication Data

ISBN: 978-1-62948-252-1

Published by Nova Science Publishers, Inc. † New York

CONTENTS

PREFACE

Within the last century, the idea that children need safeguards and protections separate from those of adults greatly impacted both domestic and international law. Although the children's rights movement has roots as early as the eighteenth century, it wasn't until the twentieth century that children were viewed as more than a labor hand or an economic value. What began as an effort to protect children from long hours of labor and its corresponding health defects, turned into an organized and influential movement. The children's rights movement promotes legal protections and safeguards for children, distinct from those of adults. After each world war, international legal instruments increasingly included protection for children across the globe. The League of Nations Declaration of 1924, and the successive United Nations' Declaration of the Rights of the Child in 1959, declared that children need safeguards and protections separate from those of adults and that these protections should begin even before birth. This book provides a superior and comprehensive analysis of significant children's rights laws. Each domestic and international practice is summarized; relevant clauses and language are defined and highlighted; and the effects of each are described. This book examines sixteen nations, across five continents: Argentina, Australia, Brazil, Canada, China, France, Germany, Greece, Iran, Israel, Japan, Lebanon, Mexico, Nicaragua, Russia, and the United Kingdom (England and Wales). For each nation, the study focuses on the domestic laws and policies that affect child health and social welfare, education and special needs, child labor and exploitation, sale and trafficking of children, and juvenile justice. This book also lists which pertinent international treaties the nation has ratified and implemented.

This book will enable researchers, legislators, and academics to compare and contrast how children are treated among the different continents and which policies and laws have had the most profound impact on the younger generations. There has been much progress in the children's rights movement, but more nations must act to protect those who most need it. Children are a nation's future and the best gift we can give to the world is to ensure a safe, healthy, educated, and able future generation.

Chapter 1 – Within the last century, the idea that children need safeguards and protections separate from those of adults greatly impacted both domestic and international law. Although the children's rights movement has roots as early as the eighteenth century, it wasn't until the twentieth century that children were viewed as more than a labor hand or an economic value. What began as an effort to protect children from long hours of labor and its corresponding health defects, turned into an organized and influential movement. The children's rights movement promotes legal protections and safeguards for children, distinct from those of adults. After each world war, international legal instruments increasingly included protection for children across the globe. The League of Nations Declaration of 1924, and the successive United Nations' Declaration of the Rights of the Child in 1959, declared that children need safeguards and protections separate from those of adults and that these protections should begin even before birth. The major global and regional legal instruments of the twentieth and twenty-first century are included in The Law Library of Congress' Children's Rights: International and National Laws and Practices, a superior and comprehensive analysis of the significant children's rights laws. Each domestic and international is summarized; relevant clauses and language are defined and highlighted; and the effects of each are described. Children's Rights examines sixteen nations, across five continents: Argentina, Australia, Brazil, Canada, China, France, Germany, Greece, Iran, Israel, Japan, Lebanon, Mexico, Nicaragua, Russia, and the United Kingdom (England and Wales). For each nation, the study focuses on the domestic laws and policies that affect child health and social welfare, education and special needs, child labor and exploitation, sale and trafficking of children, and juvenile justice. Children's Rights also lists which pertinent international treaties the nation has ratified and implemented. Children's Rights will enable researchers, legislators, and academics to compare and contrast how children are treated among the different continents and which policies and laws have had the most profound impact on the younger generations. There has been much progress in the children's rights movement, but more nations must act to protect those who most need it. As a former judge, I saw firsthand how crimes against children affected their future. Children are a nation's future. The best gift we can give to the world is to ensure a safe, healthy, educated, and able future generation. And that's just the way it is.

Chapter 2 – The growth of children's rights as reflected in international and transnational law has transformed the post-war legal landscape. This overview describes some of the major global and regional legal instruments that have contributed to this transformation, as well as specific relevant provisions in broader human-rights related instruments and in international agreements on child protection and placement.

Chapter 3 – The long awaited national Law for the Integral Protection of Children and Adolescents was enacted in 2005 to implement the UN Convention on the Rights of the Child, ratified by Argentina in 1990. In addition to adopting comprehensive protective measures for children, it lays the groundwork for a juvenile justice system, calls for institutionalized children to be integrated back into society, and establishes mechanisms to protect children from abuse and exploitation.

Chapter 4 – Australia is a signatory to all significant treaties that impact on children's rights. The rights and protection of children are governed by both Federal and state and territory law. Persons below the age of eighteen are generally considered children.

Children may be able to give consent to medical procedures where they are either over a statutory age (fourteen to sixteen depending on the jurisdiction), or, of sufficient maturity that they are able to comprehend the procedure and give informed consent. Children below the age of ten are unable to be charged with a criminal offense and children between the ages of ten to fourteen have a refutable presumption that they are incapable of forming the necessary criminal intent for an offense. Children below the age of seventeen may not volunteer to join the armed services. Education of children is compulsory. The age between which children must be educated varies across jurisdictions but is generally between the ages of five to sixteen. Australian children have a right to access health care via Australia's universal health insurance program and all jurisdictions have additional programs to encourage children and young persons to seek medical care.

Chapter 5 – The Constitution provides the principles to be followed for the protection of children and adolescents in Brazil. These principles, coupled with numerous international treaties and several pieces of enacted legislation, offer a wide range of protection for children's and adolescents' rights.

Chapter 6 – Canada has ratified the Convention on the Rights of the Child and the two optional protocols to it. Responsibility for implementation is split between the federal government and the provinces. Canada's ten provinces have nearly universal health insurance plans that cover virtually all children and maintain most social welfare agencies. Another provincial responsibility is education. Children receive tax-supported elementary and secondary education. Universities charge subsidized tuition. Minimum ages for employment are yet another provincial responsibility. On the federal level, there are many criminal laws designed to prevent child abuse. The number of related offenses and the maximum punishments for them have been greatly increased in recent years. In its national defense laws, the federal government now prohibits Canadian soldiers under the age of eighteen from being deployed in armed conflict. The federal government also created a new juvenile justice system in 2002 that gives the police and judges more options in handling cases of juveniles charged with criminal offenses than the previous law.

Chapter 7 – China has ratified major international documents with regard to children's rights protection. China's domestic legislation also provides protection for a wide range of children's rights. The reality, however, is disputable. Few accurate statistics could be obtained directly from the official source. In practice, enforcement of the treaty obligations and the legislative declarations remains a huge problem.

Chapter 8 – France is a signatory to all the significant treaties dealing with children rights. It has in place several mechanisms to monitor the implementation of the 1989 Convention on the Rights of the Child, in particular, an ombudsman for children. Pregnant women are entitled to paid maternity leave. To offset the loss of salary, they receive benefits via the public maternity insurance, often supplemented by a complementary sum payable by the employer as per a collective bargaining agreement. Several categories of family allowances are provided without any condition of employment. Children under six receive free and mandatory preventive health services in a widespread network of thousands of health-care facilities. After the age of six, children's health is monitored by school health services. Mandatory physical and psychological checkups take place when the children are ages six, nine, twelve, and fifteen. When they are of sufficient maturity, children must be informed of their medical treatment and participate in the decision- making process. School is mandatory from ages six to sixteen. Although not compulsory, preschool for children under six is widely available and strongly encouraged. Children with special educational needs are educated in mainstream classes alongside their peers wherever possible, to better incorporate them into society. There is no specific legal age under which a juvenile cannot be prosecuted. The sole criterion is that of moral discernment. Penalties, however, are adapted to the age of the child.

Chapter 9 – Germany is a party to the global conventions that protect the rights of the child, yet Germany prefers to interpret these according to the precepts of European agreements, in particular the European Human Rights Convention, and also in accordance with German Constitutional guarantees. Germany has generous systems of health care and social welfare that benefit all citizens and long-term residents, while being less generous for new immigrants. The education system differentiates between vocational and college-bound tracks, and that is sometimes criticized in international comparisons. Problems occur in particular with the children of immigrants. Stringent laws against child labor are fully enforced, as are criminal provisions against the sexual exploitation of children and human trafficking. The juvenile justice system was path-breaking in the 1920s, but more recently it has borrowed ideas from the United States, particularly on diversion.

Chapter 10 – Based on the constitutional mandate to protect and safeguard children and on its international obligations arising from ratifications of agreements on children's rights, which have the status of domestic law upon ratification, Greece has enacted various laws and has adopted a number of measures and services to promote and advance the rights of the children. The topics covered in this report are health and social welfare, education, labor and exploitation, and juvenile justice. In 2002, the Greek Parliament adopted a new law on human trafficking, and the government has allocated a number of resources in an effort to eliminate this scourge. In 2003, the juvenile system was reformed. An additional law was enacted in 2006 to combat intra-family violence, which also encompasses a prohibition of corporal punishment of children.

Chapter 11 – The Islamic Revolution of 1979 introduced drastic and fundamental changes in the social, economic and political structure of Iran. It marked the end of a 2,500 year-old monarchical regime and brought to power a religion-oriented government based on the Shiite school tenets of Islam. The change in the nature of the regime from secular to religious had its impact both on domestic legislation and international conventions, as explained below.

Chapter 12 – Israel adheres to international conventions to which it is a signatory and maintains a special set of laws to protect children. In addition to health benefits applicable to all Israeli residents, special benefits apply specifically to pregnant women and children. Special welfare benefits are also directed at assisting families with children and, particularly, the disabled. The law requires at least ten years of compulsory education and protects children from labor and sexual exploitation. The system recognizes different rules in the adjudication of juveniles.

Chapter 13 – Japan is a signatory of many international conventions which aim to protect the rights of children. There are various domestic laws to promote children's well-being. Almost all children in Japan are covered by health care insurance. Families with small children which do not have a high income level can receive an allowance from the government. Local governments support pregnant women's and infants' health and give advice to them. Schools also provide health examinations. Parents are obliged to have their children attend primary and secondary schools for nine years. The government provides this mandatory education free of charge. There are provisions which punish acts that harm children, both in special laws and in the Criminal Code. There is a juvenile justice system which is separated from the normal criminal justice system.

Chapter 14 – Despite the armed conflict that consumed the country and its institutions for a long period until 1989, Lebanon ratified the Convention on the Rights of the Child relatively quickly. The existing Lebanese laws comply with most of what is required under the Convention, and the Lebanese government adopted a number of amendments in its attempt to comply fully with the balance of such requirements.

Chapter 15 – The Mexican Constitution provides that the State has the duty to promote respect for the dignity of all children and the full exercise of their rights. It also provides that children have the right to satisfy their nutritional, health, educational, and recreational needs. Several laws have been enacted in order to implement this mandate, most importantly the federal Law on the Protection of the Rights of Children and Adolescents. In addition, Mexico is a signatory to several treaties that impact children's rights.

Chapter 16 – Nicaragua has issued many legislative enactments to comply with the international legal instruments to which it has subscribed. Chief among them are: the inclusion of the Convention on the Right of the Child as an express constitutional mandate; the promulgation of the Code of Childhood and Adolescence and the General Law on Education; extensive amendments to the Penal Code protecting minors; adoption of a new General Law on Health with its Program of Comprehensive Care for Women, Children, and Adolescents; and creation of a new Labor Code, raising the minimum working age and protecting young workers from being exploited.

Chapter 17 – Protection of children's rights is a serious problem for Russia, particularly because of the worsening demographic situation and progressive involvement of youngsters in criminal and other underground activities. Several presidential programs, together with major pieces of legislation, address this issue, which is at the center of domestic public discussions; because of insufficient budget financing and restrictions on work of nongovernmental organizations, however, legislative declarations remain largely unimplemented. It is expected that the newly created institution of a Children's Rights Ombudsman and introduction of the long delayed juvenile justice system will improve the situation. This paper analyzes legislation that regulates the protection of children's rights and evaluates government attempts to enforce relevant laws.

Chapter 18 – This report provides a basic overview of the laws regarding children's rights in a number of fields. England and Wales has a large number of laws protecting children and guaranteeing them basic rights – both for areas in which there is now an 'entitlement' such as education, as well as in areas in which they need rights to ensure protection, such as in the criminal justice system. Given the large number and complexity of these laws this report provides a broad overview of legislation and common law as it applies to children's rights in England and Wales.

In: Children's Rights
Editors: Brooke Dabney and Michael Eldridge

ISBN: 978-1-62948-252-1
© 2013 Nova Science Publishers, Inc.

Chapter 1

CHILDREN'S RIGHTS: INTERNATIONAL AND NATIONAL LAWS AND PRACTICES[*]

Ted Poe (Preface) and Reubens Medina (Introductory Note)

Within the last century, the idea that children need safeguards and protections separate from those of adults greatly impacted both domestic and international law. Although the children's rights movement has roots as early as the eighteenth century, it wasn't until the twentieth century that children were viewed as more than a labor hand or an economic value. What began as an effort to protect children from long hours of labor and its corresponding health defects, turned into an organized and influential movement.

The children's rights movement promotes legal protections and safeguards for children, distinct from those of adults. After each world war, international legal instruments increasingly included protection for children across the globe. The League of Nations Declaration of 1924, and the successive United Nations' Declaration of the Rights of the Child in 1959, declared that children need safeguards and protections separate from those of adults and that these protections should begin even before birth.

The major global and regional legal instruments of the twentieth and twenty-first century are included in The Law Library of Congress' Children's Rights: International and National Laws and Practices, a superior and comprehensive analysis of the significant children's rights laws. Each domestic and international is summarized; relevant clauses and language are defined and highlighted; and the effects of each are described.

Children's Rights examines sixteen nations, across five continents: Argentina, Australia, Brazil, Canada, China, France, Germany, Greece, Iran, Israel, Japan, Lebanon, Mexico, Nicaragua, Russia, and the United (England and Wales). For each nation, the study focuses on the domestic laws and policies that affect child health and social welfare, education and special needs, child labor and exploitation, sale and trafficking of children, and juvenile justice. Children's Rights also lists which pertinent international treaties the nation has ratified and implemented.

---

[*] This Preface and Introductory Note were released by the Law Library of Congress in 2007.

Children's Rights will enable researchers, legislators, and academics to compare and contrast how children are treated among the different continents and which policies and laws have had the most profound impact on the younger generations.

There has been much progress in the children's rights movement, but more nations must act to protect those who most need it. As a former judge, I saw firsthand how crimes against children affected their future. Children are a nation's future. The best gift we can give to the world is to ensure a safe, healthy, educated, and able future generation. And that's just the way it is.

INTRODUCTORY NOTE BY DR. REUBENS MEDINA

The Law Library of Congress is very pleased to present this multinational, comparative legal study on the rights of children. It is one of the many legal research products that are frequently generated by expressed request of a member of the United States Congress. It is not only of interest to our lawmakers but also in the interest of the public since our legislators are representatives of the people's interests. Congressman Ted Poe (TX-02) instructed the Law Library to compile the individual country studies into one electronic publication to be offered to the nation and the world as a tribute to our youth.

Ancient civilizations entrusted heads of families with omnipotent authority over their children. The rather common underlying legal assumption was that children lack the capacity to discern correctly between prescribed behavioral standards, a condition that made them legally comparable to property and therefore sellable. Academicians have debated on the boundaries of *patria potestas* (currently translatable into parental authority). As an example, the Roman 12 Tables assigned this power to the fathers. Strict interpreters sustained that this authority was extreme and a remnant of pre-existing "practices of barbarous origin and primitive character" (Table VI, Law I, II and III. S.P. Scott, The Civil Law, Vol. XII, 64-65 (The Central Trust Company 1932)). A more conciliatory approach interpreted the precepts as having gradually evolved to restrict irresponsible and abusive exercise of such authority.

It was not until the 20th Century that the legal status of children was subjected to serious reviews and corrections. The idea that children have rights finally emerged and were embodied in Family Codes and Code of Minors. They were enacted to recognize children as "developing beings whose moral status gradually changes" thus demanding a realistic understanding of their interests within the families and the larger social context (*Introduction to Philosophical Views of Children: A Brief History in the Moral and Political Status of Children* (David Archard & Colin Macleod eds., 2005)).

Children hold our hopes for a better future. Their status has been a subject of concern for lawmakers, scholars, judges, lawyers, and common citizens. National laws and regulations as well as international treaties have been dedicated to children with increased interest during the last century.

This legal study represents the current status of enforceable laws in a number of countries. Hopefully, this study will help readers have a more detailed understanding of the universal standards on the rights of children to make the relationships, between children and their parents, teachers, judges, lawyers, and adults in general, more conducive to a peaceful society.

In: Children's Rights
Editors: Brooke Dabney and Michael Eldridge

ISBN: 978-1-62948-252-1
© 2013 Nova Science Publishers, Inc.

Chapter 2

INTRODUCTION[*]

Wendy Zeldin

EXECUTIVE SUMMARY

The growth of children's rights as reflected in international and transnational law has transformed the post-war legal landscape. This overview describes some of the major global and regional legal instruments that have contributed to this transformation, as well as specific relevant provisions in broader human-rights related instruments and in international agreements on child protection and placement.

I. INTRODUCTION

It was not until the late nineteenth century that nascent children's rights' protection movement countered the widely held view that children were mainly quasi-property and economic assets. In the United States, the Progressive movement challenged courts' reluctance to interfere in family matters, promoted broad child welfare reforms, and was successful in having laws passed to regulate child labor and provide for compulsory education.

It also raised awareness of children's issues and established a juvenile court system. Another push for children's rights occurred in the 1960s and 1970s, when children were viewed by some advocates as victims of discrimination or as an oppressed group. In the international context, "[t]he growth of children's rights in international and transnational law has been identified as a striking change in the post-war legal landscape."[1] The purpose of this overview is to sketch in broad strokes some of the key provisions of major international legal instruments on children's rights that form part of that landscape.

---

[*] This Introduction was released by the Law Library of Congress July 2007.

II. GLOBAL INTERNATIONAL DOCUMENTATION ON CHILDREN'S RIGHTS

A. Declaration of the Rights of the Child 1959[2]

The U.N. Declaration of the Rights of the Child (DRC) builds upon rights that had been set forth in a League of Nations Declaration of 1924. The Preamble notes that children need "special safeguards and care, including appropriate legal protection, before as well as after birth," reiterates the 1924 Declaration's pledge that "mankind owes to the child the best it has to give," and specifically calls upon voluntary organizations and local authorities to strive for the observance of children's rights.[3] One of the key principles in the DRC is that a child is to enjoy "special protection" as well as "opportunities and facilities, by law and by other means," for healthy and normal physical, mental, moral, spiritual, and social development "in conditions of freedom and dignity." The "paramount consideration" in enacting laws for this purpose is "the best interests of the child,"[4] a standard echoed throughout legal instruments on children's rights. Among other DRC principles, a child is entitled to a name and nationality; to adequate nutrition, housing, recreation, and medical services; to an education; and, for the handicapped, to "special treatment, education and care."[5] Other principles are on protection against neglect, cruelty and exploitation, trafficking, underage labor, and discrimination.

B. Minimum Age Convention 1973[6]

The aim of the Minimum Age Convention (MAC) is to establish a general instrument on the subject of the minimum age of employment with a view to achieving the total abolition of child labor (Preamble). Thus, each State Party is to "pursue a national policy designed to ensure the effective abolition of child labor and to raise progressively the minimum age for admission to employment to a level consistent with the fullest physical and mental development of young persons" (article 1). States Parties must specify a minimum age for admission to employment or work, subject to certain exceptions set forth in the MAC. That minimum may not be less than the age of completion of compulsory schooling and, in any case, less than fifteen years, but it may initially be set at fourteen years if a state's economy and educational facilities are insufficiently developed (article 2). Exceptions to the age limits may also be permitted for light work or for such purposes as participation in artistic performances (articles 7 and 8). If the employment may be hazardous to a young person's health, safety, or morals, the minimum age is generally not to be less than eighteen years (article 3(1)).

C. U.N. Convention on the Rights of the Child 1989

The Convention on the Rights of the Child (CRC) is the most comprehensive document on the rights of children.[7] Based purely on the number of substantive rights it sets forth, as distinct from implementation measures, it is the longest U.N. human rights treaty in force and unusual in that it not only addresses the granting and implementation of rights in peacetime, but also the treatment of children in situations of armed conflict. The CRC is also significant because it enshrines, "for the first time in binding international law, the principles upon which adoption is based, viewed from the child's perspective."[8] The CRC is primarily concerned with four aspects of children's rights ("the four 'P's"): participation by children in decisions affecting them; protection of children against discrimination and all forms of neglect and exploitation; prevention of harm to them; and provision of assistance to children for their basic needs.[9] For the purposes of the CRC, a child is defined as "every human being below the age of eighteen years unless under the law applicable to the child, majority is attained earlier" (article 1).

Key accomplishments of the CRC have been described as five-fold. It creates new rights for children under international law that previously had not existed, such as the child's right to preserve his or her identity (articles 7 and 8), the rights of vulnerable children like refugees to special protection (articles 20 and 22), and indigenous children's right to practice their culture (articles 8 and 30). In some instances, this innovation takes the form of child-specific versions of existing rights, such as those in regard to freedom of expression (article 13) and the right to a fair trial (article 40). In addition, the CRC enshrines in a global treaty rights that hitherto had only been found in case law under regional human rights treaties (e.g., children's right to be heard in proceedings that affect them) (article 12). The CRC also replaced non-binding recommendations with binding standards (e.g., safeguards in adoption procedures and with regard to the rights of disabled children) (articles 21 and 23). New obligations are imposed on States Parties in regard to the protection of children, in such areas as banning traditional practices prejudicial to children's health and offering rehabilitative measures for victims of neglect, abuse, and exploitation (articles 28(3) and 39). Finally, the CRC sets forth an express ground obligating States Parties not to discriminate against children's enjoyment of CRC rights.[10] The right to participate in proceedings, it is argued, "together with the principles of non-discrimination in Article 2 and provision for the child's best interests in Article 3, form the guiding principles of the Convention, which reflect the vision of respect and autonomy which the drafters wished to create for all children."[11]

D. Optional Protocols to the CRC on Sex Trafficking, Armed Conflict

The United Nations adopted two protocols to the CRC on May 25, 2000, the Optional Protocol to the CRC on the Sale of Children, Child Prostitution, and Child Pornography 2000 (Sex Trafficking Protocol) and the Optional Protocol to the Convention on the Rights of the Child on the Involvement of Children in Armed Conflict (Child Soldiers Protocol) . The Sex Trafficking Protocol[12] (STP) addresses the problem of sex trafficking, one among many purposes for which children are bought and sold, including, in addition, forced labor, adoption, participation in armed conflicts, marriage, and organ trade. The Preamble refers to achieving "the purposes of the CRC" and to the need for States Parties to implement specific provisions, among them CRC articles 34 and 35 on broad protections against child trafficking, sexual exploitation, and abuse. The Preamble also reflects CRC language in regard to protecting children from economic exploitation and performance of hazardous or harmful work.[13] In addition, it recognizes "that a number of particularly vulnerable groups, including girl children, are at greater risk of sexual exploitation" and are disproportionately represented among the sexually exploited, and expresses concern over "the growing availability of child pornography on the Internet and other evolving technologies." The STP defines and prohibits the sale of children, child prostitution, and child pornography; obliges States Parties to make certain acts punishable under their criminal law; sets forth the bases for States Parties to assert jurisdiction over actionable practices, and strengthens their ability to pursue extradition of offenders. The STP also provides for protection of and assistance to the victimized children in the criminal justice process, the best interests of the child being the guiding principle in the children's judicial treatment.[14] For purposes of prevention and redress of offenses, the victims must have access to procedures to seek compensation for damages from those legally responsible (article 9(4)). The STP also has provisions on strengthening international cooperation in regard to sex trafficking involving children and on reporting requirements for States Parties (article 12).

The Child Soldiers Protocol [15] reaffirms in its Preamble that "the rights of children require special protection," notes "the harmful and widespread impact of armed conflict on children," and condemns their being targeted in such situations. It also refers to inclusion as a war crime in the Rome Statute of the International Criminal Court "the conscripting or enlisting children under the age of 15 years or using them to participate actively in hostilities in both international and non-international armed conflicts." The Preamble takes note of the definition of a child in article 1 of the CRC and expresses the conviction that raising the age of possible recruitment will contribute effectively to implementing the principle of the best interests of the child as a primary consideration in all actions concerning children.[16] The Child Soldiers Protocol extends the minimum age requirement for direct participation in armed conflict and conscription to eighteen (articles 1 and 2, respectively) and forbids rebel or other non-governmental armed forces "under any circumstances," to recruit or to use in hostilities persons under that age (article 4). It does not prescribe the age eighteen minimum for voluntary recruitment, but requires States Parties to raise the minimum age for it from fifteen (as set out in article 38, paragraph 3, of the CRC; i.e., to sixteen years of age) and to deposit a binding declaration setting forth the minimum age permitted for voluntary recruitment and describing safeguards adopted to ensure voluntariness (article 3(1-3), in part).[17] The Child Soldiers Protocol requires States Parties to take "all feasible measures to ensure" the demobilization or release from service of children recruited into armed conflict or used in hostilities and, "when necessary," to accord "all appropriate assistance" for the children's rehabilitation and social reintegration (article 6(1) and (3)).

III. REGIONAL DOCUMENTATION

A. African Charter on the Rights and Welfare of the Child 1990[18]

The African Charter on the Rights and Welfare of the Child (ACRWC), the first regional treaty on children's rights, builds on the 1979 Declaration on the Rights and Welfare of the African Child,[19] but most of its provisions are modeled after those of the CRC. "The main difference lies in the existence of provisions concerning children's duties [in article 31], in line with the African Human Rights Charter" (*see below*).[20] The Preamble states that "the child occupies a unique and privileged position in the African society" and requires legal protection as well as "particular care with regard to health, physical, mental, moral and social development." A child is defined as "every human being below the age of 18 years" (article 2). The ACRWC sets forth the principles of non-discrimination and the best interests of the child and also provides that children have an inherent right to life, protected by law. The death sentence is not to be applied to crimes committed by children (articles 3-5). Children have a right to a name and nationality as well as to freedom of expression, association and peaceful assembly; thought, religion, and conscience; privacy; education; and rest and leisure (articles 6-12).[21] Special measures of protection are to be taken for handicapped children and children should enjoy physical, mental, and spiritual health (articles 13-14). Children should also be protected against all forms of economic exploitation and from performing work likely to be hazardous (article 15) and against all forms of torture, maltreatment, and abuse (article 16); harmful social and cultural practices (article 21); all forms of sexual exploitation or abuse (article 27); the use of narcotics and illicit drugs (article 28); and abduction, sale, trafficking, and use in begging (article 29).

B. European Convention on the Exercise of Children's Rights 1996

The European Convention on the Exercise of Children's Rights (ECECR) stresses in the Preamble the aim of promoting the rights and "best interests" of children.[22] To that end, it states that children should have the opportunity to exercise their rights, particularly in family proceedings affecting them; they should be provided with relevant information (defined as information appropriate to the child's age and understanding, given to enable the child to exercise his or her rights fully, unless contrary to the welfare of the child) and their views should be given "due weight"; and, "where necessary," States as well as parents, should engage in the protection and promotion of those rights and best interests (Preamble). The ECECR applies to children who have not reached the age of eighteen (article 1(1)). The ECECR procedural rights include the child's right to be informed and to express his or her views in proceedings; the right to apply for the appointment of a special representative; and "other possible procedural rights," e.g., the right to apply to be assisted by an appropriate person of their choice to help them express their views, the right to appoint their own representative, and the right to exercise some or all of the rights of parties to the proceedings (articles 3-5).

IV. Specific Provisions in Other International and Regional Instruments

A. Universal Declaration of Human Rights 1948[23]

The Universal Declaration of Human Rights contains two articles that specifically refer to children. Article 25(2) states: "[m]otherhood and childhood are entitled to special care and assistance. All children whether born in or out of wedlock shall enjoy the same social protection."[24] Article 26 calls for the right to education for all, and deals both with access to and the aims of education. Thus, education is to be free, at least in the elementary and fundamental stages; elementary education is to be compulsory; and education should be "directed to the full development of the human personality and to the strengthening of respect for human rights and fundamental freedoms." Nevertheless, "[p]arents have a prior right to choose the kind of education that shall be given to their children."

B. International Covenant on Economic, Social and Cultural Rights 1966[25]

The Preamble to the International Covenant on Economic, Social and Cultural Rights (ICESCR), insofar as it recognizes the indivisibility of human rights, is applicable to children's rights as well. Thus, it notes that "recognition of the inherent dignity and of the equal and inalienable rights of all members of the human family is the foundation of freedom, justice and peace in the world" and that "these rights derive from the inherent dignity of the human person."[26] Specific references to children are found in articles 10 and 12. Under article 10, "[t]he widest possible protection and assistance should be accorded to the family, ... particularly for its establishment and while it is responsible for the care and education of dependent children" (item 1, in part). It further stipulates that "special measures of protection and assistance" should be taken on behalf of the young without any discrimination; that they should be protected from economic and social exploitation; that employing them in morally or medically harmful or dangerous work or in work likely to hamper their normal development should be punishable by law; and that age limits should be set below which the paid employment of child labor is prohibited and punishable by law (item 3). Article 12 addresses the right of all to "enjoyment of the highest attainable standard of physical and mental health," to be fully realized by, among other measures, States Parties' providing "for the reduction of the stillbirth-rate and of infant mortality and for the healthy development of the child" (item 2(a)). The ICESCR also provides for the right of everyone to education (article 13(1)) and stipulates "primary education shall be compulsory and available free to all" (article 13(2a)).

C. International Covenant on Civil and Political Rights 1966[27]

The International Covenant on Civil and Political Rights (ICCPR) contains general provisions from which children are entitled to benefit as well as certain specific provisions on safeguards for children in the administration of justice and as members of a family unit. Thus, article 2 obliges States Parties "to respect and to ensure to all individuals within its territory and subject to its jurisdiction" the rights recognized in the ICCPR, "without distinction of any kind;" to adopt laws to give effect to those rights; and to provide effective remedies where there are violations. Article 14(1) incorporates a more specific reference to rights of the young: "any judgement rendered in a criminal case or in a suit at law shall be made public except where the interest of juvenile persons otherwise requires or the proceedings concern matrimonial disputes or the guardianship of children." Furthermore, criminal proceedings "should take account of [juveniles'] age and the desirability of promoting their rehabilitation" (article 14(4)) and the penal system should segregate juvenile offenders from adults and accord them treatment "appropriate to their age and legal status" (article 10(3)).[28] Like the ICESCR, the ICCPR recognizes the family as entitled to societal and state protection (article 23(1)), and so States Parties are to respect the liberty of parents to ensure their children's religious and moral education in conformity with their own convictions (article 18(4)). If a marriage is dissolved, provision must be made for the protection of any children (article 23(4)). Article 24 of the ICCPR is specifically devoted to children. It stipulates that "every child shall have, without any discrimination as to race, colour, sex, language, religion, national or social origin, property or birth, the right to such measures of protection as are required by his status as a minor, on the part of his family, society and the State." It further prescribes that every child must be registered immediately after birth and have a name and that every child has the right to acquire a nationality.

D. Convention on the Rights of Persons with Disabilities 2006[29]

The Convention on the Rights of Persons with Disabilities contains a number of specific provisions on children. Aside from recalling various key human rights conventions, including the CRC, the Preamble specifically recognizes that "women and girls with disabilities are often at greater risk, both within and outside the home, of violence, injury or abuse, neglect or negligent treatment, maltreatment or exploitation" (q). It further states, "children with disabilities should have full enjoyment of all human rights and fundamental freedoms on an equal basis with other children,"recalling obligations of States Parties to the CRC (r). Among the general principles of the Convention is "respect for the evolving capacities of children with disabilities" and for the children's right to preserve their identities (article 3(h)) It is a general obligation of the States Parties to "closely consult with and actively involve persons with disabilities, including children with disabilities, through their representative organizations" in developing and implementing legislation and policies to execute the Convention as well as in other decision-making processes on issues concerning the disabled (article 4, item 3).

Under article 6, item 1, of the Convention, States Parties, recognizing that disabled women and girls are subject to multiple discrimination, are to take measures to ensure that they fully and equally enjoy all human rights and fundamental freedoms. Article 7, which is entirely devoted to children with disabilities, prescribes that States Parties are to take all necessary measures to ensure the children's full enjoyment "of all human rights and fundamental freedoms on an equal basis with other children," and the "best interests of the child" are to be "a primary consideration" "in all actions concerning children." In addition, States Parties must ensure that disabled children "have the right to express their views freely on all matters affecting them, their views being given due weight in accordance with their age and maturity, on an equal basis with other children, and to be provided with disability and age-appropriate assistance to realize that right."

The Convention also stipulates that States Parties must "take all appropriate measures to prevent all forms of exploitation, violence and abuse by ensuring, inter alia, appropriate forms of ... age-sensitive assistance and support for persons with disabilities and their families and caregivers" as well as protection services that are age-sensitive (article 16, item 2). Recovery from abuse and reintegration in society are also to take into account age-specific needs (article 16, item 4). In addition, States Parties should adopt effective legislation and policies focused on children to ensure identification, investigation, and, where appropriate, prosecution of acts of exploitation, violence, and abuse against disabled children (article 16, item 5). The Convention provides that children with disabilities are to be registered right after birth and "have the right from birth to a name, the right to acquire a nationality and, as far as possible, the right to know and be cared for by their parents" (article 18, item 2).

States Parties are obliged to take measures to ensure that disabled children retain their fertility on an equal basis with others (article 23, item 1 (c)); that their best interests are paramount in such matters as guardianship, wardship, trusteeship, and adoption; and that they have equal rights in family life. To realize the latter, "and to prevent concealment, abandonment, neglect and segregation of children with disabilities, States Parties shall undertake to provide early and comprehensive information, services and support to children with disabilities and their families" (article 23, items 2-3). States Parties must further ensure that children are not separated from their parents against their will, except when it is determined to be in their best interest. However, "[i]n no case shall a child be separated from parents on the basis of a disability of either the child or one or both of the parents" (article 23, item 4). The Convention stipulates that, to realize the right of the disabled to an education, States Parties must ensure that "children with disabilities are not excluded from free and compulsory primary education, or from secondary education, on the basis of disability" and that, in particular, they deliver education to children "who are blind, deaf or deafblind ... in the most appropriate languages and modes and means of communication for the individual, and in environments which maximize academic and social development" (article 24, items 2 (a) and 3 (c))., States Parties are to provide health services for the disabled that include early identification and intervention and those "designed to minimize and prevent further disabilities, including among children" (article 25 (b)). States Parties must also take appropriate measures to ensure that women and girls with disabilities, in particular, have access to social protection and poverty reduction programs (article 28, item 2 (b)). Disabled children must also be ensured "equal access with other children to participation in play, recreation and leisure and sporting activities, including those activities in the school system" (article 30, item 5 (d)).

E. European Convention on Human Rights 1950[30]

The Convention for the Protection of Human Rights and Fundamental Freedoms, also known as the European Convention on Human Rights (ECHR), the first international human rights agreement to establish supervisory and enforcement machinery, obliges States Parties to "secure everyone within their jurisdiction" the rights and freedoms it sets forth (article 1). The ECHR uses throughout the term "everyone" (or, where appropriate, "no one"); as a result, children have successfully brought suit either on their own behalf or as co-applicants with their parents.[31] Specific references to the young are found in two articles of the ECHR and concern legal proceedings. Article 5(1)(d), on the lawful procedures for depriving a minor of his or her liberty, permits the lawful detention of a minor for the purpose of educational supervision or for bringing him before the competent legal authority. Article 6(1) stipulates that everyone is entitled to a fair and public hearing and that judgment will be pronounced publicly, but the hearing may be held in private when required by the interests of juveniles or the protection of the parties' private life. Protocol No. 7 to the ECHR provides that while spouses enjoy equality of rights and responsibilities in their relations with their children, this does not prevent States "from taking such measures as are necessary in the interests of the children" (article 5).[32]

F. African Charter on Hum an and People's Rights 1981 (Banjul Charter) and Protocol[33]

The African Charter on Human and People's Rights (hereinafter ACHPR) (also known as the Banjul Charter) encompasses civil and political as well as economic, social, and cultural rights. In regard to children, it emphasizes the rights of the family and of duties towards the family rather than the rights and duties of individual family members, which can be viewed as a reflection of African customary law. Thus, the ACHPR makes it incumbent on the individual "[t]o preserve the harmonious development of the family and to work for the cohesion and respect of the family; to respect his parents at all times, to maintain them in case of need" (article 29(1)). The ACHPR does not set forth any additional specific rights for children, relying instead on existing international protections regarding children's rights[34] (in article 18(3)). As in other international human rights documents, however, rights in the ACHPR are mentioned in connection with "the individual" or "every individual."

The Protocol to the African Charter on Human and Peoples' Rights on the Rights of Women in Africa[35] makes numerous specific references to children and to girls in particular. The Preamble calls for the condemnation and elimination of "any practice that hinders or endangers the normal growth and affects the physical, emotional and psychological development of women and girls." States Parties are to enact and implement legislative measures to prohibit all forms of such harmful practices (article 2(1)(b)); protect women and girls against rape and all other forms of violence, including trafficking; and "ensure that in times of conflict and/or war, such acts are considered war crimes and are punished as such" (article 4(c) and (d)). States Parties should also condemn harmful practices such as medicalization of female genital mutilation and scarification that affect the fundamental human rights of women and girls and are contrary to recognized international standards, and take measures against them, such as rehabilitation of the victims and granting of asylum to those at risk (article 6(b-d)). States Parties should afford effective protection to women and children in emergency and conflict situations (article 11(4)) as well. In furtherance of the right to education and training, "all appropriate measures" should be taken to eliminate discrimination against women and girls, with specific positive action to be taken to promote girls' education and training "at all levels and in all disciplines" as well as their retention in schools and other training institutions (article 12).

G. American Convention on Human Rights (Pact of San José, Costa Rica)[36]

The American Convention on Human Rights (ACHR) obliges States Parties to respect the rights and freedoms recognized in its provisions and "to ensure to all persons subject to their jurisdiction the free and full exercise of those rights and freedoms, without any discrimination for reasons of race, color, sex, language, religion, political or other opinion, national or social origin, economic status, birth, or any other social condition. The term "person" used in the ACHR means "every human being" (article 1). Thus, every person has the right to a legal personality, to life, to humane treatment, to personal liberty, and to a fair trial, among many other rights set forth. However, parents or guardians "have the right to provide for the religious and moral education of their children or wards that is in accord with their own convictions" (article 12(4)), and "public entertainments may be subject by law to prior censorship for the sole purpose of regulating access to them for the moral protection of childhood and adolescence," notwithstanding the right to freedom of thought and expression (article 13(4)).

The ACHR stipulates that provision must be made for the protection of children "solely on the basis of their own best interests" when a marriage is dissolved and that equal rights must be recognized by law for children born in and out of wedlock (article 17(4) & (5)). Everyone also has the right to a given name and to the surnames of one or both parents (article 18).

The ACHR has a separate provision on the rights of the child: "[e]very minor child has the right to the measures of protection required by his condition as a minor on the part of his family, society, and the state (article 19)." This article is listed among those that may not be suspended in time of war, public danger, or other emergency (article 27(2)).

H. Convention on the Elimination of all Forms of Discrimination against Women 1979[37]

The Convention on the Elimination of All Forms of Discrimination Against Women (CEDAW) has been described as an international bill of rights for women. It defines what constitutes discrimination against women and establishes an agenda for States Parties to act to end it.[38]

The Preamble, in invoking the Universal Declaration of Human Rights, notes its affirmation of the principle of the inadmissibility of discrimination and its proclamation "that all human beings are born free and equal in dignity and rights and that everyone is entitled to all the rights and freedoms set forth therein, without distinction of any kind, including distinction based on sex."

This kind of statement forms the backdrop for certain rights set forth in CEDAW, even though girls specifically are mentioned only once: the obligation of States Parties to ensure the reduction of female student drop-out rates and the organization of programs for girls and women who have left school prematurely (article 10, in part). States Parties are also to take appropriate steps "to modify the social and cultural patterns of conduct of men and women, with a view to achieving the elimination of prejudices and customary and all other practices which are based on the idea of the inferiority or the superiority of either of the sexes or on stereotyped roles for men and women" (article 5(a)).

CEDAW refers to the interests of children being paramount in relation to the common responsibility of men and women for their children's upbringing and development (article 5(b)) as well as in regard to States Parties' ensuring the same rights and responsibilities between men and women as parents in matters relating to their children and in matters of guardianship, wardship, trusteeship, and adoption of children (article 16 (1)(d) and (f)). CEDAW also proscribes betrothal and marriage of children and calls for action to specify a minimum age for marriage and to make marriage registration compulsory (article 16(2)).

V. CHILD PROTECTION AND PLACEMENT AGREEMENTS

A. Hague Convention on Jurisdiction, etc., for the Protection of Children 1996[39]

The Hague Convention on Jurisdiction, Applicable Law, Recognition, Enforcement and Cooperation in Respect of Parental Responsibility and Measures for the Protection of Children (1996 Convention) covers a wide range of civil child protection measures, "from orders concerning parental responsibility and contact to public measures of protection or care, and from matters of representation to the protection of children's property."[40] The Preamble confirms "that the best interests of the child are to be a primary consideration." Article 2 stipulates that the Convention is applicable "to children from the moment of their birth until they reach the age of 18 years." The 1996 Convention provides a structure to resolve disputes over contact and custody issues when parents are separated and living in different countries and has uniform rules to determine which country's authorities are competent to take the necessary protection measures. Provisions on recognition and enforcement ensure that primacy be given to decisions taken by the authorities of the country where the child has his or her habitual residence, reinforcing provisions of the 1980 Hague Convention (*see below*). There are also provisions on cooperation procedures to better protect unaccompanied minors who cross borders and are in vulnerable situations and children placed in alternative care across frontiers. The latter includes arrangements such as foster care and the Islamic law institution of *Kafala*, a functional equivalent of adoption falling outside the scope of the 1993 Intercountry Adoption Convention (*see below*).[41]

B. Hague Convention on Jurisdiction, etc., Relating to Adoptions 1965[42]

The Hague Convention on Jurisdiction, Applicable Law and Recognition of Decrees Relating to Adoptions (1965 Convention), the first Hague Convention on the issue, apparently has no contracting parties at present. The Convention is applicable "to all international adoptions, not only where a child originated from another country but also to adoptions where the only international aspect is the foreign nationality of the child."[43] It has been characterized as incorporating four important provisions. The authorities are not to grant an adoption "unless it will be in the interest of the child." Before granting an adoption, the authorities should conduct "a thorough inquiry" relating to the adopter(s), the child, and the child's family. The inquiry should be carried out "as far as possible ... in cooperation with public or private organizations qualified in the field of inter-country adoptions" and with the help of specially trained or qualified social workers (article 6). Furthermore, the national law of the child is to be applied in decisions pertaining to consent and consultation issues, rather than that of the adopter, family, or spouse (article 5, paragraph 1).[44] The 1965 Convention also allows States Parties to make a declaration at the time of signature, ratification, or accession but revocable at any time, specifying provisions of domestic law prohibiting adoptions founded upon certain specified grounds, e.g., the existence of a previous adoption of the child or the age of the adopter and that of the child (article 13).

C. European Convention on the Adoption of Children 1967[45]

The European Convention on the Adoption of Children (ECAC) applies to the legal adoption of children under the age of eighteen, not currently or previously married, and not deemed in law to have come of age earlier (article 3). Its provisions are only minimum standards; States Parties may adopt provisions more favorable to the adopted child (article 16).[46] The ECAC ensures that national child protection laws apply not only to adoptions of children from the States Parties, but also to those of children from other States. The essential provisions are on adoption practices that each Party should undertake to incorporate in national legislation. Under them, adoption must be granted by a judicial or administrative authority in order to be valid (article 7) and the competent authority should not grant an adoption unless it "will be in the interest of the child" (article 8(1)). The authority is to make appropriate inquiries into such matters as the child's views with respect to the adoption and the mutual suitability of the child and the adopter (article 9). After the adoption, the child should generally be able to acquire the adopter's surname and be treated as having rights of succession (article 10 (3) and (5)). States Parties should prohibit any improper financial advantage arising from a child being given up for adoption (article 15). Four supplementary provisions, requiring only the States' Parties' consideration, stipulate, inter alia, that provision be made to enable adoption to be completed without the adopter's identity being disclosed to the child's family (article 20(1)) and to require or permit adoption proceedings to take place in camera (article 20(2)). Children are not accorded the right to know the identity of their former parents.[47]

D. Inter-American Convention on Conflict of Laws Concerning the Adoption of Minors 1984[48]

The Inter-American Convention on Conflict of Laws Concerning the Adoption of Minors (IAC) applies to the adoption of minors in the form of full adoption, adoptive legitimation, and "other similar institutions" when the domicile of the adopter and the habitual residence of the adoptee are in different States Parties (article 1). Such adoptions are irrevocable (article 12). A State Party may declare that the IAC also applies to "any other form of international adoption of minors" (article 2); revocation of such adoptions will be governed by the law of the adoptee's habitual residence at the time of adoption (article 12). The IAC states that the law of the minor's habitual residence also governs capacity, consent, and other requirements for adoption, as well as adoption procedures and formalities (article 3). The IAC protects the identity of the birth parents, with certain exceptions regarding medical data (article 7). The adoptee and the adopter (and the adopter's family) generally have the same rights of succession as those of legitimate family members (article 11). In cases where conversion of a simple adoption into full adoption, adoptive legitimation, or similar institutions is permitted, the adoptee's consent is required if he or she is over fourteen years of age (article 13, paragraph 2)). If an adoption is annulled, the minor's interests are to be protected (article 14). Although the IAC terms and the laws applicable under it are to be interpreted "consistently and in favor of the validity of the adoption and the best interests of the adoptee" (article 19), a State Party's authorities may refuse to apply those laws when they are "manifestly contrary to its public policy" (article 18).

E. Hague Convention on the Protection of Children in Intercountry Adoption 1993[49]

The Hague Convention on the Protection of Children and Cooperation in Respect of Intercountry Adoption (1993 Convention), has three stated aims: to establish safeguards to ensure that intercountry adoptions are in the best interest of the child and in accordance with the child's fundamental rights; to establish a system of safeguards to avoid abuses such as trafficking in children; and to secure recognition in States Parties of adoptions made in accordance with the Convention (article 1). The underlying principle of the 1993 Convention is that "although it is difficult to define the best interests of the child, the child's interests should always take priority over those of the prospective adopters," but the application of this principle has proved problematic.[50] The 1993 Convention asserts that authorities must ensure, taking into account the age and degree of maturity of the child, that he or she has been counseled and informed of the effects of the adoption and of his or her consent to the adoption, where such consent is required; that consideration has been given to the child's wishes and opinions; that the child's consent to the adoption has been given freely, in the required legal form, and in writing; and that consent has not been induced by payment or compensation of any kind (article 4(d)). Information on the child's origin, in particular the identity of the parents as well as the medical history, should be preserved, but access by the child to that information is permitted only insofar as it is allowed by the law of the State where it is held (article 30). Personal data gathered or transmitted under the 1993 Convention's provisions is to be used "only for the purposes for which they were gathered or transmitted," without prejudice to article 30 (article 31).[51]

F. Hague Convention on the Civil Aspects of International Child Abduction 1980[52]

The Hague Convention on the Civil Aspects of International Child Abduction (1980 Convention) governs issues related to parental kidnapping or the removal of children under the age of sixteen across international borders and involving the jurisdiction of different countries' courts. Its stated objectives are to secure the prompt return of children wrongfully removed to or retained in any contracting state and to ensure that the rights of custody and of access under the law of one contracting state are effectively respected in the other contracting states (article 1). Removal or retention of a child is deemed wrongful if: a) it is in breach of custody rights attributed to a person, an institution, or any other body, either jointly or alone, under the law of the State in which the child was habitually resident immediately before the removal or retention; and b) at the time of removal or retention those rights were exercised, or would have been but for the removal or retention (article 3, paragraph 1).

G. The European Convention Concerning the Custody of Children 1980[53]

The European Convention on the Recognition and Enforcement of Decisions Concerning the Custody of Children (the Luxembourg Convention) seeks to protect the rights of custody and access to children in the international context. It calls upon the central authorities designated by States Parties to provide "free, prompt, non-bureaucratic assistance" in determining the whereabouts and restoring custody of an improperly removed child.[54] They must also avoid prejudice to the interests of the child or of the applicant in restoring child custody, among other requirements. Like the 1980 Convention, the Luxembourg Convention defines a child as being under the age of sixteen (article 1(a)). Also, under both instruments, the right of action lies with the custody holder.[55] The Luxembourg Convention uses the term "improper removal" to refer to "the removal of a child across an international frontier in breach of a decision relating to his custody" given in a State Party and enforceable in that State (article 1(d)), in contrast to the 1980 Convention's term "wrongful removal or retention" of a child and the CRC's term "the illicit transfer and non-return of children abroad" (article 11).[56]

H. Worst Forms of Child Labour Convention 1999[57]

The Worst Forms of Child Labour Convention (WFCLC) refers in the Preamble to the need to adopt new instruments for the prohibition and elimination of the worst forms of child labour, "to complement the Convention and the Recommendation Concerning Minimum Age for Admission to Employment, 1973, which remain fundamental instruments on child labour." For the purposes of the WFCLC, the term "child" applies to all persons under the age of eighteen (article 2). The "worst forms of child labour" comprise: (a) all forms of slavery or practices similar to it, such as the sale and trafficking of children and forced labor (including forced recruitment for armed conflict); (b) the use, procuring, or offering of a child for prostitution or for pornography or pornographic performances; c) the use, procuring, or offering of a child for illicit activities such as drug trafficking; and (d) work that is likely to harm children's health, safety, or morals (article 3). Each State Party is to adopt measures to: prevent the engagement of children in the worst forms of child labor; to provide direct assistance for the removal of children from such labor and for their rehabilitation and social integration; to ensure access to free basic education and, wherever possible and appropriate, to vocational training for all children removed from the worst forms of child labor; to identify and reach out to children at special risk; and to take account of the special situation of girls (article 7(2)).

I. International Convention for the Protection of All Persons from Forced Disappearance 2006[58]

The International Convention for the Protection of All Persons from Forced Disappearance stipulates in general that "no one shall be subjected to enforced disappearance" and that "no exceptional circumstances whatsoever" may be invoked as a justification for it (article 1). "Enforced disappearance" is defined in article 2, for the purposes of the Convention, as

the arrest, detention, abduction or any other form of deprivation of liberty by agents of the State or by persons or groups of persons acting with the authorization, support or acquiescence of the State, followed by a refusal to acknowledge the deprivation of liberty or by concealment of the fate or whereabouts of the disappeared person, which place such a person outside the protection of the law.

The Convention prescribes that States Parties may establish aggravating circumstances, without prejudice to other criminal procedures, particularly when the commission of an enforced disappearance involves minors, among other categories of especially vulnerable persons (article 7, item 2 (b)).

Article 25 of the Convention focuses on the enforced disappearance of children. It provides for each State Party to take measures to prevent and punish under its criminal law the following acts:

> 1. (a) The wrongful removal of children who are subjected to enforced disappearance, children whose father, mother or legal guardian is subjected to enforced disappearance or children born during the captivity of a mother subjected to enforced disappearance;
> (b) The falsification, concealment or destruction of documents attesting to the true identity of the children referred to in subparagraph (a) above.

States Parties are obliged to search for and identify the children referred to in item 1(a) above and to return them to their families "in accordance with legal procedures and applicable international agreements," and to assist one another in taking such measures (items 2 and 3). To protect the best interests of such children as well as

> their right to preserve, or to have re-established, their identity, including their nationality, name and family relations as recognized by law, States Parties which recognize a system of adoption or other form of placement of children shall have legal procedures in place to review the adoption or placement procedure, and, where appropriate, to annul any adoption or placement of children that originated in an enforced disappearance (item 4).

Article 25 further affirms that "in all cases, and in particular in all matters relating to this article, the best interests of the child shall be a primary consideration," and that children capable of forming their own views have a right to express them freely, with the views being given due weight in accordance with the child's age and maturity (item 5).

VI. Other Initiatives

Among other developments regarding children's rights are an international call for action to end violence against children and a resolution adopted by the U.N. General Assembly on the establishment of a Human Rights Council.[59]

Prepared by Wendy Zeldin
Senior Legal Research Analyst
July 2007

End Notes

[1] Stephen R. Arnott, Family Law: Autonomy, Standing, and Children's Rights, 33 WILLIAM MITCHELL LAW REVIEW 809 (2007). Arnott notes that "the very term 'children's rights' is both broad and loose," id. at 808.

[2] The U.N. Declaration of the Rights of the Child comprises a Preamble and ten principles. G.A. Res. 1386 (XIV), 14 U.N. GAOR Supp. (No. 16) at 19, U.N. Doc. A/4354. For an online text of the Declaration, see the Office of the U.N. High Commissioner for Human Rights (UNHCHR) Web site, http://www.unhchr.ch/html/menu3/b/25.htm (last visited July 20, 2007) (unofficial source). A list of the Status of Ratification of the Principal International Human Rights Treaties as of July 14, 2006, is available at http://www2.ohchr.org/english/bodies/docs/status.pdf (last visited Dec. 3, 2007).

[3] GERALDINE VAN BUEREN, THE INTERNATIONAL LAW ON THE RIGHTS OF THE CHILD 10-11 (Dordrecht/Boston/London, Martinus Nijhoff Publishers, 1995. 35 International Studies in Human Rights).

[4] DRC, principle 2, supra note 2.

[5] The 1924 Declaration stated children "must be the first to receive relief"; the DRC specifies more pragmatically that they are to be "among the first" to receive protection and relief (principle 8). VAN BUEREN, supra note 3, at 11.

[6] The Minimum Age Convention, comprising a Preamble and 18 articles, was adopted by the 58th Session of the General Conference of the International Labour Organisation on June 26, 1973 , and entered into force on June 19, 1976; I.L.O. No. 138. For an online text, see the Office of the U.N. High Commissioner of Human Rights (OHCHR) Web site, http://www.ohchr.org/english/law/ageconvention.htm (last visited July 25, 2007) (unofficial source).

[7] The Convention on the Rights of the Child, with a Preamble and 54 articles, was adopted by the U.N. General Assembly on November 20, 1989, and entered into force on September 2, 1990. G.A. Res. 44/25, annex, 44 U.N. GAOR Supp. (No. 49) at 167, U.N. Doc. A/44/49 (1989); 28 I.L.M. 1448 (1989). For an online text, see the OHCHR Web site, http://www.ohchr.org/english/law/crc.htm (last visited July 23, 2007); it includes the 1995 amendment to article 43, paragraph 2 (G.A. Res. 50/155 (Dec. 21, 1995)), which entered into force on November 18, 2002. For the status of signatures, ratifications, and accessions, see the OHCHR Web site, http://www.ohchr.org/english/bodies/ratification/11.htm (last visited Nov. 28, 2007). The United States (and Somalia) has signed but not ratified the CRC; it insisted that ratification of the two CRC Protocols on sex trafficking and on child soldiers (see below) not be considered a legal assumption by the United States of CRC obligations.7 Both Protocols permit CRC signatories to sign and ratify the Protocols without having ratified the CRC, under article 13(1) in each document. Inclusion of such a provision has been characterized as an attempt to obtain U.S. support for the Protocol; the United States ratified the Protocols on December 23, 2002. See Cris R. Revaz, The Optional Protocols to the UN Convention on the Rights of the Child on Sex Trafficking and Child Soldiers, 9 HUMAN RIGHTS BRIEF 13 (Fall 2001). For an in-depth analysis of Part I of the Convention (articles 1-41), see SHARON DETRICK, A COMMENTARY ON THE UNITED NATIONS CONVENTION ON THE RIGHTS OF THE CHILD (The Hague/Boston/London, Martinus Nijhoff Publishers, 1999); see also Convention on the Rights of the Child, AMNESTY INTERNATIONAL USA, http://www.amnestyusa.org/Children/ Convention_on_the_Rights_of_the_Child/page.do?id =1101777& n1=3&n2=78&n3=1272 (last visited July 24, 2007).

[8] VAN BUEREN, supra note 3, at 16, 101.

[9] Id. at 15. Van Bueren calls these "the four 'P's"; other scholars refer to the Convention as being concerned with the three types of children's rights, called the three 'P's: provision, protection, and participation. See, for example, Jean Koh Peters, How Children Are Heard in Child Protective Proceedings, in the United States and Around the World in 2005: Survey Findings, Initial Observations, and Areas for Further Study [Special Issue on Legal Representation of Children], 6 NEVADA LAW JOURNAL 971 (Spring 2006).

[10] VAN BUEREN, supra note 3, at 16; Ursula Kilkelly, The Best of Both Worlds for Children's Rights? Interpreting the European Convention on Human Rights in the Light of the UN Convention on the Rights of the Child, HUMAN RIGHTS QUARTERLY 311 (2001), available at http://muse.jhu.edu/journals/human rights quarterly/v023/23.2kilkelly.pdf.

[11] Kilkelly, supra note 10.

[12] The Sex Trafficking Protocol comprises a preamble and 17 articles. G.A. Res. A/RES/54/263 of 25 May 2000. It entered into force on January 18, 2002. For an online text, see the OHCHR Web site, http://www.ohchr.org/english/law/crcsale.htm (last visited Nov. 28, 2007). The status of ratifications and reservations to the STP is available via hyperlinks on the same Web site.

[13] Revaz, supra note 7.

[14] Id.

[15] The Child Soldiers Protocol, comprising a Preamble and 13 articles, entered into force on February 12, 2002. G.A. Res. A/RES/54/263 of 25 May 2000. For an online text, see the OHCHR Web site, http://www.ohchr. org/english/law/crc-conflict.htm (last visited July 23, 2007). The status of ratifications and reservations to the Child Soldiers Protocol is available via hyperlinks in the left column of that same Web site. 16 Id.

[17] According to article 3(5), "the requirement to raise the age in paragraph 1 of the present article does not apply to schools operated by or under the control of the armed forces of the States Parties, in keeping with articles 28 and 29 of the Convention on the Rights of the Child." See also Revaz, supra note 7.

[18] The African Charter on the Rights and Welfare of the Child, with a Preamble and 48 articles, was adopted on July 11, 1990, and entered into force on November 29, 1999. OAU Doc. CAB/LEG/24.9/49 (1990). For an online text, see the African Union Web site, http://www.africa-union.org/official_documents/Treaties_% 20Conventions_%20Protocols/A.%20C.%20ON%20THE%20RIGHT%20AND%20WELF%20OF%20CHIL D.pdf (last visited July 20, 2007) (unofficial source). For a list of signatures, ratifications, and accessions, see the African Union Web site, http://www.africa-union.org/root/AU/Documents/Treaties/ List/African%20 Charter%20on%20the%20Rights%20and%20Welfare%20of%20the%20Child.pdf(last visited July 30, 2007).

[19] VAN BUEREN, supra note 3, at 24-25 and n.171. For an online text, see Organization of African Unity (OAU), Declaration on the Rights and Welfare of the African Child, AHG/St. 4 (XVI) Rev. 1 1979, DECLARATION AND RESOLUTIONS ADOPTED BY THE SIXTEENTH ORDINARY SESSION OF THE ASSEMBLY OF HEADS OF STATE AND GOVERNMENT (July 17-20, 1979), http://www.africa-union.org/root/au/ Documents/Decisions/hog/pHoGAssembly1979.pdf (last visited July 24, 2007).

[20] International Norms and Standards Relating to Disability, UNITED NATIONS ENABLE, http://www.un. org/esa/socdev/enable/comp303.htm (last visited July 25, 2007). VAN BUEREN, supra note 3, at 24-25, notes "the high risk of conditionality" of the concept of children's responsibilities set forth in the two Charters and criticizes the responsibility "to respect parents and elders at all times" as being "too unquestioning and general." She adds, "[w]here family members are abusing or exploiting children, to maintain that children are obliged to respect the abuser is a dangerous precedent."

[21] Article 11 on education is the longest article in the ACRWC. It also provides, among other measures, that States Parties are to in particular to provide free and compulsory basic education (art. 11(3))

[22] The European Convention on the Exercise of Children's Rights, C. E.T.S. No. 160, has a Preamble and 26 articles. It was opened for signature on January 25, 1996, and entered into force on July 1, 2000. For an online text, see the COE Web site, http://conventions.coe.int/Treaty/Commun/ QueVoulezVous.asp? NT=160 &CL=ENG, and, for an explanatory report, http://conventions.coe.int/Treaty/EN/ Reports/ HTML /160.htm (both last visited July 27, 2007). See also Kilkelly, supra note 10; Ursula Kilkelly, Children's Rights: a European Perspective, 4:2 JUDICIAL STUDIES INSTITUTE JOURNAL 68 (2004), available at http://www.jsijournal.ie/html/Volume%204%20No.%202/4%5B%5D_Kilkelly_Children's%20Rights%20A %20European%20P erspective.pdf; and SANDY RUXTON, WHAT ABOUT US? CHILDREN'S RIGHTS IN THE EUROPEAN UNION: NEXT STEPS (Nov. 2005), available at http://www.crin.org/ docs/Ruxton%20Report WhatAboutUs.pdf. ["CRIN" is the Child Rights Information Network.]

[23] The Universal Declaration of Human Rights, with a Preamble and 30 articles, was adopted by the U.N. General Assembly on December 10, 1948. G.A. Res. 217 A (III), U.N. Doc. A/810 at 71 (Dec. 10, 1948). For an online text, see the United Nations Web site, http://www.un.org/Overview/rights.html (unofficial source) (last visited July 24, 2007).

[24] This gives no recognition, however, to the role of fatherhood, and the "twinning of the exclusive role of women and children continues to resound throughout international law." VAN BUEREN, supra note 3, at 18.

[25] The International Covenant on Economic, Social and Cultural Rights, with a Preamble and 31 articles, was adopted by the U.N. General Assembly on December 16, 1996, and entered into force on January 3, 1976. G.A. Res. 2200A (XXI), 21 U.N.GAOR, 21st Sess., Supp. (No. 16) at 49, U.N. Doc. A/6316 (Dec. 16, 1966), 993 U.N.T.S. 3. For an online text, see the OHCHR Web site, http://www.ohchr.org/english/law/cescr.htm (last visited July 23, 2007).

[26] Id. See also VAN BUEREN, supra note 3, at 19.

[27] The International Covenant on Civil and Political Rights, with a Preamble and 53 articles, was adopted by the U.N. General Assembly on December 16, 1966, and entered into force on March 23, 1976. G.A. Res. 2200A (XXI), 21 U.N. GAOR, 21st Sess. Supp. (No. 16) at 52, U.N. Doc. A/6316 (Dec. 16, 1966), 999 U.N.T.S. 171. For an online text, see the OHCHR Web site, http://www.ohchr.org/english/law/ccpr.htm (last visited July 26, 2007).

[28] VAN BUEREN, supra note 3, at 20. She notes that the Covenant prohibits imposition of the death penalty for crimes committed by persons under the age of 18 as the result of an initiative from Japan, citing to U.N. Doc. A/C.3/L 650.

[29] The Convention on the Rights of Persons with Disabilities has a Preamble and 50 articles. It was adopted by the U.N. General Assembly on December 13, 2006, and was opened for signature on March 30, 2007. G.A. Res. 61/106, U.N. Doc. A/RES/61/106 (Jan. 24, 2007). For an online text, see GENERAL ASSEMBLY, 1 RESOLUTIONS AND DECISIONS ADOPTED BY THE GENERAL ASSEMBLY DURING ITS SIXTY-FIRST SESSION: VOLUME I, RESOLUTIONS, 12 SEPTEMBER – 22 DECEMBER 2006 65-80 (New York, United Nations, 2007) (Supplement No. 49 (A/61/49), available at http://daccessdds.un.org/doc/UNDOC/GEN/N07/295/65/PDF/N0729565.pdf?OpenElement), or the OHCHR Web site, http://www.ohchr.org/Documents/Publications/newCoreTreatiesen.pdf (last visited Dec. 2, 2007). The Optional Protocol to the Convention, adopted on the same date, mainly refers to procedural matters and does not refer to children's rights per se. According to the UN ENABLE Web site, the Convention had a record number of signatories (82) for a U.N. Convention on its opening day and is also "the first human rights convention to be open for signature by regional integration organizations." Convention on the Rights of Persons with Disabilities, UN ENABLE, http://www.un.org/disabilities/default.asp?navid=8&pid=150 (last visited Dec. 3, 2007). As of December 3, 2007, ten countries had ratified the Convention; the total number required for its entry into force is 20. DISABILITY: Three More Countries Ratify Rights Convention, CRIN Web site, Dec. 3, 2007, available at http://www.crin.org/resources/infodetail.asp?id=15727. The ten countries include Bangladesh, Croatia, Cuba, Gabon, Hungary, India, Jamaica, Panama, South Africa, and Spain. U.N. Convention on the Rights of Persons with Disabilities, CRIN Web site, http://www.crin.org/Law/instrument.asp?InstID=1048 (last visited Dec. 3, 2007).

[30] The Convention for the Protection of Human Rights and Fundamental Freedoms, C.E.T.S. No. 005, with a Preamble and 59 articles, was adopted on November 4, 1950, and entered into force on September 3, 1953. There have been 11 Protocols to the Convention, but as from November 1, 1998, Protocol 9 was repealed and Protocol 10 lost its purpose. For an online text as amended by Protocol 11 (E.T.S. No. 155, in force November 1, 1998), see the Council of Europe Web site, http://conventions.coe.int/Treaty/en/Treaties/Html/005.htm (last visited July 26, 2007). Other documents, such as the status of ratifications and an explanatory report, are also available through links provided on the same Web site, at http://conventions.coe.int/Treaty/Commun/QueVoulezVous.asp?NT=005&CL=ENG (last visited July 26, 2007).

[31] VAN BUEREN, supra note 3, at 22. She mentions several cases in fn. 153 and discusses them elsewhere in the text.

[32] Id. at 22, n.154.

[33] The Banjul Charter, in a Preamble and 68 articles, was adopted June 27, 1981, and entered into force October 21, 1986. OAU Doc. CAB/LEG/67/3 rev. 5, 21 I.L.M. 58 (1982). For an online text, see the African Commission on Human and People's Rights Web site, http://www.achpr.org/english/_info/charter_en.html (unofficial source) (last visited July 26, 2007).

[34] VAN BUEREN, supra note 3, at 24.

[35] The Protocol was adopted by the African Union on July 11, 2003, and entered into force on November 25, 2005. For an online text, see the Human Rights Education Associates Web site, http://www.hrea.org/erc/Library/display.php?doc_id=806&category_id=31&category_type=3 (last visited July 25, 2007).

[36] The American Convention on Human Rights, with a Preamble and 82 articles, was adopted on November 22, 1969, in San José, Costa Rica, and entered into force on July 18, 1978. OAS, Treaty Series, No. 36; U.N. Registration 08/27/79 No. 17955. For an online text of the Convention, see Organization of American States (OAS) Web site, http://www.oas.org/juridico/english/treaties/b-32.html (unofficial source) (last visited July 26, 2007); for the status of ratifications, see OAS Web site http://www.oas.org/juridico/english/Sigs/b-32.html (last visited July 26, 2007).

[37] CEDAW, comprising a Preamble and 30 articles, was adopted by the U.N. General Assembly on December 18, 1979, and entered into force on September 3, 1981. G.A. Res. 34/180, 34 U.N. GAOR Supp. (No. 46) at 193, U.N. Doc. A/34/46. For an online text, see the U.N. Division of the Advancement of Women Web site, http://www.un.org/womenwatch/daw/cedaw/text/econvention.htm#article1 (last visited July 27, 2007). A list of the status of signatures, ratifications, and accessions is available on the same Web site, at http://www.un.org/womenwatch/daw/cedaw/states.htm (last visited July 27, 2007).

[38] Convention on the Elimination of all Forms of Discrimination Against Women: Text of the Convention, U.N. Division of the Advancement of Women: Department of Social and Economic Affairs Web site, http://www.un.org/womenwatch/daw/cedaw/cedaw.htm (last visited July 27, 2007).

[39] The 1996 Convention was adopted on October 19, 1996, and entered into force January 1, 2002. 35 I.L.M. 1391, 1396 (1996). It comprises a brief Preamble and 63 articles. For an online text, see the Hague Conference on Private International Law (HCCH) Web site, http://hcch.e-vision.nl/index_en.php?act=conventions.text &cid=70 (last visited July 27, 2007). See also How Children's Voices Are Heard in Protective Proceedings, REPRESENTING CHILDREN WORLDWIDE (RCW) (2005), available at http://www.law.yale.edu/rcw/ (the study covers 250 jurisdictions), and Gloria Folger DeHart, The Relationship Between the 1980 Child Abduction Convention and the 1996 Protection Convention, 33:1 JOURNAL OF INTERNATIONAL LAW AND POLITICS 83 (2000), available at http://www3.law.nyu.edu/journals/jilp/issues/33/pdf/33f.pdf. The entire issue of the JILP is devoted to the 1980 Convention, marking its twentieth anniversary.

[40] The Hague Convention of 1996 on the International Protection of Children, HCCH Web site, http://hcch.e-vision.nl/upload/outline34e.pdf (last visited July 27, 2007). The article summarizes the Convention's contents.

[41] Id.

[42] The Hague Convention on Jurisdiction, Applicable Law and Recognition of Decrees Relating to Adoptions, Hague No. 13, with a brief Preamble and 24 articles, was concluded on November 15, 1965, and entered into force on October 23, 1978. In accordance with its article 23, it will cease to have effect on October 23, 2008. For an online text, see the HCCH Web site, http://hcch.e-vision.nl/index_en.php?act=conventions.text&cid=75 (last visited July 27, 2007).

[43] VAN BUEREN, supra note 3, at 98.

[44] Id.

[45] The European Convention on the Adoption of Children was opened for signature on April 24, 1967, and entered into force on April 26, 1968. C.E.T.S. No. 058. It comprises a Preamble and 28 articles. For an online text, see the COE Web site, http://conventions.coe.int/Treaty/en/Treaties/Html/058.htm (last visited July 27, 2007). Links to a chart of signatures and ratifications and other information are available via the same Web site, at http://conventions.coe.int/Treaty/Commun/QueVoulezVous.asp?NT=058&CL=ENG (last visited July 27, 2007).

[46] VAN BUEREN, supra note 3, at 99.

[47] Summary of the Treaty, the COE Web site, http://conventions.coe.int/Treaty/en/Summaries/Html/058.htm (last visited July 27, 2007); VAN BUEREN, supra note 3, at 99.

[48] The Inter-American Convention, in 29 articles, was adopted by the OAS Member States on May 24, 1984, and in force as of May 26, 1988. O.A.S.T.S. No. 62. For an online text of the Inter-American Convention, see the OAS Web site, http://www.oas.org/juridico/english/sigs/b-48.html (last visited July 30, 2007) (scroll to the end of the page for the hyperlink to the treaty text). The URL also lists the status of signatures and ratifications to the Convention.

[49] The Hague Convention on the Protection of Children and Cooperation in Respect of Intercountry Adoption, comprising a Preamble and 48 articles, was concluded on May 29, 1993, and entered into force on May 1, 1995. 32 I.L.M. 1134 (1993). For an online text, see the HCCH Web site, http://www.hcch.net/index en.php?act=conventions.text&cid=69 (last visited July 27, 2007). See also Hans Van Loon, Hague Convention of 29 May 1993 on Protection of Children and Cooperation in Respect of Intercountry Adoption, 3 THE INTERNATIONAL JOURNAL OF CHILDREN'S RIGHTS 463 (1995), available at http://www.iss-ssi.org/Resource_Centre/Tronc_CI/thcvloon.pdf.

[50] VAN BUEREN, supra note 3, at 99-100.

[51] Id. at 122 notes that the 1993 Convention's approach reinforces that taken in the IAC guaranteeing the secrecy of the adoption "where called for." She also refers to the non-binding 1986 Declaration on Social and Legal Principles Relating to the Protection and Welfare of Children with Special Reference to Foster Placement and Adoption Nationally and Internationally, which states: "[t]he need of a foster or an adopted child to know about his or her background should be recognised by persons responsible for the child's care unless this is contrary to the child's best interests."

[52] The Hague Convention on the Civil Aspects of International Child Abduction, Hague No. 28, was adopted by the Hague Conference on Private International Law on October 25, 1980, and entered into force on December 1, 1983. T.I.A.S. No. 11,670, 1343 U.N.T.S. 89; 19 I.L.M. 1501 (1980). It has a brief Preamble and 45 articles. For an online text, see the HCCH Web site, http://hcch.e-vision.nl/index_en.php?act=conventions.text&cid=24 (last visited July 26, 2007) (unofficial source). For an online description of the Convention and links to other sites and information, see the U.S. Department of State Bureau of Consular Affairs Web site, http://travel.state.gov/family/abduction/hague_issues/hague_issues_578.html (last visited July 26, 2007). For a list of "Party Countries and Effective Dates with U.S.," see http://travel.state.gov/family/abduction/hague issues/hague issues 1487.html (last visited July 26, 2007). See also Gloria Folger DeHart, The Relationship Between the 1980 Child Abduction Convention and the 1996 Protection Convention, 33:1 JOURNAL OF

INTERNATIONAL LAW AND POLITICS 83 (2000), available at http://www3.law.nyu.edu/journals/jilp/issues/33/pdf/33f.pdf. The entire JILP issue is on the 1980 Convention.

[53] The European Convention on the Recognition and Enforcement of Decisions Concerning the Custody of Children, comprising a Preamble and 30 articles, was concluded in Luxembourg on May 20, 1980. E.T.S. No. 105. For an online text, see the COE Web site, http://conventions.coe.int/Treaty/EN/Treaties/Html/105.htm (last visited July 30, 2007).

[54] DETRICK, supra note 7, at 208.

[55] This is because children are rarely in a position to initiate legal proceedings in situations of child abduction. VAN BUEREN, supra note 3, at 90-92.

[56] DETRICK, supra note 7, at 208-209.

[57] The Worst Forms of Child Labour Convention, in a Preamble and 16 articles, was adopted by the General Conference of the International Labour Organisation on June 17, 1999, and entered into force on November 19, 2000. For an online text, see the OHCHR Web site, http://www.ohchr.org/english/law/childlabour.htm (last visited July 30, 2007).

[58] The International Convention for the Protection of All Persons from Forced Disappearance has a Preamble and 45 articles. It was adopted on December 20, 2006. G.A. Res. 61/177, U.N. Doc. A/RES/61/177 (Jan. 24, 2007). For an online text, see 1 RESOLUTIONS AND DECISIONS ADOPTED BY THE GENERAL ASSEMBLY DURING ITS SIXTY-FIRST SESSION: VOLUME I, RESOLUTIONS, 12 SEPTEMBER – 22 DECEMBER 2006 supra note 29, at 408-418, or International Convention for the Protection of All Persons from Forced Disappearance, United Nations Treaty Collection database, available at http://untreaty.un. org/English/notpubl/ IV 16 english.pdf (last visited Dec. 6, 2007).

[59] News Release, NGO Advisory Council for the UN Study on Violence Against Children, International Call for Action to End Violence Against Children: Establish a Special Representative to the UN Secretary General on Violence Against Children (May 18, 2007), Child Rights Information Network, available at http://www.crin. org/resources/infodetail.asp?id=13401; Resolution Adopted by the General Assembly [without Reference to a Main Committee (A/60/L.48)] 60/251, Human Rights Council, the OHCHR Web site, http://www.ohchr.org/ english/bodies/hrcouncil/docs/A.RES.60.251_En.pdf (last visited July 27, 2007).

In: Children's Rights
Editors: Brooke Dabney and Michael Eldridge

ISBN: 978-1-62948-252-1
© 2013 Nova Science Publishers, Inc.

Chapter 3

ARGENTINA: CHILDREN'S RIGHTS[*]

Graciela Rodriguez-Ferrand

EXECUTIVE SUMMARY

The long awaited national Law for the Integral Protection of Children and Adolescents was enacted in 2005 to implement the UN Convention on the Rights of the Child, ratified by Argentina in 1990. In addition to adopting comprehensive protective measures for children, it lays the groundwork for a juvenile justice system, calls for institutionalized children to be integrated back into society, and establishes mechanisms to protect children from abuse and exploitation.

I. INTRODUCTION

Although the last years have seen consistent economic growth and diminished poverty and unemployment rates in Argentina, the rights of some of the most impoverished children have yet to be fully established. About seven percent of the population lives on the equivalent of less than US$1 a day.[1]

Most poor children have no access to the early learning activities that would prepare them for primary school. Primary education is almost universal, and literacy rates are high, but many students repeat grades or drop out of secondary school.[2] Updated statistics about the status of children, which could be used to guide policymakers, are not regularly available.[3]

After years of advocacy, in 2005 a national Law for the Integral Protection of Children and Adolescents was enacted. It lays the basis for a juvenile justice system and calls for institutionalized children to be integrated back into society. Each province will create mechanisms to protect children from abuse and exploitation.[4]

---

[*] This document was released by the Law Library of Congress August 2007.

A national program called *"Plan Familia"* has been launched to assist poor families, ensuring that their children attend school and receive primary health care. The project will eventually reach 500,000 families.[5]

II. IMPLEMENTATION OF INTERNATIONAL RIGHTS OF THE CHILD

Argentina ratified the United Nations Convention on the Rights of the Child[6] (CRC) in 1990, and since 1994, it has been included in the National Constitution.[7] In spite of this very important step, it took some time for the country to engage in a process of legislative reform that would implement the legal and financial commitments undertaken under the CRC towards the protection of children's rights. It was only in 2005 that Congress enacted Law 26061[8] on the Comprehensive Protection of the Rights of Children and Adolescents.

The General Protection System created by Law 26061 is a set of public policies that consider girls, boys, and adolescents as subjects with rights. Its purpose is the comprehensive protection of children and adolescents, in order to guarantee the full exercise and enjoyment of the rights granted under the national legal system and the international treaties to which the country is a party. These rights cover education, health, culture, recreation, and other matters.[9]

This is the first comprehensive statute for the protection of children in the country, with a clear definition of the responsibilities of the family, society, and the government with regard to the universal rights of the children as provided under the CRC. Law 26061 was regulated by Decree 415/2006.[10]

Argentina also ratified the Optional Protocol to the CRC on the Involvement of Children in Armed Conflict[11] and the Optional Protocol to the CRC on the Sale of Children, Child Prostitution and Child Pornography.[12]

III. CHILD HEALTH AND SOCIAL WELFARE

While mortality rates, both maternal and infant, have considerably decreased in recent years, they still remain high, especially with regard to children from a lower socio-economic background; those living in rural or poor areas, in particular in the northern provinces; and indigenous children.[13]

Law 26061 requires that the government and its entities have to provide: a) access to health services while respecting cultural and family standards recognized by the family and society that do not pose a threat to their health and safety;[14] b) comprehensive health, rehabilitation, and integration programs; c) assistance and orientation programs for families; and d) informational campaigns to promote the rights of the child through the media.[15]

The Law also requires health services to be rendered with priority to children, adolescents, and pregnant women.[16]

The lack of financing for social security programs has severely impacted all Argentine health institutions. In addition to overcoming what has been described by the Pan American Health Organization (PAHO) as a sanitary emergency, the gap between the richest and poorest in the society have not been addressed.[17]

The Federal Plan of Health 2004-2007 proposed, among other items, the development of preventive and promotional programs, emphasizing primary care and respecting the growing network of provincial and township level health care programs. It also proposes protecting the financing of established programs.

The Program of Maternal and Infant Health Care protects women and children in populations at risk. It emphasizes prenatal care, care during delivery, and control of the health and development of children. Vaccine coverage increased progressively during the 1980-2002 period. Since 1990, vaccine coverage has been above eighty percent in all provinces, and since 1995 it has been greater than eighty-five percent. In 2002, the national coverage was 93.8% for the Sabin polio vaccine (3rd dose), 92.5% for the Diptheria Pertussis and Tetnus vaccine (3rd dose), and 95% for the measles vaccine.[18]

The program to fight against human retrovirus and AIDS provides to the uninsured population: antiretroviral drugs free of charge, support for the determination of viral load, and development of informative actions directed to the general public, focused on high-risk groups.[19]

IV. EDUCATION

According to the National Law on Education,[20] *Ley Nacional de Educación*, the Argentine education system is structured as follows:

- Initial Education: consisting of kindergartens for children between three and five years of age, and being obligatory for the latter.
- General Basic Education (*EGB*): nine grades of obligatory education. It is understood to be a comprehensive pedagogic unit organized in different cycles.
- Secondary School (*Educación Polimodal*): after finishing the EGB. It has a minimum duration of three years.
- Higher Education: Professional and academic education. Its duration is set by universities or corresponding agencies.
- Special Education: includes initial education, EGB, job pre-training workshops, and job training workshops.[21]

While school enrollment for both primary and secondary education has increased, there is still limited access to education, and there are high drop-out and repetition rates, especially at the secondary school level. Children from marginalized urban and rural areas, indigenous children, and children from migrant families, particularly illegal migrants, are especially affected.[22] Due to economic constrains, the country has suffered a reduction in education spending which also particularly affects poorer children.[23]

In compliance with the commitments under the CRC,[24] Law 26061 regulates the right of the children to education as a fundamental human right.[25] It provides for the right of children to public and free education, to help them reach their full development as human beings and citizens. The right to education must be exercised respecting the children's creativity, culture, and language of origin.[26] The law also secures the right to access to and permanent attendance at an educational facility close to their residence.[27]

In case a child is missing his or her identification documents, the child will be provisionally registered in the educational institution, while the competent authorities proceed to expeditiously provide the child with such documentation.[28]

Children and adolescents with special needs or with disabilities are granted all the rights under the law to a comprehensive education, in addition to the special rights derived from their condition.[29]

Even though neither Law 26061 nor its regulatory Decree 415/06 provides for a definition of child and adolescent, the Civil Code (Codigo Civil de la Republica Argentina y Legislacion Complementaria, 47th ed., LexisNexis Abeledo Perrot, Buenos Aires, 2006, arts. 126-128) does provide for a distinction between minors between fourteen and eighteen years old (*menores impuberes*) and minors between eighteen and twenty-one years old (*menores adultos*), who are assigned a different set of rights.

It is specifically provided that public education is free at all levels, including education for children with special needs.[30]

V. CHILD LABOR AND EXPLOITATION

It has been noted that child protection requires not only adequate laws, but also a committed police force and judiciary to implement them. In addition to good legislation that is properly enforced, the legal environment needs to be child friendly and sensitive to the needs of child victims of commercial sexual exploitation.[31]

Argentina has ratified all the international instruments related to child labor and exploitation, such as the International Labour Organization Convention No. 182 on the Worst Forms of Child Labour (ILO Convention 182)[32] and the Inter-American Convention on International Trafficking of Minors.[33]

Decree No. 719/2000[34] of August 25, 2000, has established the National Commission for the Elimination of Child Labor within the Ministry of Labor, Employment, and Training of Human Resources, in order to coordinate, evaluate, and implement measures aimed at preventing and eliminating child labor. The International Labor Organization (ILO), UNICEF, and the International Program on the Elimination of Child Labor (IPEC) are to act in an advisory capacity to the Commission. Law No. 25072[35] of December 9, 1998, covers the prevention of the ill-treatment of children and adolescents and the topic of domestic violence.

Although Argentina has made considerable advances in its legislation, child labor has increased, in large part due to the economic situation. Child labor is defined as work performed by children outside their homes if the children are aged five to fourteen years. It includes both rural and urban area occupations and does not exclude tasks done for tips or done customarily as assistance to relatives or neighbors.[36]

In 1995, 225,000 children worked, compared with the 482,803 children who worked in 2000, an increase of over ninety-one percent. Using a definition of child labor that considers as work "to do the housework when adults are outside," the number of working children aged five to fourteen increases almost three fold to about 1,503,925.[37]

In 2000, Argentina established a National Plan of Action against the Commercial Sexual Exploitation of Children (*Plan de Acción a Favor de los Derechos de la Infancia Objeto de Explotación Sexual Comercial*).[38] It was developed jointly by the department responsible for

Criminal Policies and Services to the Community within the Office of the Attorney General (*Procuración General de la Nación, Fiscalía General de la Política Criminal y Servicios a la Comunidad*), the Secretariat for Criminal Policies and Penal Affairs in the Ministry of Justice and Human Rights (*Ministerio de Justicia y Derechos Humanos de la Nación, Secretaría de Política Criminal y Asuntos Penitenciarios*), the National Council for Children and the Family (*Consejo Nacional del Menor y la Familia*), and the National Council for Women (*Consejo Nacional de la Mujer*).

The National Plan was developed with six action areas: awareness raising and prevention; information and training; strengthening of networks; strengthening girls, boys, and adolescents; legislation and legal practices; and research. There are specific objectives and activities assigned to each action area.[39]

Argentina also ratified ILO Convention No. 138 concerning Minimum Age for Admission to Employment in 1996, in addition to ILO Convention No. 182 concerning the Prohibition and Immediate Action for the Elimination of the Worst Forms of Child Labor in 2001.[40] In spite of these actions, a growing number of children under fourteen are subject to economic exploitation; the problem is especially serious in particular in rural areas, because of the economic crisis. It has also been noted by writers in the field that there is a lack of data and information with regard to this issue.[41]

The phenomenon of child prostitution, especially in big cities, is increasing. Although the National Plan of Action to Combat Commercial Sexual Exploitation of Children has been in place since 2000, coordinated policies and programs on this issue have yet to be fully funded. Research undertaken for UNICEF Argentina has shown this increase in the extent of child and adolescent prostitution in the country.

While statistics are not available, the research concludes that young persons' participation in prostitution is not insignificant or represented merely in isolated cases. Research has also found that the use of young persons in the production of pornographic materials and sex tourism, as well as in homosexuality and transvestitism for the purposes of prostitution, is not unknown in Argentina."[42]

As a party to the Optional Protocol to the CRC on the involvement of children in armed conflict,[43] Argentina has forbidden the enrollment of children younger than eighteen in armed conflicts, according to a statement included as a declaration at the time of ratification of the Protocol.[44]

VI. SALE AND TRAFFICKING OF CHILDREN

Sale of children, child prostitution, and child pornography are criminalized under a number of pieces of legislation which give effect to relevant international obligations, including the Optional Protocol to the CRC on the Sale of Children, Child Prostitution, and Child Pornography, which was implemented by Law 25087/1999,[45] amending the Criminal Code,[46] as well as Law 26061.[47]

The Criminal Code criminalizes the prostitution of minors of eighteen years of age or younger,[48] but it only sanctions those who "promote or facilitate" prostitution, and not the client who exploits the minor. This approach does not comply with the commitments assumed under the international above-mentioned instruments.[49]

The provisions penalizing child pornography[50] are also deficient and do not fulfill the international law standards, since they do not penalize the possession, import, export, sale, or offer of child pornographic material. Nor is the distribution of such material through the Internet or other virtual means of communication penalized.[51]

The National Counsel for Children, Adolescents, and the Family implements a number of programs to assist children, including programs aimed at the prevention of domestic violence, maltreatment, and sexual abuse of children; the rehabilitation of victims; the provision of legal assistance to child victims and to those in conflict with the law; assistance to children to return home or to return to school; and assistance to parents, to learn about their responsibilities.[52]

VII. JUVENILE JUSTICE

Law 26061 provides that the government has to guarantee both children and adolescents, in addition to all the rights provided by the national constitution, the CRC, and international treaties to which the country is a party, in any judicial or administrative proceeding, the following rights: a) to be heard before a competent authority; b) to have as a primary consideration the child's opinion at the time the decision is made; c) to have legal counsel, preferably specialized in children's issues, from the beginning of the judicial or administrative proceeding and paid for by the government if the child has no economic resources; d) to actively participate throughout the proceedings; and e) to appeal before the superior courts if needed.[53]

In spite of the enactment of Law 26061, the juvenile justice system still needs to be fully reformed to implement the mandates of that Law and of the CRC. The current Law 22278 of 1980,[54] as amended by Law 22803[55] on the Criminal Regime of Minors, does not provide a punitive juvenile regime that considers the special needs of children and adolescents, as well as the necessary measures needed to reinstate that child in society after a criminal violation has occurred.[56]

Law 22278 is based on the doctrine of "irregular situation," and does not make a clear distinction between children in need of care and protection and those in violation of the law. Under the current law, a judge can order the detention of children without due process based only on their social situation, and this decision cannot be appealed.[57]

The conception of childhood under the current Law is thought to be unconstitutional, because it implies that the child is considered an object of "judicial protection," entailing the annulment of all the legal safeguards enjoyed by adults, the judicialization of poverty, and the invention of the "social risk" category as a justification for coactive state intervention.[58]

There is a 2005 draft bill on Juvenile Justice[59] pending Congressional approval that would fulfill these commitments. It establishes limits on juvenile criminal responsibility and procedures to be followed, in accordance with article 40, paragraph 3, of the CRC.[60]

CONCLUSION

The ratification of the CRC by Argentina meant a turning point in the advancement of the rights of children and adolescents in the country. Adverse circumstances, such as the economic and social crisis in the country, however, have resulted in a deterioration of general living conditions in the society at large and for children in particular since the 1990s. The passage of Law 26061 in 2005, on the Comprehensive Protection of the Rights of Children and Adolescents, is another milestone, but a need has been expressed to couple it with a comprehensive new public policy approach towards the child; specific policies, especially on the criminal responsibility of minors with a basic guarantee of due process; and strengthening of institutions so that children are given due priority.[61]

Prepared by Graciela Rodriguez-Ferrand
Senior Foreign Law Specialist
August 2007

End Notes

[1] UNICEF, Argentina, 2007, THE STATE OF THE WORLD'S CHILDREN, available at http://www.unicef.org/infobycountry/ argentina.html.

[2] Id.

[3] Id.

[4] Id.

[5] Plan Familia. PLANES DE GOBIERNO, http://www.presidencia.gov.ar/plan.aspx?cdArticulo=1582 (Web site of the President of Argentina) (last visited Aug. 14, 2007).

[6] LAW 23849 adopting the U.N. Convention on the Rights of the Child, Sept. 27, 1990, BOLETIN OFICIAL (B.O.) Oct. 10, 1990.

[7] CONSTITUCION DE LA NACION ARGENTINA, Buenos Aires, 1994, art. 75, para. 22.

[8] Law 26061 on the Comprehensive Protection of the Rights of Children and Adolescents, Oct. 26, 2005, B.O. Oct. 26, 2005.

[9] Id., art. 1.

[10] Decree 415/2006 on the Regulation of Law 26061, Apr. 17, 2006, B.O. Apr. 18, 2006.

[11] Law 25616 on the Ratification of the Optional Protocol of the CRC on the Involvement of Children in Armed Conflict, July 17, 2002, B.O. Aug. 12, 2002.

[12] Law 25763 on the Ratification of the Optional Protocol of the CRC on the Sale of Children, Child Prostitution and Child Pornography, July 23, 2003, B.O. Aug. 25, 2003.

[13] UNICEF, supra note 1.

[14] Law 26061 on the Comprehensive Protection of the Rights of Children and Adolescents, Oct. 26, 2005, B.O. Oct. 26, 2005, art. 14.

[15] Id.

[16] Id.

[17] PAHO, Argentina, Health Situation and Trends Summary, http://www.paho.org/English/DD/AIS/cp_032.htm (last visited Aug. 15, 2007).

[18] Programa Materno Infantil, http://www.msal.gov.ar/htm/Site/promin/UCMISALUD/index.htm (last visited Aug. 15, 2007).

[19] PAHO, supra note 17.

[20] Law 26206 on National Law on Education, Dec. 14, 2006, B.O. Dec. 28, 2006.

[21] Id.

[22] Netherlands Institute of Human Rights Web site, http://sim.law.uu.nl/SIM/CaseLaw/uncom.nsf/0/3567bf5c 062c819e41256c5d0043aa0b?OpenDocument (last visited Aug. 15, 2007).

[23] Id.

[24] CAMPAÑA ARGENTINA POR EL DERECHO A LA EDUCACIÓN. 22 AL 29 DE ABRIL 2007 SEMANA DE ACCIÓN MUNDIAL, available at http://www.casacidn.org.ar/leer.php/131.

[25] Law 26061 on the Comprehensive Protection of the Rights of Children and Adolescents, Oct. 26, 2005, B.O., Oct. 26, 2005, art. 15.

[26] Id., art. 15.

[27] Id.

[28] Id.

[29] Id.

[30] Id., art. 16.

[31] Informe Global de Monitoreo de las acciones en contra de la explotacion sexual comercial de ninos, ninas y adolescentes -2006, at 18, available at http://www.ecpat.net/eng/A4A 2005/americas.html.

[32] Convention concerning the Prohibition and Immediate Action for the Elimination of the Worst Forms of Child Labour (ILO Convention 182), 38 INT'L LEGAL MATERIALS 1207 (1999) (an unofficial source). Entered into force Nov. 19, 2000. Argentina ratified by Law 25255, July 20, 2000, ratification effective Feb. 5, 2001. Consultado el 13 de septiembre de 2006, available at http://www.ilo.org/ilolex/english/ convdisp1.htm.

[33] InterAmerican Convention on International Trafficking of Minors, available at the OAS Web site, httpwww.oas.org/juridico/spanish/tratados/b-57.html (last visited Aug. 15, 2007). Argentina adhered to the Convention on Feb. 28, 2000, Consultado el 13 de septiembre de 2006, available at http://www.oas.org/juridico/spanish/firmas/b-57.htm.

[34] DECREE 719/2000, Aug. 25, 2000, B.O. Aug. 30, 2000.

[35] LAW 25072 Dec. 9, 1998, B.O. Jan. 11, 1999.

[36] PAHO, supra note 17.

[37] Id.

[38] ECPAT International, Argentina, NATIONAL PLANS OF ACTION, Jan. 9, 2004, available at http://www.ecpat.net/eng/ecpat inter/Country/National plans of action/Argentina.html.

[39] Id.

[40] Law 24650, June 24, 1996, B.O. July 1, 1996. ILO Convention Concerning Minimum Age for Admission to Employment.

[41] Netherlands Institute, supra note 22.

[42] UNICEF, supra note 1.

[43] Law 25616 on the Ratification of the Optional Protocol of the CRC on the Involvement of Children in Armed Conflict, July 17, 2002, B.O. Aug. 12, 2002.

[44] Id.

[45] Law 25087 on the Amendement of the Criminal Code, Apr. 14, 1999, B.O. May 14, 1999.

[46] 1 CODIGO PENAL Y LEYES COMPLEMENTARIAS (6th ed., Editorial Astrea, Buenos Aires, 2007).

[47] Law 26061 on the Comprehensive Protection of the Rights of Children and Adolescents, Oct. 26, 2005, B.O., Oct. 26, 2005, art. 9.

[48] 1 CODIGO PENAL Y LEYES COMPLEMENTARIAS, art. 125 bis (6th ed., Editorial Astrea, Buenos Aires, 2007).

[49] Informe Global de Monitoreo de las acciones en contra de la explotacion sexual comercial de ninos, ninas y adolescentes -2006, available at http://www.ecpat.net/eng/A4A_2005/americas.html.

[50] 1 CODIGO PENAL Y LEYES COMPLEMENTARIAS, art. 128 (6th ed., Editorial Astrea, Buenos Aires, 2007).

[51] Informe Global, supra note 49.

[52] United Nations, Commission on Human Rights, Report Submitted by Mr. Juan Miguel Petit, Special Rapporteur on the Sale of Children, Child Prostitution and Child Pornography, in Accordance with Commission on Human Rights Resolution 2002/92, Jan. 6, 2003, available at http://www.hri.ca/fortherecord2003/ documenttation/commission/e-cn4-2003-79.htm.

[53] Law 26061 on the Comprehensive Protection of the Rights of Children and Adolescents, Oct. 26, 2005, B.O. Oct. 26, 2005, art. 27.

[54] LAW 22278 ON THE CRIMINAL REGIME OF MINORS of Aug. 25, 1980 in B.O. Aug. 28, 1980 as amended by LAW 22803 of May, 5, 1983 in B.O. May 9, 1983.

[55] Id.

[56] E.GARCIA MENDEZ, INFANCIA Y DEMOCRACIA EN LA ARGENTINA, LA CUESTION DE LA RESPONSABILIDAD PENAL DE LOS ADOLESCENTES (Fundacion Sur, Editores del Puerto, 2004).

[57] J.A. VERGARA LUQUE, REGIMEN PENAL DE LA MINORIDAD (Ediciones Juridicas Cuyo, Mendoza, 2004).

[58] The Implementation of the Rights of Children and Adolescents in Argentina. Current Scenario, challenges and recommendtions, COLECTIVO DE ONG'S DE INFANCIA Y ADOLESCENCIA, ARGENTINA, 2002, at 9, available at http://www.oijj.org/contador.php?url=doc/documental 705 en.pdf&&tabla=1&cod= 705&codcont =4217.

[59] REGIMENT LEGAL APLICABLE A LAS PERSONAS MENORES DE 18 ANIOS DE EDAD INFRACTORAS DE LA LEY PENAL, Bill 6789-D-05 in Camara de Diputados, available at http://www1. hcdn.gov.ar/folio-cgi-bin/om_isapi.dll?clientID=2485252296&advquery=6789-D-05&infobase=tp.nfo&   rec ord={AF7B}&softpage=Browse_Frame_Pg42&x=29&y=19&zz=.

[60] Argentina: Report Submitted under article 44 of the CRC in CRC/C/15/Add.187, Oct. 9, 2002.

[61] Comite Argentino de Seguimienbto y Aplicacion de la Convencion Internacional de los Derechos del Nino, Breve Analisis de las politicas de Infancia en Argentina, sus paradigmas y la construccion de la nueva ley, http://www.casacidn.org.ar/leer.php/97 (last visited Aug. 15, 2007).

In: Children's Rights
Editors: Brooke Dabney and Michael Eldridge

ISBN: 978-1-62948-252-1
© 2013 Nova Science Publishers, Inc.

Chapter 4

AUSTRALIA: CHILDREN'S RIGHTS[*]

Lisa White

EXECUTIVE SUMMARY

Australia is a signatory to all significant treaties that impact on children's rights.

The rights and protection of children are governed by both Federal and state and territory law. Persons below the age of eighteen are generally considered children.

Children may be able to give consent to medical procedures where they are either over a statutory age (fourteen to sixteen depending on the jurisdiction), or, of sufficient maturity that they are able to comprehend the procedure and give informed consent.

Children below the age of ten are unable to be charged with a criminal offense and children between the ages of ten to fourteen have a refutable presumption that they are incapable of forming the necessary criminal intent for an offense.

Children below the age of seventeen may not volunteer to join the armed services.

Education of children is compulsory. The age between which children must be educated varies across jurisdictions but is generally between the ages of five to sixteen.

Australian children have a right to access health care via Australia's universal health insurance program and all jurisdictions have additional programs to encourage children and young persons to seek medical care.

I. INTRODUCTION

Australia has a federal constitutional system in which legislative, executive, and judicial powers are shared or distributed between the Federal Government and those of the six States – New South Wales (NSW), Victoria (Vic), Queensland (Qld), South Australia (SA), Tasmania (Tas), and Western Australia (WA) – and two internal self-governing territories – the Australian Capital Territory (ACT) and the Northern Territory (NT).

---

[*] This document was released by the Law Library of Congress August 2007.

Australia includes a number of external territories of these only Norfolk Island and Territory of Cocos (Keeling) Islands and the Territory of Christmas Island, are inhabited.

Of these external territories only Norfolk Island is essentially self-governing (for example, Norfolk Island has its own health and social security systems); the Federal Government, however, retains a veto power over legislation in some areas.

Thus the other external territories (and Norfolk Island in some areas) are governed by federal legislation. In many instances the Federal government has adopted Western Australian legislation and entered into an agreement with the Western Australian government for the Western Australian government to administer the adopted legislation and provide government services to these territories.[1]

Who Is a Child?

Under Australian law the age of majority is eighteen;[2] in many areas of law, however, a person under the age of eighteen may make decisions or be deemed old enough to be legally responsible for their actions.

Government Services for Youths

Federal, state and territory governments offer a range of services specifically aimed at children and young people. Services range from health services to general information and project to increase community participation by children and young people. Details of the programs are available on the Federal government department of Health and Ageing website.[3]

Each state and territory has a government office or statutory authority responsible for the coordination of government policies affecting children and youths.[4]

Three states have established independent bodies to review and advise on issues relevant to children. These are: New South Wales (Commission for Children and Young People);[5] Queensland (Commission for Children and Young People and Children's Guardian);[6] and Tasmania (Commissioner for Children).[7]

Within the Federal government this role is assumed by the Human Rights and Equal Opportunity Commission (HREOC) a national independent statutory government body established under the Human Rights and Equal Opportunity Commission Act 1986 (Cth) (HREOC Act).[8]

II. IMPLEMENTATION OF THE RIGHTS OF THE CHILD

Among other relevant treaties and agreements the following child-specific treaties have entered into force in Australia:

- Convention on the Civil Aspects of International Child Abduction [1987] ATS 2. Entry into force for Australia: 1 January 1987.[9]

- Convention on Protection of Children and Co-operation in respect of Intercountry Adoption (The Hague, 29 May 1993). [1998] ATS 21. Entry into force for Australia: 1 December 1998.[10]
- Convention on the Recognition and Enforcement of Decisions Relating to Maintenance Obligations. [2002] ATS 2. Entry into force for Australia: 1 February 2002.[11]
- Convention on Jurisdiction, Applicable Law, Recognition, Enforcement and Cooperation in respect to Parental Responsibility and Measures for the Protection of Children (under the auspices of the Hague Convention) [2003] ATS 19. Entry into force for Australia: 1 August 2003.[12]
- Optional Protocol to the Convention on the Rights of the Child on the Involvement of Children in Armed Conflict [2006] ATS 12 Entry into force for Australia: 26 October 2006.[13]
- International Convention for the Suppression of the Traffic in Women and Children, 1921. (ATS 1922 no. 10) Entry into force for Australia: 28 June 1922.
- Protocol to amend the Convention for the Suppression of the Traffic in Women and Children of 30 September 1921, and the Convention for the Suppression of the Traffic in Women of Full Age, 1933, (ATS 1947 No. 17). Entry into force for Australia 24 April 1950.
- Convention on the Rights of the Child [1991] ATS 4. Entry into force for Australia: 16 January 1991.[14]
- Optional Protocol to the Convention on the Rights of the Child on the Sale of Children, Child Prostitution and Child Pornography [2007] ATS 6. Entry into force for Australia, 8 February 2007.[15]
- Protocol To Prevent, Suppress And Punish Trafficking In Persons, Especially Women And Children, Supplementing The United Nations Convention Against Transnational Organised Crime 2000 [2005] ATS 27. Entry into force for Australia: 14 October 2005.[16]

III. Child Health and Social Welfare Family Law

In determining family law matters the Family Court will consider the wishes of a child when determining what is "in the best interests of the child." The "best interests of the child" will be the court's paramount consideration when making parenting, location and recovery orders.[17]

In some jurisdictions children's rights and the child's right to participate in decision making have been specifically incorporated into legislation. For example: in Queensland, a 'Charter of Rights for Child in Care' is included as a schedule to the Child Protection Act 1999 (Qld),[18]

NSW has non-binding principles for children to participate in decision making regarding their care and protection.[19]

General Access to Health Care

Australia has a universal health insurance program called Medicare.[20] People (including children) who reside in Australia (excluding Norfolk Island) are eligible to participate in Medicare if they:

- hold Australian citizenship;
- have been issued a permanent visa;
- hold New Zealand citizenship; or
- have applied for a permanent visa (excluding an application for a parent visa). Norfolk Island does not participate in the Medicare program.

Medicare is funded by the Federal government from general revenue and partially funded via a taxation surcharge for those earning above a specified income threshold. This surcharge is discounted if the taxpayer has private health insurance.

Medicare provides free medical treatment as a public patient in a public hospital and free or subsidized treatment for some medical and optometrist services and dental care. Medicare may also support (via partial rebate of practitioner's fees) treatments by allied health professionals such as physiotherapists, dietitians, and speech pathologists.[21]

Australian states and territories have the primary responsibility for Australia's public hospital systems; the Federal government, however, has the power to pass legislation for sickness and hospital benefits and therefore contributes to the funding of hospitals.[22] Licensing of private hospitals is undertaken by states or territories while some regulatory power is retained by the Federal government via its power to authorize the hospital to receive health insurance benefits.[23]

Federal funding of state and territory hospitals is governed by Australian Health Care Agreements signed between each state or territory and the Commonwealth.[24] These agreements identify the amount of Federal funding that will be provided to the state or territory's hospital system and require that: public hospital services be provided free of charge to public patients; access to public hospital services be on the basis of clinical need and within a clinically appropriate period; and that equitable access to public hospital services be provided regardless of geographical location.[25]

Australia has several specialist hospitals that are dedicated to provide pediatric and neonatal.care.[26]

Access by Youths to Medical Services

All states and territories have initiatives designed to encourage children and young people to seek healthcare. In many instances individual health centers will not require a child or young person to pay or to provide their Medicare card (thus permitting children or young people to seek healthcare in the absence of parental knowledge).[27]

The Federal, state, and territory governments have (in conjunction) undertaken several immunization programs that are directly relevant to children and young people. These include:[28]

- human papillomavirus (HPV) vaccination program;
- meningococcal C program;
- chickenpox (varicella) program;
- pneumococcal program; and
- Hepatitis A program (for Aboriginal and Torres Strait Islander children in the NT, WA, SA and QLD).

The following vaccines are recommended and provided free of charge:

- Hepatitis B;
- Diphtheria, tetanus and whooping cough (pertussis);
- Hib (*Haemophilus influenzae* type b);
- polio;
- measles, mumps and rubella (German measles); and
- rotavirus

The following vaccines are also free of charge for Aboriginal and Torres Strait Islander children:

- pneumococcal; and
- Hepatitis A.

Consent to Medical Treatment

The age of consent for medical treatment differs across jurisdictions; for example, in Western Australia the age of consent remains at eighteen[29] (the general age of majority in Australia), in NSW and South Australia, however, the age of consent for making decisions regarding medical treatment has been amended by legislation to fourteen and sixteen respectively.[30]

Generally treatment provided to children below the age of sixteen requires the consent of their parents or guardians. Parents may only consent to treatement that is in the best interests of the child.[31]

In all jurisdictions the consent of the child alone may be sufficient in circumstances where the child has "sufficient understanding and intelligence to enable him or her to understand fully what is proposed" (Gillick test).[32] In South Australia this test has been modified by statute to be: if the child consents, and (1) the medication practitioner is satisfied that the child is capable of understanding the nature, consequences, and risks of the treatment, and that the treatment is in the best interests of the child's health and wellbeing; (2) and that this opinion of the medical practitioner is supported by the written opinion of another medical practitioner who has also examined the child.[33]

A parent may not consent to certain treatments of children. Where a treatment involves major, invasive and irreversible surgery (not for the purpose of curing a malfunction or disease, e.g. sterilization or gender reassignment), neither a child nor a parent may consent and it is necessary to obtain the consent of both the court[34] and the parents.[35]

Children should only participate in medical research with the consent of both the child and the parent in circumstances where the research is not contrary to the best interests of the child.[36]

Mortality Rates

In its 2007 report The State of the World's Children' UNICEF has provided the following statistics on Australia:[37]

Under-5 mortality rate, 200538	Infant mortality rate (under 1), 200539	Neonatal mortality rate, 200040
6	5	3

Financial Support to People with Children

The Federal government provides financial support to people with children (called family assistance). This financial support includes:

- Family Tax Benefit Part A – financial assistance;
- Family Tax Benefit Part B – additional financial assistance to families with one income;
- Child Care Benefit – financial assistance for child care;
- Child Care Tax Rebate – tax rebate for working persons incurring child care costs;
- Baby Bonus – one-off payment to off-set the costs of a new child (including adopted and still born children);
- Maternity Immunisation Allowance - payment for children aged eighteen to twenty-four months and who are fully immunized or have an approved exemption from immunization;
- Large Family Supplement – where the applicant has three or more children and receives the Family Tax Benefit for three or more children;
- Multiple Birth Allowance – applicable for births of three or more children;
- Double Orphan Pension – additional financial aid to provide assistance to raise children who are orphans;
- Jobs, Education and Training (JET) Child Care fee assistance – extra help with the cost of approved child care for eligible parents undertaking activities such as work, job search, training, study or rehabilitation as part of an activity agreement, to help them enter or re-enter the workforce.

IV. EDUCATION, INCLUDING SPECIAL NEEDS

Child Care – General

Capital grants for non-profit child care centers and for research into child care centers may be funded by the Federal government.[41] Child care services are jointly funded by Federal and state/territory governments.[42]

Preschool education is the responsibility of the states and territories, and services are provided by government, community and private providers. The Australian Government provides some funding for Indigenous preschool services.[43]

Education - General

Australian schooling varies across each state and territory; in general, however, schooling consists of a preparatory year followed by twelve years of primary and secondary school. In the final year of secondary school (year twelve) students study for a government endorsed certificate that is recognized by all Australian universities and vocational education and training institutions. School hours are Monday to Friday generally from 9:00am to 3:30pm.[44]

Australia has developed a national curriculum framework across eight "Key Learning Areas": English, Mathematics, Studies of Society and the Environment, Science, Arts, Languages Other Than English, Technology and Personal Development, Health and Physical Education.[45]

Funding of Australian schools (both public and private) is from both state and territory governments and the Federal Government.[46] Federal government funding of schools is legislated for four year periods.[47]

State and territory legislation, in general, will govern matters such as: the obligation of the state to provide public education;[48] the compulsory curriculum;[49] compulsory attendance at school and exemption for attendance at certain classes;[50] government schools, including: their establishment[51] and obligation to provide free instruction,[52] their format (such as primary, secondary, for disability children, for advanced children, or focusing on technology or agriculture),[53] their secular and religious education,[54] admission[55] and discipline;[56] registration of non-government schools and home schooling;[57] and certificates of education or study to be awarded.[58]

Relevant Legislation

Primary state and territory legislation governing education are as follows:

Australian Capital Territory: Education Act 2004 (ACT); Education Regulation 2005 (ACT).

New South Wales: Education Act 1990 (NSW); Education Regulations 2001 (NSW).

Northern Territory: Education Act (NT); Education (Board of Studies) Regulations (NT), Education (College and School Councils) Regulations (NT).

Queensland: Education (General Provisions) Act 2006 (QLD); Education (General Provisions) Regulation 2006 (QLD); Education (Accreditation of Non-State Schools) Act 2001 (QLD); Education (Accreditation of Non-State Schools) Regulation 2001 (QLD); Education (Capital Assistance) Act 1993 (QLD); Education (Capital Assistance) Regulation 2005 (QLD); Education (Overseas Students) Act 1996 (QLD); Education (Overseas Students) Regulation 1998 (QLD); Education (Queensland Studies Authority) Act 2002 (QLD); Education (Queensland Studies Authority) Regulation 2002 (QLD).

South Australia: Education Act 1972 (SA); Education (Councils - Transitional) Regulations 2001 (SA); Education (Registration of Non-Government Schools) Regulations 1998 (SA); Education Regulations 1997(SA).

Tasmania: Education Act 1994 (Tas); Education Regulations 2005 (Tas); Education Providers Registration (Overseas Students) Act 1991 (Tas); Education Providers Registration (Overseas Students) Regulations 2005 (Tas).

Victoria: Education and Training Reform Act 2006 (Vic); Education and Training Reform Regulations 2007 (Vic).

Western Australia: School Education Act 1999 (WA); School Education Regulations 2000 (WA); Education Service Providers (Full Fee Overseas Students) Registration Act 1991 (WA); Education Service Providers (Full Fee Overseas Students) Registration Regulations 1992 (WA).

Federal: Australian Technical Colleges (Flexibility in Achieving Australia's Skills Needs) Act 2005 (establishes Australian Technical Colleges for Year 11 and Year 12 students); Student Assistance Act 1973 (Cth) (funds the student financial assistance schemes, ABSTUDY and the Assistance for Isolated Children Scheme); Indigenous Education (Targeted Assistance) Act 2000 (Cth) (legislative basis and appropriates funding for Indigenous education programs); Education Services for Overseas Students Act 2000 (Cth) (regulates the education and training sector's involvement with overseas students studying in Australia on student visas); Education Services for Overseas Students Regulations 2001 (Cth).

Education - Special Needs

In accordance with the Disability Discrimination Act 1992 (Cth) (DDA) it is unlawful for any person (including a child) to be discriminated against by an educational authority on the basis of a disability. Educational authority includes: all public and private educational institutions, primary and secondary schools, and tertiary institutions such as "Technical and Further Education" (TAFE),[59] private colleges and universities. Generally the DDA covers discrimination in the areas of admission, access, and harassment.

Disability Standards for Education 2005 (Cth),[60] made under the DDA, are legal standards applicable to education providers to ensure their compliance with the DDA. The Standards cover the following areas:

- enrollment (Part 4);
- participation (Part 5);
- curriculum development, accreditation and delivery (Part 6); and
- student support services (Part 7).

The Standards also require education providers to develop policies and programs that eliminate harassment and victimization.[61]

In general neither the DDA nor the Disability Standards for Education Standards require changes to be made where such changes would impose unjustifiable hardship on a person or organization.[62]

V. CHILD LABOR AND EXPLOITATION

Employment of Children

The minimum age of employment and regulation of children in employment varies across each state and territory.[63]

For example NSW has no minimum age of employment and employment of children is only regulated in certain industries.[64] Thus, in NSW, employment of children under fifteen years of age in entertainment, exhibition, still photography or door-to-door sales is regulated by the Office for Children - Children's Guardian (OCCG).[65] Employers in these industries must be authorized to employ children and comply with the legislated Code of Practice.[66]

In contrast, Victoria has a minimum age of employment and children below the age of thirteen may not be employed generally (exceptions exist for family businesses, entertainment industry and children above the age of eleven delivering newspapers, advertising material or delivers for a registered pharmacist), and any employed child (including children within family businesses) must only perform 'light work', work certain hours and be granted specified rest periods.[67]

Children within the Australian Defence Force (ADF)

The ADF maintains a minimum voluntary recruitment age of seventeen years (with exceptions for entrants to military schools, apprentices and members of Service cadet programs).[68] All personnel wishing to join the ADF must provide evidence of their age and all minors require written informed consent from their parents or guardians.[69] ADF commanders are directed to take all feasible measures to ensure that minors do not participate in hostilities.[70]

VI. SALE AND TRAFFICKING OF CHILDREN

Criminal law is governed by both Federal and state and territory law. Therefore offenses against children will be a crime under both federal and state and territory law.

Under Federal law it is an offense to traffic in children, and slavery and sexual servitude are offenses with victims under the age of eighteen being an aggravating circumstance,[71] for example:

- trafficking (domestic or international) of children. Maximum penalty of twenty-five years imprisonment.[72]
- slavery. Maximum penalty of twenty-five years imprisonment;[73]
- sexual servitude – where a person is engaged to provide sexual services subject to force or threats and is not free to cease or leave: Maximum penalty fifteen years imprisonment, or nineteen years if the victim is under eighteen years of age;[74] and
- deceptive recruiting – where a person deceptively induces another person to provide sexual services. Maximum penalty seven years imprisonment, or nine years if the victim is under eighteen years of age.[75]

It is also an offense to: supply drugs (or other controlled substances) to children or to children for the purposes of trafficking,[76] to procure children to traffic drugs,[77] to expose children (below the age of fourteen) to the unlawful manufacture of drugs,[78] or to use a carriage service to possess, control, produce, supply or obtain child pornography or child abuse material, or use a carriage service to procure or groom a child (below the age of sixteen).[79]

It is also an offense of genocide to forcibly transfer children,[80] and a war crime to use, conscript or enlist children below the age of fifteen.[81]

VII. Juvenile Justice

The standard age for criminal responsibility in all Australian jurisdictions is ten years of age.[82] For children between the ages of ten and fourteen years there is a refutable presumption that they are incapable of forming the criminal intent necessary to be guilty of a crime (*doli incapax*).[83]

Criminal law and procedure varies across each jurisdiction in Australia, generally, however, there are separate laws, procedures and courts for children.[84] For example, in NSW, any statement, confession, admission, or information made by a child to police without the presence of their guardian, lawyer, or other responsible adult is presumptively not admissible as evidence and may only be admitted where the court is satisfied that there was sufficient reason for the absence of the adult and that with, after consideration of all the circumstances, the statement or information should be admitted as evidence.[85]

Children are prosecuted and sentenced in a children's court in relation to crimes committed when a child,[86] or may be processed via alternative proceedings such as youth justice conferences, cautions, and warnings.[87] Criminal proceedings against a child can not commence until the Court has explained to the child the nature of any allegations made against the child, and the facts that must be established before the child can be found guilty of the offence with which the child is charged.[88]

Traditionally criminal proceedings against a child are not open to the public and names are suppressed from publication.[89] A person under the age of twenty-one may be sentenced to a term of imprisonment as a 'juvenile offender' that is to serve all or part of their imprisonment within a juvenile detention facility.[90] Children may also be subject to community service orders (including an order to remove graffiti).[91]

Convictions of children of summary offenses below the age of sixteen are not recorded and the court has discretion whether or not to record convictions of summary offenses of children aged between sixteen and eighteen and convictions of indictable offenses of children below the age of sixteen.[92]

Prepared by Lisa White
Foreign Law Specialist
August 2007

End Notes

[1] Western Australia is the closest state to the external territories of Cocos (Keeling) Territory and Christmas Island Territory. see: Department of Foreign Affairs and Trade, AUSTRALIA'S COMBINED SECOND AND THIRD REPORTS UNDER THE CONVENTION ON THE RIGHTS OF THE CHILD MARCH 2003, available at http://www.dfat.gov.au/hr/downloads/australia_2nd_3rd_reports_convention_rights_child.pdf, p.3.

[2] For example, see Minors (Property and Contracts) Act 1970 (NSW) § 9; Age of Majority Act 1974 (Qld) § 5(2).

[3] See http://www.health (last visited July 25, 2007).

[4] Victoria: Office for Youth, Department of Victorian Committees, see http://www.youth.vic.gov.au (last visited July 25, 2007); South Australia: Office for Youth, Government of South Australia, see http://svc031.wic138 dp.serverweb.com/youth/Home/tabid/161/Default.aspx (last visited July 25, 2007); Australian Capital Territory, Office for Children, Youth and Family, Department of Disability, Housing and Community Services. Northern Territory: Office of Youth Affairs, Department of Chief Minister, see http://www.nt. gov.au/dcm/youth_affairs/home.shtml (last visited July 25, 2007).

[5] The Commission for Children and Young People is an independent organization that administers the Commission for Children and Young People Act 1998 (NSW) and reports directly to the NSW Parliament

[6] See Commission for Children and Young People and Child Guardian website at: http://www.ccypcg.qld.gov .au/index.html (last visited Aug. 3, 2007).

[7] See Commissioner for Children Tasmania website, http://www.childcomm.tas.gov.au/ (last visited Aug. 2, 2007).

[8] Further information on HREOC is available from their website.

[9] Opened for signature Oct. 25, 1980, T.I.A.S. No. 11670, 1343 U.N.T.S. 89 (entered into force Dec. 1, 1983), 19 Int'l Legal Materials 1501 (1980). Available from the Hague Conference on Private International Law website at: http://hcch.evision.nl/index_en.php?act=conventions.text&cid=24 (last visited Aug. 6, 2007).

[10] Opened for signature May 29, 1993, 1870 U.N.T.S. 167 (entered into force May 1, 1995), 32 Int'l Legal Materials 1139 (1993). Available from the Hague Conference on Private International Law website at: http://hcch.e-vision.nl/index_en.php?act=conventions.text&cid=69&zoek=children (last visited Aug, 6, 2007).

[11] 1021 U.N.T.S. 209, 11 Int'l Legal Materials 1286 (1972). Also available from the Hague Conference on Private International Law website at: http://hcch.e-vision.nl/index_en.php?act=conventions.text&cid= 38&zoek= children (last visited Aug. 6, 2007).

[12] Available from the Hague Conference on Private International Law website at: http://hcch.evision.nl/index en.php?act=conventions.text&cid=70&zoek=children (last visited Aug. 6, 2007).

[13] G.A. Res. 54/263, U.N. Doc. A/RES/54/263 (May 25, 2000), 39 Int'l Legal Materials 1285 (2000). Available from the United Nations Office of the High Commissioner for Human Rights website at: http://www.unhchr. ch/html/menu2/6/protocolchild.htm (last visited Aug. 6, 2007).

[14] G.A. Res. 44/25, annex, 44 U.N. GAOR Supp. (No. 49), at 167, U.N. Doc A/44/49 (1989). 28 Int'l Legal Materials 1456 (1989). Available from the United Nations Office of the High Commissioner for Human Rights website at: http://www.ohchr.org/english/law/crc.htm (last visited July 23, 2007).

[15] G.A. Res. 54/263, U.N. GAOR, 54th Sess., Annex II, U.N. Doc. A/RES/54/263 (May 25, 2000). Available from the United Nations Office of the High Commissioner for Human Rights website, http://www.ohchr.org/ english/law/crc-sale.htm (last visited Aug. 6, 2007).

[16] G.A. Res. 55/25 (Nov. 15, 2000). Available from the United Nations Office of the High Commissioner for Human Rights website, http://www.ohchr.org/english/law/protocoltraffic.htm (last visited Aug. 6, 2007).

[17] Family Law Act 1975 (Cth) §§ 60B, 65CA, 67L, 67V, & 68F.

[18] Child Protection Act 1999 (Qld) Sch. 1.

[19] Children and Young Persons (Care and Protection) Act 1998 (NSW) § 9.

[20] Medicare Australia Act 1973 (Cth).

[21] Under the Enhanced Primary Care program, fees to visit some allied health practitioners and some dental visits will be rebated by Medicare where the allied health professional or dentist is registered with Medicare and the patient's attendance at the allied health professional is recommended by the patient's general practitioner in relation to a chronic condition or complex health need or dental problem that is aggravating a chronic medical condition. See: Australian Government Department of Health and Ageing website, http://www.health.gov.au/epc (last visited July 24, 2007).

[22] Australian Constitution § 51(xxiiiA); Health Care (Appropriation) Act 1998 (Cth).

[23] National Health Act 1953 (Cth); Health Insurance Act 1973 (Cth).

[24] See Australian Government, Department of Health and Ageing website, http://www.health.gov.au/internet/wcms/Publishing.nsf/Content/Australian+Health+Care+Agreements-1 (last visited Aug. 1, 2007).

[25] See Australian Health Care Agreement between the Commonwealth of Australia and the Australian Capital Territory 2003-2008 Part 2, available at http://www.health.gov.au/internet/wcms/publishing.nsf/ Content/ B02C99D554742175CA256F18004FC7A6/$File/australian capitalterritory.pdf. See also Health Care (Appropriate) Act 1998 (Cth).

[26] For information on Australia's specialist hospitals, see Australian Government website HealthInsite, http://www.healthinsite.gov.au/topics/Children_s_Hospitals. (last visited Aug. 3, 2007).

[27] Called 'innovative health services for homeless youth' (IHSHY), funding provided by the Federal Government is matched by State and Territory Governments for the purpose of providing health services for homeless and at risk young people. Details of locations and services provided are available on the Australian Government Department of Health and Aging website, http://www.health.gov.au/internet/wcms/ publishing.nsf/ Content/health-pubhlth-strateg-youth-ihshya.htm#act (last visited July 25, 2007).

[28] See Australian Government, Department of Health and Ageing: Immunisation programs and initiatives: Children website, http://www.immunise.health.gov.au/internet/immunise/publishing.nsf/Content/programs#children (last visited Aug.2, 2007).

[29] Age of Majority Act 1972 (WA) § 5. Also see: Western Australian Government, CONSENT TO TREATMENT POLICY FOR THE WESTERN AUSTRALIAN HEALTH SYSTEM, Department of Health 2006, available at http://www.safetyandquality.health

[30] Minors (Property and Contracts) Act 1970 (NSW) § 49; Consent to Medical Treatment and Palliative Care Act 1995 (SA) s 6.

[31] Department of Health and Community Services v JWB and SMB (Marion´s case) (1992), 175 CLR 218 at 240.

[32] Gillick v West Norfolk AHA (1986), AC 112 (HL) approved by the High Court of Australia in Department of Health and Community Services v JWB and SMB (Marion´s case) (1992), 175 CLR 218. See: M. Harrison, What's New in Family Law? Parental Authority and its Constraints the Case of 'Marion', FAMILY MATTERS no.32 August 1992, pp.10- 12, available from the Australian Institute of Family Studies, http://www.aifs.gov.au/institute/pubs/fm1/fm32mh.html (last visited August 3, 2007).

[33] Consent to Medical Treatment and Palliative Care Act 1995 (SA) § 12:

[34] The relevant court will be a court exercising jurisdiction under the Family Law Act 1975 (Cth) or as authorized by legislation, e.g., New South Wales Guardianship Tribunal, granted jurisdiction to consent to the carrying out of a "special medical treatment" by the Children and Young Persons (Care and Protection) Act 1998 (NSW) § 175.

[35] Gillick v West Norfolk AHA (1986), AC 112 (HL) approved by the High Court of Australia in Department of Health and Community Services v JWB and SMB (Marion´s case) (1992), 175 CLR 218.

[36] Australian Government, National Health and Research Council, Human Research Ethics Handbook, Commonwealth, Australia, 2001 NS 4.1 available at the National Health and Resaerch Council website at: http://www.nhmrc.gov.au/publications/hrecbook/misc/contents.htm.

[37] Available from the UNICEF website, http://www.unicef.org/sowc07/docs/sowc07.pdf (last visited Aug. 2, 2007).

[38] Under-five mortality rate - Probability of dying between birth and exactly five years of age expressed per 1,000 live births.

[39] Infant mortality rate - Probability of dying between birth and exactly one year of age expressed per 1,000 live births.

[40] Neonatal mortality rate – Probability of dying during the first 28 completed days of life expressed per 1,000 live births.

[41] Child Care Act 1972 (Cth).

[42] State and territory governments generally fund and regulate kindergartens (year before school), centre-based long day care and occasional care services, while the Federal government is responsible for the national child care

policy and funds long day care childcare places and provides subsidies for family day care arrangements and outside school hours care via the Child Care Benefit. For example see State Government of Victoria, Department of Human Services, Office for Children website, http://www.office-for-children.vic.gov.au/childrens-services/home (last visited Aug. 3, 2007).

[43] See Australian Parliament Library, Social Policy Resources: Education and Training Resources Guide, http://www.aph.gov.au/library/intguide/sp/speducation.htm#39 (last visited Aug. 2, 2007).

[44] Australian Government, Study in Australia, : http://www.studyinaustralia.gov.au/Sia/en/What ToStudy/ Schools/ SchoolSystem.htm (last visited Aug. 3, 2007).

[45] Id.

[46] Australian Government, School Education Summary, http://www.dest.gov.au/sectors/school_education/School_education_summary2.htm (last visited Aug. 3, 2007).

[47] Schools Assistance (Learning Together Achievement through Choice and Opportunity) Act 2004 (Cth); Schools Assistance Regulations 2005 (Cth).

[48] Education Act 1990 (NSW) § 4.

[49] Id §§ 7-18A.

[50] Id §§ 22-26.

[51] Id § 27.

[52] Id § 31.

[53] Id § 29.

[54] Id §§ 30, 32, 33.

[55] Id § 34.

[56] Id § 35.

[57] Id §§ 37 -83.

[58] Id §§ 84-96.

[59] "Technical and Further Education" is the designation for a preparatory course for or a course in trade, technical, or other skilled occupations. Technical and Further Education Commission Act 1990 (NSW); also Employment, Education and Training Act 1988 (Cth) § 3(1).

[60] Standards are subordinate legislation in accordance with Disability Discrimination Act 1992 (Cth) § 31, available att ComLaw website, http://www.comlaw.gov.au/ComLaw/Legislation/ LegislativeInstrument1.nsf/0/CB9CCD31BB70C3ADCA256FD50023EA BF/$file/F2005L00767.pdf.

[61] Disability Standards for Education 2005 (Cth) Part 8.

[62] Id. Standard 10.1.

[63] Workplace Relations Act 1996 (Cth) § 16(2).

[64] In addition NSW has regulated employment of children under the federal employment legislation to ensure they do not suffer detriment from being employed under the federal system rather than under a NSW award. Industrial Relations (Child Employment) Act 2006 (NSW) Pt 2. As has Queensland and South Australia see: Child Employment Act 2006 (Qld); Child Employment Regulation 2006 (Qld); Fair Work Act 1994 (SA) § 98A; Child Labour Award 2006 (SA).

[65] Children and Young Persons (Care and Protection) Act 1988 (NSW), Chp. 13 & Sch. 2; Children and Young Persons (Care and Protection – Child Employment) Regulation 2005 (NSW). Also see: NSW Office of Children's Guardian website at: http://www.kidsguardian.nsw.gov.au/child_employment.php (last visited July 31, 2007).

[66] Children and Young Persons (Care and Protection – Child Employment) Regulation 2005 (NSW

[67] Child Employment Act 2003 (Vic).

[68] Defence Instruction (General) PERS 33–4 (4 July 2005) (DI(G) PERS 33-4). Issue No. Pers B/9/2005/, NAVY PERS 61–4; ARMY PERS 116–17; AIR FORCE PERS 29–30 § 4, available at http://www.defencejobs.gov.au/mediaUpload/mediaUpload/RecruitmentandEmploymentofMembersUnder18inADF.pdf (last visited Aug. 1, 2007).

[69] DI(G) PERS 33-4 §§ 5,6.

[70] DI(G) PERS 33-4 § 10.

[71] Criminal Code Act 1995 (Cth).

[72] Id §§ 271.4, 271.7.

[73] Id § 270.3.

[74] Id §§ 270.6, 270.8.

[75] Id §§ 270.7, 270.8.

[76] Id §§ 309.2-309.4, 311.6, 311.17-21.

[77] Id §§ 309.4, 309.7, 309.8, 309.12, 309.13, 309.14 & 309.15.

[78] Id §§ 310.1-310.4.

[79] Id §§ 474.19, 474.20, 474.23, 474.26 & 474.27.

[80] Id § 268.7.

[81] Id §§ 268.68, 268.88.

[82] For example, see Crimes Act 1914 (Cth) § 4M; Criminal Code Act 1995 (Cth) § 7.1; Criminal Code 2002 (ACT) §25; Children (Criminal Proceedings) Act 1987 (NSW) § 5; Criminal Code Act (NT) § 38(1); Criminal Code Act 1899 (Qld) § 29(1); Young Offenders Act 1993 (SA) § 5; Criminal Code Act 1924 (Tas) § 18(1); Children and Young Persons Act 1989 (SA) § 127; Criminal Code Act Compilation Act 1913 (WA) § 29. Also see: Australian Government, Australian Institute of Criminology, Crime Fact Info. No. 106 THE AGE OF CRIMINAL RESPONSIBILITY, Sept. 13, 2005, available at http://www.aic.gov.au/publications/ cfi/cfi106. pdf.

[83] Crimes Act 1914 (Cth) § 4N, Criminal Code Act 1995 (Cth) § 7.2. In some jurisdictions this is common law, for example in South Australia, Victoria and New South Wales, ie. established by case law. See: R v CRH 18/12/96 Court of Criminal Appeal, NSW. 2(b) Criminal Code 2002 (ACT) §26; Criminal Code Act (NT) § 38(2); Criminal Code Act 1899 (Qld) § 29(2); Criminal Code Act 1924 (Tas) § 18(2); Criminal Code Act Compilation Act 1913 (WA) § 29.

[84] There are provisions protect children who are victims during criminal proceedings. For example see: Protection of children in proceedings for sexual offences, Criminal Act 1914 (Cth) Part IAD.

[85] Children (Criminal Proceedings) Act 1987 (NSW) § 13.

[86] For example: Children's Court Act 1987 (NSW). See: Children (Criminal Proceedings) Act 1987 (NSW) § 28 for jurisdiction of the children's court. In NSW the Children's Court does not have jurisdiction over proceedings in relation to an unrelated traffic offense or a 'serious children's indictable offence', eg. homicide or an offence punishable by imprisonment for life or for 25 years.

[87] Young Offenders Act 1997 (NSW).

[88] Children (Criminal Proceedings) Act 1987 (NSW) §§ 12(1), (2).

[89] Id. §§ 10, 11.

[90] Children (Detention Centres) Act 1987 (NSW).

[91] Children (Community Service Orders) Act 1987 (NSW).

[92] Children (Criminal Proceedings) Act 1987 (NSW) § 14.

In: Children's Rights
Editors: Brooke Dabney and Michael Eldridge
ISBN: 978-1-62948-252-1
© 2013 Nova Science Publishers, Inc.

Chapter 5

BRAZIL: CHILDREN'S RIGHTS*

Eduardo Soares

EXECUTIVE SUMMARY

The Constitution provides the principles to be followed for the protection of children and adolescents in Brazil. These principles, coupled with numerous international treaties and several pieces of enacted legislation, offer a wide range of protection for children's and adolescents' rights.

I. INTRODUCTION

This report covers the international treaties to which Brazil is a signatory in the field of protection of children and presents a summary of the relevant legislation enacted, including Constitutional principles, in the areas of child health and social welfare, child education, child labor and exploitation, sale and trafficking of children, and juvenile justice.

II. IMPLEMENTATION OF INTERNATIONAL RIGHTS OF THE CHILD

Brazil is a founding member of the United Nations (UN) and a signatory of the Universal Declaration of Human Rights, which was adopted and proclaimed by General Assembly resolution 217A(III) of December 10, 1948.[1] Article 25(2) of the Universal Declaration enunciates that motherhood and childhood are entitled to special care and assistance and that all children, whether born in or out of wedlock, shall enjoy the same social protection.

In 1959, this theme was expanded and the UN proclaimed by General Assembly resolution 1386(XIV) of November 20, 1959, the Declaration of the Rights of the Child.[2] The declaration

---

* This document was released by the Law Library of Congress January 2009.

served as the basis for the future Convention on the Rights of the Child,[3] which would be adopted, thirty years later, by UN General Assembly resolution 44/25 of November 20, 1989.

On November 21, 1990, Brazil issued Decree[4] No. 99,710,[5] ratifying Legislative Decree No. 28 of September 14, 1990, which approved the UN Convention on the Rights of the Child, fully incorporating it onto Brazil's positive law. Additionally, on March 8, 2004, Brazil issued Decree No. 5,007,[6] promulgating the UN Optional Protocol to the Convention on the Rights of the Child on the Sale of Children, Child Prostitution, and Child Pornography[7] and Decree No. 5,006,[8] promulgating the UN Optional Protocol to the Convention on the Rights of the Child on the Involvement of Children in Armed Conflict.[9]

Brazil also ratified the International Covenant on Civil and Political Rights of 1966,[10] and on July 6, 1992, this covenant was promulgated through Decree No. 592.[11] On September 13, 2002, Brazil issued Decree No. 4,377,[12] promulgating the Convention on the Elimination of All Forms of Discrimination against Women,[13] and on July 30, 2002, issued Decree No. 4,316,[14] promulgating the Optional Protocol to the Convention on the Elimination of All Forms of Discrimination against Women.[15]

At the Organization of American States, Brazil is a State-party to the Inter-American Convention on the International Return of Children,[16] adopted in Montevideo on July 15, 1989, and to this effect issued, on August 3, 1994, Decree No. 1,212,[17] promulgating the Convention. Brazil approved the Inter-American Convention on Conflict of Laws Concerning the Adoption of Minors[18] on June 19, 1996, through Legislative Decree No. 60, and then promulgated it by Decree No. 2,429 of December 17, 1997.[19] On August 20, 1998, Brazil also issued Decree No. 2,740,[20] promulgating the Inter-American Convention on International Traffic in Minors.[21]

Decree No. 3,087 of June 21, 1999,[22] promulgated the Hague Convention on Protection of Children and Cooperation in Respect of Inter-Country Adoption,[23] and Decree No. 3,413 of April 14, 2000,[24] promulgated the Hague Convention on the Civil Aspects of International Child Abduction.[25] Additionally, on September 16, 1999, Brazil issued Decree No. 3,174,[26] which designated the central authorities in charge of carrying out the duties imposed by the Hague Convention on Protection of Children and Cooperation in Respect of Inter-Country Adoption; instituted the National Program on Cooperation on International Adoption; and created the National Council of Brazilian Central Administrative Authorities.

On September 12, 2000, Brazil issued Decree No. 3,597,[27] which promulgated the International Labor Organization's (ILO) Convention No. 182 on the Worst Forms of Child Labor[28] and ILO Recommendation No. 190,[29] concerning the prohibition and Immediate Action for the Elimination of the Worst Forms of Child Labor. Additionally, on February 15, 2002, Decree No. 4,134[30] was issued promulgating ILO Convention No. 138,[31] Concerning Minimum Age for Admission to Employment and ILO Recommendation No. 146.[32]

III. CHILD HEALTH

A. Constitutional Principles

The Brazilian Constitution, enacted on October 5, 1988, determines, *inter alia,* that health is a social right[33] and that it is the duty of the family, the society and the State to ensure to children and adolescents, with absolute priority, the right to life, health, nourishment, education, leisure, professional training, culture, dignity, respect, freedom, and family and community life, as well as to guard them from all forms of negligence, discrimination, exploitation, violence, cruelty, and oppression.[34]

In addition, article 229 of the Constitution dictates that it is the duty of the parents to assist, raise, and educate their underage children.

Paragraph 1 of article 227 of the Constitution further establishes that the State must promote full health assistance programs for children and adolescents, allows the participation of non-governmental entities, and determines that the following precepts must be regarded by the State:[35]

I.   allocation of a percentage of public health care funds to mother and child assistance;
II.   creation of preventive and specialized care programs for the physically, sensorially, or mentally handicapped, as well as programs for the social integration of handicapped adolescents, including training for a profession and for community life and facilitating access to public places and services, by eliminating prejudice and architectural obstacles.

Paragraph 2 determines that the law must regulate construction standards for public sites and buildings and for the manufacturing of public transportation vehicles, in order to ensure adequate access to the handicapped.

Paragraph 3 establishes that the right to special protection must include the following aspects:

i.   a minimum age of fourteen years for admission to work, with due regard to the provisions of article 7, XXXIII of the Constitution that prohibits night, dangerous, or unhealthy work for minors under eighteen years of age as well as any work for minors under fourteen years of age, except as an apprentice;
ii.   a guarantee of social security and labor rights;
iii. a guarantee of access to school for the adolescent worker;
iv.   a guarantee of full and formal knowledge of the determination of an offense,
v.   equal rights in the procedural relationships, and technical defense by a qualified professional, in accordance with the provisions of the specific protection legislation;
vi.   compliance with the principles of brevity, exceptionality, and respect for the peculiar conditions of the developing person, when applying any measures that restrain freedom;
vii. government fostering, by means of legal assistance, of tax incentives and subsidies, as provided by law, for the protection, through guardianship, of orphaned or abandoned children or adolescents;
viii. prevention and specialized assistance programs for children and adolescents addicted to narcotics or related drugs.

Paragraph 4 mandates that the law must severely punish abuse, violence, and sexual exploitation of children and adolescents; Paragraph 5 clarifies that adoption must be assisted by the Government, as provided by law, which must establish cases and conditions for adoption by foreigners. Paragraph 6 decrees that children born inside or outside wedlock or who have been adopted must have the same rights and qualifications and that any discriminatory designation of their filiation is forbidden.

In addition, health in Brazil is considered to be a right of all and a duty of the State, which is guaranteed both by social and economic policies aimed at reducing the risk of illness and other hazards and by universal and equal access to actions and services for its promotion, protection, and recovery.[36]

The Constitution also establishes that health actions and services are of public importance and that it is incumbent upon the government to provide, in accordance with the law, for their regulation, supervision, and control. The Government may execute this duty directly or through third parties, whether they are individuals or private legal entities.[37]

Article 198 of the Constitution determines that health actions and public services are to be integrated in a regionalized and hierarchical network and constitute a single system (*Sistema Único de Saúde*) organized according to the directives established in the Constitution.

B. Legislation

On September 19, 1990, as established in the Constitution, Brazil issued Law No. 8,080, regulating, in all its territory, the actions and health services, carried out separately or together, permanently or intermittently, by individuals or public or private legal entities.[38]

The law determines that health is a fundamental right of the human being and that the State must provide the indispensable conditions for its full exercise.[39] The law further determines that the duty of the State to guarantee health consists of the planning and execution of economic and social policies aimed at reducing the risks of diseases and other hazards and the establishment of conditions to guarantee the universal and equal access to the actions and services for its promotion, protection, and recovery.[40]

Moreover, article 4 of Law No. 8,080 explains that, according to article 198 of the Constitution, the body of actions and health services, provided by organs and public institutions, federal, state, or municipal, whether directly or indirectly funded by the government, constitute the Single System of Health (*Sistema Único de Saúde*). In 1990, Brazil enacted the Child and Adolescent Statute through Law No. 8,069 of July 13, which provides for the full protection of the child and the adolescent.[41] For the purposes of the law, a child is considered to be a person less than twelve years of age and an adolescent is a person between twelve and eighteen years of age.[42] In some exceptional cases foreseen in the statute, it also applies to persons between the ages of eighteen and twenty-one.

Additionally, article 5 of the Brazilian Civil Code[43] determines that minority ceases at the completion of eighteen years of age, when the person is then fully capable of practicing all acts of civil life. Paragraph 1 of article 5 further establishes that the minor's incapacity may also cease by the concession of the parents, or one of them in the absence of the other, through a public instrument, independently of judicial sanction or judicial decision of a sixteen year-old minor;[44] by marriage;[45] effective exercise of public employment;[46] graduation from an institution of higher education;[47] commercial or civil establishment, or the existence of employment relation, that provides a sixteen year-old minor with economic support.[48]

For criminal purposes, the Brazilian Penal Code dictates that minors under eighteen years of age are not criminally chargeable and are subject to the rules established in special legislation.[49]

In accordance with articles 6 and 227 of the Constitution, the statute establishes that the family, the community, the society in general, and the government have the duty to guarantee, with absolute priority, the enforcement of the right to life, health, food, education, sports, leisure, professionalization, culture, dignity, respect, freedom, and close family and community association.[50]

Article 7 of the statute proclaims that the child and the adolescent have the right to protection of life and health through the implementation of social public policies that enable satisfactory conditions for births and for the health and harmonious development of children.

In 1991, Brazil created the National Council for the Rights of the Child and the Adolescent (*Conselho Nacional dos Direitos da Criança e do Adolescente*).[51] The Council is responsible, *inter alia*, for the elaboration of the general norms of the national policy on the rights of children and adolescents and the inspection of the execution of actions established in the directives contained in articles 87 and 88 of the Child and Adolescent Statute.[52]

IV. CHILD SOCIAL WELFARE

A. Constitutional Principles

The Brazilian Constitution declares that social assistance must be rendered to whomever may need it, regardless of their contribution to social welfare. The objectives are the protection of adolescents; promotion of the integration into the labor market; habilitation and rehabilitation of the handicapped and their integration into community life; and the guarantee of a monthly benefit of one minimum wage to the handicapped and to the elderly who prove their incapability of providing for their own support or having it provided for by their families, as set forth by law.[53]

B. Legislation

The Child and Adolescent Statute guarantees to the pregnant woman pre-natal and post-natal assistance through the Single System of Health.[54] Hospitals and other health institutions that deal with pregnant women, whether public or private, must keep medical records for a period of eighteen years;[55] identify the newborn child by his footprint (*impressão plantar*) and the mother's fingerprint or other forms of identification used by the competent administrative authorities; perform exams aimed at the diagnosis and remediation of abnormalities of the newborn's metabolism, as well as provide orientation to the parents; provide a declaration of birth containing all the information concerning the child's delivery and the development of the newborn child; and keep accommodations that make it possible for the mother and the newborn child to stay together.[56]

Article 11 of the statute guarantees medical assistance to children and adolescents by the Single System of Health and the universal and equal access to actions and services for the promotion, protection and recovery of health. A handicapped child or adolescent is entitled to specialized treatment; it is the duty of the government to provide free medicines, prostheses, or any other means related to medical treatment, habilitation, or rehabilitation for the needy.

The statute determines that health institutions must provide the necessary conditions for one parent or guardian to the stay at any time when a child or an adolescent is hospitalized.[57] According to the statute, the Single System of Health must promote medical and dental assistance programs for the prevention of illnesses that ordinarily affect the young and campaigns of health education for parents, educators, and students. The statute also requires the vaccination of children, as recommended by public health authorities.[58]

On March 31, 1993, the government enacted Law No. 8,642,[59] creating the National Program for the Full Attention to the Child and the Adolescent (*Programa Nacional de Atenção Integral à Criança e ao Adolescente*), and Decree No. 1,056,[60] of February 11, 1994, regulates this law. The purpose of the program is to articulate all the actions in support of children and adolescents.[61] The priority areas of the program are the mobilization for community participation; full attention to children between zero and six years of age; basic education; attention to the adolescent and education for the job market; protection to the health and safety of the child and the adolescent; assistance to handicapped children; culture, sports, and leisure for children and adolescents; and training of professionals specializing in the development of children and adolescents.[62]

Law No. 8,742 of December 7, 1993, organizes social assistance in Brazil (*Lei Orgânica da Assistência Social*). The objective of social assistance is to provide protection for the family, motherhood, childhood, adolescence, and the elderly; to support needy children and adolescents; to promote integration into the job market; to provide for the habilitation and rehabilitation of handicapped people and the promotion of their integration into the community; and to guarantee a monthly minimum wage to the handicapped or to any elderly person that has been proven to have no means to provide for his own maintenance and whose his family cannot take care of him.[63]

V. EDUCATION

A. Constitutional Principles

In Brazil, education is considered a right of all and a duty of the State and of the family, which must be promoted and fostered with the cooperation of the society, with a view to the full development of the person and his preparation for the exercise of citizenship and qualification for work.[64]

Article 206 of the Constitution establishes the principles to be used as the basis for education:

I.   equal access to school;
II. freedom to learn, teach, research, and expression of thought, art, and knowledge;
III. pluralism of pedagogic ideas and conceptions and coexistence of public and private teaching institutions;
IV. free public education in official schools;
V.   appreciation of the value of teaching professionals, guaranteeing, in accordance with the law, career plans for public school teachers, with a professional minimum salary

and hiring exclusively by means of public entrance examinations consisting of tests and presentation of academic and or professional credentials;

VI. democratic administration of public education, in the manner prescribed by law;

VII. guaranteed standards of quality.

Article 208 determines that the government's duty to provide education must be fulfilled by ensuring the following:[65]

I. mandatory and free elementary education, including the assurance of its free offer to all those who did not have access to it at the proper age;

II. progressive promotion of access to free high school education throughout the country;

III. specialized schooling for the handicapped, preferably in the regular school system;

IV. assistance to children up to the age of six in day-care centers and preschools;

V. access to higher levels of education, and opportunities for research and artistic creation according to individual capacity;

VI. provision of regular night courses to meet the needs of the student;

VII. assistance to elementary school students through supplementary programs providing school material, transportation, food, and health assistance.

Additionally, the article specifies that access to compulsory and free education is a public subjective right;[66] that the competent authority must be held liable for any failure of the Government in providing compulsory education or providing it irregularly;[67] and that the Government has the power to take a census of elementary school students, call them for enrollment, and ensure that parents or guardians see to their children's attendance at school.[68]

B. Legislation

The Child and Adolescent Statute sanctions the above-listed constitutional principles. In article 53, it says that children and adolescents have the right to education, with a view to the full development of the person and his preparation for the exercise of citizenship and qualification for work. It also assures equal access to school; the right to be respected by their educators; the right to contest evaluation criteria, with the right to appeal, for higher school entrance; the right to be organized and to participate in student entities; and access to public and free schools near their residences. Moreover, parents and guardians have the right to be informed of the pedagogic process, as well as to participate in the development of educational policy proposals.[69]

On December 20, 1996, Brazil issued Law No. 9,394[70] (*Lei de Diretrizes e Bases*), which establishes the directives and the basis for education. According to the Law, the term "education" includes the formative processes that take place in life in the family, in human associations, at work, at institutions of education and research, within social movements, in the organizations of civil society, and at cultural events.[71] Law No. 9,394 directs school education, developed predominantly through teaching at the appropriate institutions,[72] and states that school education must be linked to the job market and the social experience.[73]

In articles 2 and 3, the Law defines the principles and the purpose of education. Article 2 specifies that education is a duty of the family and of the government; that it is inspired by the principles of freedom and is based on the ideals of human solidarity; and that its purpose is the full development of the student, his preparation for the exercise of citizenship, and his qualification to work. Article 3 enunciates the constitutional principles applied to education (described above).

In 2001, the government created a School Allowance Program (*Bolsa Escola*)[74] designed to keep children in school. The program is the federal government's financial participation in municipal programs that work through the schools to guarantee a minimum income.[75] The federal government supports the programs that have as beneficiaries the families residing within the municipality, that have a certain family income defined by the federal government, and that have responsibility for children between six and fifteen years of age regularly enrolled in educational institutions, with a school attendance rate of eighty-five percent or more.[76]

VI. CHILD LABOR AND EXPLOITATION

Based on principles elaborated in the Constitution, the Child and Adolescent Statute sanctions the prohibition of any work for minors less than fourteen years of age, except as apprentices,[77] and dictates that the protection of the work of adolescents is regulated by special legislation.[78] Article 62 defines apprenticeship as technical-professional education administered according to the directives and on the basis of the education legislation in force. Article 64 lays out the principles to be followed in technical-professional education. The statute also assures labor and social security rights for apprentice adolescents older than fourteen years[79] and protected work for handicapped adolescent.[80] In addition, it establishes that the adolescent worker has the right to acquire a profession and protection at work, which must respect the peculiar conditions of a developing person and equip them with adequate professional qualifications for the job market.[81]

On December 19, 2000, the government enacted Law No. 10,097[82] to supplement the section (arts. 402 to 441) of the Consolidation of Labor Laws[83] that regulates the protection of the work of minors to conform the section to both the Constitution and the Child and Adolescent Statute.

In 2001, the Ministry of Labor and Employment issued an administrative act (*Portaria*)[84] listing eighty-one working activities prohibited to minors of less than eighteen years of age. The act prohibits, for instance, work by minors in both civil construction and heavy machinery construction; in industrial operations of paper, plastic, or metal recycling; with infected animals; in fabrication of fireworks, and in slaughter houses.

VII. SALE AND TRAFFICKING OF CHILDREN

The Constitution decrees that the law must severely punish any abuse, violence, and sexual exploitation of children and adolescents.[85]

According to the Brazilian Penal Code, it is a crime to benefit or profit from the prostitution of a third party, which is punished with up to four years in prison and a fine,[86] and if the victim is older than fourteen and less than eighteen years of age, or if the perpetrator is the victim's ancestor, descendant, spouse, partner, sibling, tutor, guardian, or a person responsible for the minor's education, treatment, or custody, the punishment is increased to up to six years in prison and a fine.[87] If violence or a serious threat is used, the punishment increases to up to eight years and a fine, plus the corresponding punishment for the violent acts.[88]

Article 231 of the Penal Code can also be applied to punish, with up to eight years in prison and a fine, whoever promotes, intermediates, or facilitates the entrance, in Brazilian territory, of a person coming to the country to exercise prostitution or the departure of a person to exercise prostitution abroad. If the victim is older than fourteen and less than eighteen years of age, or if the perpetrator is the victim's ancestor, descendant, spouse, partner, sibling, tutor, or guardian, or a person responsible for the minor's education, treatment, or custody, the punishment is increased to up to ten years in prison and a fine.[89] If violence or a serious threat is used, the punishment increases to up to twelve years and a fine, plus the corresponding punishment for the violent acts.[90]

Additionally, giving an offspring less than eighteen years of age to a person in whose company, the parent knows or should know, the minor is morally or materially in danger is punished with up to two years in prison.[91] If the perpetrator carries out the offense to obtain profit or if the minor is sent abroad, the punishment is increased to up to four years in prison.[92] Assisting in the sending of a minor abroad for profit is also punished with up to four years in prison, even if there is no moral or material danger.[93]

Pursuant to article 5 of the Child and Adolescent Statute, no child or adolescent must be the object of any form of negligence, discrimination, exploitation, violence, cruelty, or oppression, and any attempt, by action or omission, to violate the fundamental rights of a child or adolescent must be punished according to the law.

The statute punishes with up to six years in prison whoever promotes or helps in the process of sending a child or adolescent abroad without observing the legal requirements or with the purpose of obtaining profit.[94] If violence, a serious threat, or fraud is used, the punishment increases to up to eight years in prison plus the corresponding punishment for the violent acts.[95]

The presentation, production, sale, supply, disclosure, or publication, by any means of communication, including the Internet, of photographs or images of pornography or sex scenes involving a child or an adolescent is punished with up to six years in prison and a fine.[96]

The statute also assigns the same punishment to whoever negotiates, authorizes, facilitates, or by any means, is an intermediate in the participation of a child or adolescent in the production of images of pornography or sex scenes;[97] provides the means or services for the storage of the photographs, scenes, or images of pornography or sex scenes involving a child or an adolescent;[98] or provides, by any means, access via the Internet to the photographs or images of pornography or sex scenes involving a child or adolescent.[99] The punishment is increased to up to eight years in prison if the perpetrator carries out the crime making use of an office, position, or function,[100] or with the purpose of obtaining profit.[101]

Additionally, the Child and Adolescent Statute determines that to subject a child or an adolescent to prostitution or sexual exploitation is punished with up to ten years in prison and a fine.[102] The same punishment is also applied to the owner, manager, or person in charge of a location at which a child or an adolescent is prostituted or sexually exploited.[103]

VIII. JUVENILE JUSTICE

Article 228 of the Constitution specifies that minors under eighteen years of age may not be held criminally liable and must be subject to the rules of special legislation for minors.

The Brazilian Penal Code thus provides that minors under eighteen years of age are not criminally chargeable and are subject to the rules established in special legislation (*Estatuto da Criança e do Adolescente*).[104] The Penal Code also determines that if the perpetrator of a crime is less than twenty-one years of age, the punishment for the crime is attenuated.[105] In addition, a curator is nominated if the person being indicted[106] or accused[107] of a crime is a minor.

According to the Child and Adolescent Statute, conduct described as a crime or a misdemeanor is considered to be an act of infraction if carried out by a minor.[108] The statute confirms the provision of the Penal Code that minors under eighteen years of age are not criminally chargeable and adds that minors are subject to the provisions contained in that law.[109]

Article 106 ascertains that no adolescent will be deprived of his liberty except in cases involving acts of infraction, or a written order issued by the competent judicial authority. The adolescent has the right to know the identity of those who apprehend him and must be informed of his rights.[110] The apprehension of a minor and the place where he is being held must be immediately communicated to the competent judicial authority, his family, or a person indicated by him.[111] A maximum confinement of forty-five days can be determined before a final decision on the acts of infraction is issued.[112]

Moreover, no adolescent will be deprived of his liberty without due process,[113] and it is guaranteed that the adolescent will have the full and formal knowledge that an act of infraction is being attributed to him by means of service or the equivalent;[114] the right to confront victims and witnesses and produce all evidence necessary for his defense;[115] the right to be defended by an attorney;[116] free and full judicial assistance to the needy according to the law;[117] the right to be personally questioned by the competent authority;[118] and the right to ask for the presence of his parents or guardian during all phases of the procedure.[119]

Once the practice of an act of infraction is verified, the competent authority may apply the following measures to an adolescent: [120]

I.   a warning;
II.   the obligation to repair the damage;
III. community service;
IV.   assisted freedom;
V.   insertion of the minor in a semi-free regime;
VI.   confinement in an educational institution;
VII. application of the provisions of article 101, I to VI of the Child and Adolescent Statute.

The measure applied must take into account the adolescent's capacity to execute it and the seriousness of the infraction;[121] under no circumstance is forced labor allowed.[122] The disabled and the mentally challenged adolescent must receive individual treatment in a place appropriate to his condition.[123]

The law further describes the concept of a warning,[124] what composes the obligation to repair the damage,[125] community service,[126] assisted freedom,[127] a semi-free regime,[128] and confinement.[129]

Article 124 provides that a minor that has been deprived of his freedom has the rights, *inter alia*, to be treated with respect and dignity;[130] to receive a weekly visit;[131] and to correspond with his family and friends.[132] The government is charged with the duty to take care of the physical integrity of confined minors as well as to adopt the necessary restraint and security measures.[133]

Before the beginning of the appropriate judicial procedure to verify an infraction, a member of the Public Prosecutor's Office may grant remission, as a form of exclusion of the procedure, based on the circumstances and consequences of the facts and of the social context, as well as on the adolescent's personality and his greater or smaller participation in the infraction.[134] If granted, the remission suspends or extinguishes the judicial procedure.[135]

The Child and Adolescent Statute guarantees to all children and adolescents access to the Public Defender's Office (*Defensoria Pública*), the Public Prosecutor's Office, and all organs of the judiciary.[136] Judicial assistance is free and will be provided to those who need it through a Public Defender or a nominated lawyer.[137] The judicial actions under the jurisdiction of the Childhood and Youth Courts (*Justiça da Infância e da Juventude*) are free of charge, except in the case of bad faith.[138]

In judicial proceedings, a minor of less than sixteen years of age is represented and a minor that is more than sixteen and less than twenty-one years old is assisted by his parents, tutors, or guardian, according to the Civil Code and the Civil Procedure Code.[139] The judicial authority will nominate a special guardian for the child or adolescent every time that there is a conflict between the child's interests and his parents or guardian' interests or if the child lacks the due legal assistance.[140] The law also prohibits the disclosure of the judicial, police, and administrative acts involving an infraction committed by a minor.[141] Any news regarding the act cannot identify the child or adolescent by photograph or name, including name and surname initials, nickname, filiation, kinship, or residence.[142]

The Child and Adolescent Statute authorizes the states and the Federal District to create specialized and exclusive courts for children and youth.[143] Such courts are competent, *inter alia*, to receive representations initiated by the Public Prosecutor's Office for the verification of acts of infraction carried out by an adolescent and the application of the pertinent punishment,[144] to grant remission as a form of suspension or extinction of the judicial procedure,[145] to receive adoption requests and related matters,[146] to apply administrative punishments in case of breach of a rule for the protection of a child or adolescent;[147] and to hear cases involving requests for child custody and guardianship in general.[148]

In light of recent violent acts of infraction carried out by minors, Congress is currently studying a proposal for a law that decreases from eighteen to sixteen the age that a minor is criminally responsible for his actions.[149]

Conclusion

The Brazilian Constitution especially grants rights and establishes principles designed to protect minors. In a special chapter dedicated to the family, the child, the adolescent, and the elderly, the law of the land clearly stipulates that it is the duty of the family, the society, and the State to ensure to children and adolescents, with absolute priority, the right to life, health, nourishment, education, leisure, professional training, culture, dignity, respect, freedom, and family and community life, as well as to guard them from all forms of negligence, discrimination, exploitation, violence, cruelty, and oppression.[150]

In response to these constitutional principles, plus the many international treaties and conventions to which Brazil is either a signatory or a party, many pieces of legislation have been enacted and policy programs developed, offering a wide range of legal protection to children's and adolescents' rights. The enactment of the Child and Adolescent Statute in 1990 consolidated the many rights and duties that were scattered throughout different pieces of legislation and reflects the effort made by the government to promote the protection of children and adolescents.

Prepared by Eduardo Soares
Foreign Law Specialist
August 2007

Addendum – Amendment of the Child and Adolescent Statute

On November 25, 2008, Law No. 11,829[151] was promulgated to improve the fight against child pornography and to criminalize pedophilia on the Internet. It amended articles 240 and 241 of the Child and Adolescent Statute and included a definition of child pornography.

According to article 240 of the Child and Adolescent Statute, to produce, reproduce, direct, photograph, film or register, by any means, an explicit sex or pornographic scene involving a child or adolescent, is punishable upon conviction with four to eight years in prison and a fine. The same punishment is applicable to whoever negotiates, facilitates, recruits, coerces, or by any other way intermediates the participation of a child or adolescent in the mentioned scenes, or participates in such scenes.[152] The punishment is increased by one-third if the person commits the described crime during the exercise of public functions or under the pretense of such exercise;[153] by taking advantage of domestic relations, cohabitation or hospitality;[154] or by being related to the minor by blood or by law up to the third degree, or by adoption, guardianship or employment.[155]

Article 241 punishes with up to eight years in prison and a fine whoever sells or offers for sale, a photograph, video, or any other means that contains an explicit sex or pornographic scene involving a child or adolescent. Whoever facilitates the participation of minors in such scenes;[156] provides the means or services for the storage of such photographs or scenes;[157] or furnishes, by any means, access, through the world wide web or Internet, to the mentioned photographs or scenes,[158] is also punished in the same way.

Article 241 punishes with up to six years in prison and a fine whoever offers, exchanges, makes available, transmits, distributes, publishes, or publicizes by any means a photograph, video, or any other source that contains an explicit sex or pornographic scene involving a child or adolescent.[159]

Article 241-B, punishes with up to four years in prison and a fine the acquisition, possession or storage, by any means, of a photograph, video, or any other source that contains an explicit sex or pornographic scene involving a child or adolescent. Paragraph 2 of article 241-B lists the exceptional circumstances that allow a person to possess or store such material.

To simulate the participation of child or adolescent in an explicit sex or pornographic scene, by means of adulteration, montage, or modification of video or any other format of visual representation is punished with up to three years in prison and a fine.[160]

The enticement, harassment, instigation, or constraint, by any means of communication, of a child, with the purpose of practicing with the child lustful acts is punished with up to three years in prison and a fine.[161] The same punishment is applied to whoever facilitates or induces the access of a child to material containing an explicit sex or pornographic scene with the purpose of practicing lustful acts with the child;[162] or entices, harasses, instigates, or constrains a child, with the purpose of inducing the child to expose herself in a pornographic or sexually explicit way.[163]

Finally, Law No. 11,829 created article 241-E determining that, for the purpose of the crimes described in the Child and Adolescent Statute, the expression "an explicit sex or pornographic scene" encompasses any situation that involves a child or adolescent in explicit sexual activities, real or simulated, or the exhibition of the sexual organs of a child or adolescent for sexual purposes.

Updated by Eduardo Soares
Foreign Law Specialist
January 2009.

End Notes

[1] Universal Declaration of Human Rights, G.A. Res. 217 A (III), U.N. Doc. A/810 at 71 (Dec. 10, 1948), available at official website of the United Nations, http://www.un.org/Overview/rights

[2] The U.N. Declaration of the Rights of the Child, G.A. Res. 1386 (XIV), 14 U.N. GAOR Supp. (No. 16) at 19, U.N. Doc. A/4354, official website of the United Nations, http://www.unhchr.ch/html/menu3/b/25.htm (last visited Aug. 3, 2007).

[3] Convention on the Rights of the Child, G.A. Res. 44/25, annex, 44 U.N. GAOR Supp. (No. 49) at 167, U.N. Doc. A/44/49 (1989); 28 I.L.M. 1448 (1989), official website of the United Nations, available at http://www.unhchr.ch/html/menu3/b/k2crc.htm.

[4] Art. 84, VIII of the Brazilian Constitution determines that the President of the Republic has the exclusive power to conclude international treaties, conventions, and acts, ad referendum of the National Congress.

[5] Decreto No. 99.710 de 21 de Novembro de 1990, website of the Brazilian Presidency, available at http://www.planalto.gov.br/ccivil_03/decreto/1990-1994/D99710.htm.

[6] Decreto No. 5.007 de 8 de Março de 2004, website of the Brazilian Presidency, available at http://www.planalto.gov.br/ccivil_03/_Ato2004-2006/2004/Decreto/D5007.htm.

[7] Optional Protocol to the Convention on the Rights of the Child on the Sale of Children, Child Prostitution, and Child Pornography, official website of the United Nations, http://www.unhchr.ch/html/menu2/dopchild.htm (last visited Aug. 3, 2007).

[8] Decreto No. 5.006 de 8 de Março de 2004, website of the Brazilian Presidency, available at http://www. planalto.gov.br/ccivil_03/_Ato2004-2006/2004/Decreto/D5006.htm.

[9] Optional Protocol to the Convention on the Rights of the Child on the Involvement of Children in Armed Conflict, official website of the United Nations, http://www.unhchr.ch/html/menu2/6/protocolchild.htm (last visited Aug. 3, 2007).

[10] International Covenant on Civil and Political Rights, G.A. Res. 2200A (XXI), 21 U.N. GAOR, 21st Sess. Supp. (No. 16) at 52, U.N. Doc. A/6316 (Dec. 16, 1966), 999 U.N.T.S. 171, official website of the United Nations, available at http://www.unhchr.ch/html/menu3/b/a_ccpr.htm.

[11] Decreto No. 592 de 6 de Julho de 1992, website of the Brazilian Presidency, available at http://www.planalto.gov.br/ccivil_03/decreto/1990-1994/D0592.htm.

[12] Decreto No. 4.377 de 13 de Setembro de 2002, website of the Brazilian Presidency, available at http://www.planalto.gov.br/ccivil_03/decreto/2002/D4377.htm.

[13] Convention on the Elimination of All Forms of Discrimination against Women, 1249 U.N.T.S. 13, official website of the United Nations, http://www.un.org/womenwatch/daw/cedaw/text/econvention.htm (last visited Aug. 3, 2007).

[14] Decreto No. 4.316 de 30 de Julho de 2002, website of the Brazilian Presidency, available at http://www.planalto. gov.br/ccivil_03/decreto/2002/D4316.htm.

[15] Optional Protocol to the Convention on the Elimination of All Forms of Discrimination against Women, official website of the United Nations, http://www.un.org/womenwatch/daw/cedaw/protocol/text.htm (last visited Aug. 3, 2007).

[16] Inter-American Convention on the International Return of Children, O.A.S.T.S. No. 70, official website of the Organization of American States, http://www.oas.org/juridico/english/treaties/b-53.html (last visited Aug. 3, 2007).

[17] Decreto No. 1.212 de 3 de Agosto de 1994, website of the Brazilian Presidency, http://www.planalto. gov.br/ccivil_03/decreto/1990-1994/D1212.htm.

[18] Inter-American Convention on Conflict of Laws Concerning the Adoption of Minors, O.A.S.T.S. No. 62, official website of the Organization of American States, http://www.oas.org/juridico/english/treaties/b-48.html (last visited Aug. 3, 2007).

[19] Decreto No. 2.429 de 17 de Dezembro de 1997, website of the Brazilian Presidency, http://www. planalto.gov.br/ccivil_03/decreto/D2429.htm.

[20] Decreto No. 2.740 de 20 de Agosto de 1998, website of the Brazilian Presidency, http://www. planalto.gov.br/ccivil_03/decreto/D2740.htm.

[21] Inter-American Convention on International Traffic in Minors, O.A.S.T.S. No. 79, official website of the Organization of American States, http://www.oas.org/juridico/english/treaties/b-57.html (last visited Aug. 3, 2007).

[22] Decreto No. 3.087 de 21 de Junho de 1999, website of the Brazilian Presidency, available at http://www.planalto. gov.br/ccivil_03/decreto/D3087.htm.

[23] Hague Convention on Protection of Children and Cooperation in Respect of Inter-Country Adoption, 32 I.L.M. 1134 (1993), official website of the Hague Conference on Private International Law, available at http://www.hcch.net/index_en.php?act=conventions.text&cid=69.

[24] Decreto No. 3.413 de 14 de Abril de 2000, website of the Brazilian Presidency, available at http://www.planalto.gov.br/ccivil_03/decreto/D3413.htm.

[25] Hague Convention on the Civil Aspects of International Child Abduction, 19 I.L.M. 1501 (1980), official website of the Hague Conference on Private International Law, available at http://www.hcch.net/index_en. php?act=conventions.text&cid=24.

[26] Decreto No. 3.174 de 16 de Setembro de 1999, website of the Brazilian Presidency, available at http://www.planalto.gov.br/ccivil_03/decreto/D3174.htm.

[27] Decreto No. 3.597 de 12 de Setembro de 2000, website of the Brazilian Presidency, available at http://www. planalto.gov.br/ccivil 03/decreto/D3597.htm.

[28] Worst Form of Child Labor Convention, I.L.O. No. 182, official website of the International Labor organization, http://www.ilocarib.org.tt/childlabour/c182.htm (last visited Aug. 3, 2007).

[29] Recommendation Concerning the Prohibition and Immediate Action for the Elimination of the Worst Forms of Child Labor, I.L.O. Recommendation No. 190, official website of the International Labor organization, http://www.ilo.org/public/ english/standards/relm/ilc/ilc87/com-chir.htm (last visited Aug. 3, 2007).

[30] Decreto No. 4.134 de 15 de Fevereiro de 2002, website of the Brazilian Presidency, available at http://www.planalto.gov.br/ccivil_03/decreto/2002/D4134.htm.

[31] Convention concerning Minimum Age for Admission to Employment, I.L.O. No. 138, official website of the International Labor organization, http://www.ilo.org/ilolex/cgi-lex/convde.pl?C138 (last visited Aug. 3, 2007).

[32] Minimum Age Recommendation, I.L.O. Recommendation No. 146, official website of the International Labor Organization, http://www.ilocarib.org.tt/childlabour/r146.htm (last visited Aug. 3, 2007).

[33] Constituição Federativa do Brasil de 1988 [C.F.], art. 6, website of the Brazilian Presidency, http://www.planalto. gov.br/ccivil_03/Constituicao/Constituiçao.htm (last visited Aug. 3, 2007).

[34] Id. art. 227.

[35] Translation of all constitutional passages modified by the author from the version available in FEDERAL SENATE SPECIAL SECRETARIAT FOR PRINTING AND PUBLISHING, UNDERSECRETARIAT OF TECHNICAL PUBLICATIONS, CONSTITUTION OF THE FEDERATIVE REPUBLIC OF BRAZIL (Brasília, 2002).

[36] C.F., art. 196.

[37] Id. art. 197.

[38] Lei No. 8.080 de 19 de Setembro de 1990, art. 1, website of the Brazilian Presidency, http://www.planalto.gov.br/ccivil_03/Leis/L8080.htm.

[39] Id. art. 2.

[40] Id. §1.

[41] Estatuto da Criança e do Adolescente, Lei No. 8.069 de 13 de Julho de 1990, art. 1, website of the Brazilian Presidency, http://www.planalto.gov.br/ccivil/LEIS/L8069.htm.

[42] Id. art. 2.

[43] Código Civil, Lei No. 10.406 de 10 de Janeiro de 2002, website of the Brazilian Presidency, http://www.planalto.gov.br/ccivil 03/LEIS/2002/L10406.htm.

[44] Id. art. 5(§1)(I).

[45] Id. (II).

[46] Id. (III).

[47] Id. (IV).

[48] Id. (V).

[49] Código Penal, Decreto-Lei No. 2.848 de 7 de Dezembro de 1940, art. 27, website of the Brazilian Presidency, http://www.planalto.gov.br/ccivil_03/Decreto-Lei/Del2848compilado.htm.

[50] Id. art. 4.

[51] Lei No. 8.242 de 12 de Outubro de 1991, art. 1, website of the Brazilian Presidency, http://www.planalto.gov.br/ccivil_03/LEIS/L8242.htm.

[52] Id. art. 2.

[53] C.F., art. 203.

[54] Estatuto da Criança e do Adolescente, Lei No. 8.069 de 13 de Julho de 1990, art. 8, website of the Brazilian Presidency, http://www.planalto.gov.br/ccivil/LEIS/L8069.htm.

[55] Id. art. 10(I).

[56] Id. art. 10.

[57] Id. art.12.

[58] Id. art.14.

[59] Lei No. 8.642 de 31 de Março de 1993, website of the Brazilian Presidency, http://www.planalto. gov.br/ccivil 03/Leis/1989 1994/L8642.htm.

[60] Decreto No. 1.056 de 11 de Fevereiro de 1994, website of the Brazilian Presidency, http://www.planalto.gov.br/ccivil_03/decreto/1990-1994/D1056.htm.

[61] Id. art. 1.

[62] Id. art. 2.

[63] Lei No. 8.742 de 7 de Dezembro de 1993, art. 2, website of the Brazilian Presidency, http://www.planalto.gov.br/ccivil_03/Leis/L8742.htm.

[64] C.F., art. 205.

[65] Id. art. 208.

[66] C.F., art. 208(§1).

[67] Id. (§2).

[68] Id. (§3).

[69] Estatuto da Criança e do Adolescente, Lei No. 8.069 de 13 de Julho de 1990, art. 53 (§1), website of the Brazilian Presidency, http://www.planalto.gov.br/ccivil/LEIS/L8069.htm.

[70] Lei No. 9.394 de 20 de Dezembro de 1996, website of the Brazilian Presidency, http://www. planalto.gov. br/ccivil_03/Leis/L9394.htm.

[71] Id. art. 1.

[72] Id. (§1).

[73] Id. (§2).

[74] Lei No. 10.219 de 11 de Abril de 2001, website of the Brazilian Presidency, http://www.planalto. gov.br/ccivil_03/Leis/LEIS_2001/L10219.htm.

[75] Id. (§1).

[76] Id. art. 2(II).

[77] Estatuto da Criança e do Adolescente, Lei No. 8.069 de 13 de Julho de 1990, art. 60, website of the Brazilian Presidency, http://www.planalto.gov.br/ccivil/LEIS/L8069.htm.

[78] Id. art. 61.

[79] Id. art. 60.

[80] Id. art. 66.

[81] Id. art. 69.

[82] Lei No. 10.097 de 19 de Dezembro de 2000, art. 1, website of the Brazilian Presidency, http://www.planalto. gov.br/ccivil_03/Leis/L10097.htm.

[83] Decreto-Lei No. 5.452 de 1 de Maio de 1943, arts. 402, 403, 428, 429, 430, 431, 432 and 433, website of the Brazilian Presidency, https://www.planalto.gov.br/ccivil_03/decreto-lei/Del5452.htm.

[84] Portaria No. 20 de 13 de Setembro de 2001, official website of the Ministry of Labor and Employment, http://www.mte.gov.br/legislacao/portarias/2001/p_20010913_20.pdf.

[85] C.F., art. 227(§4).

[86] Código Penal, Decreto-Lei No. 2.848 de 7 de Dezembro de 1940, art. 230, website of the Brazilian Presidency, http://www.planalto.gov.br/ccivil_03/Decreto-Lei/Del2848compilado.htm.

[87] Id. (§1).

[88] Id. (§2).

[89] Id. art. 231(§1).

[90] Id. (§2).

[91] Id. art. 245.

[92] Id. (§1).

[93] Id. (§2).

[94] Estatuto da Criança e do Adolescente, Lei No. 8.069 de 13 de Julho de 1990, art. 239, website of the Brazilian Presidency, http://www.planalto.gov.br/ccivil/LEIS/L8069.htm.

[95] Id. (§1).

[96] Id. art. 241.

[97] Id. (§1)(I).

[98] Id. (II).

[99] Id. (III).

[100] Id. art. 241(§2)(I).

[101] Id. (§2)(II).

[102] Id. art. 244-A.

[103] Id. (§1).

[104] C.P. art. 27

[105] Id. art. 65(I).

[106] Código de Processo Penal, Decreto-Lei No. 3.689 de 3 de Outubro de 1941, art. 15, website of the Brazilian Presidency, http://www.planalto.gov.br/ccivil_03/Decreto-Lei/Del3689Compilado.htm.

[107] Id. art. 262.

[108] Estatuto da Criança e do Adolescente, Lei No. 8.069 de 13 de Julho de 1990, art. 103, website of the Brazilian Presidency, http://www.planalto.gov.br/ccivil/LEIS/L8069.htm.

[109] Id. art. 104.

[110] Id. art. 106(§1).

[111] Id. art. 107.

[112] Id. art. 108.

[113] Id. art. 110.

[114] Id. art. 111(I).

[115] Id. (II).

[116] Id. (III).

[117] Id. (IV).

[118] Id. (V).

[119] Id. (VI).

[120] Id. art. 112.

[121] Id. (§1).

[122] Id. (§2).

[123] Id. (§3).

[124] Id. art. 115.

[125] Id. art. 116.

[126] Id. art. 117.

[127] Id. art. 118.

[128] Id. art. 120.

[129] Id. art. 121.

[130] Id. art. 124(V).

[131] Id. (VII).

[132] Id. (VIII).

[133] Id. art. 125.

[134] Id. art. 126.

[135] Id. art. 126(§1).

[136] Id. art. 141.

[137] Id. (§1).

[138] Id. (§2).

[139] Id. art. 142.

[140] Id. art. 142(§1).

[141] Id. art. 143.

[142] Id. (§1).

[143] Id. art. 145.

[144] Id. art. 148(I).

[145] Id. (II).

[146] Id. (III).

[147] Id. (VI).

[148] Id. (§1)(a).

[149] Maioridade Penal, VEJA, Feb. 2007, available at http://veja.abril.com.br/idade/exclusivo/ perguntas_respostas/maioridade_penal/index.shtml.

[150] C.F., art. 227.

[151] Lei No. 11.829, de 25 de Novembro de 2008, available at the website of the Brazilian Presidency, http://www.planalto.gov.br/ccivil_03/_Ato2007-2010/2008/Lei/L11829.htm.

[152] Estatuto da Criança e do Adolescente, Lei No. 8.069 de 13 de Julho de 1990 [E.C.A.], art. 240(§1), available at the website of the Brazilian Presidency, http://www.planalto.gov.br/ccivil/LEIS/L8069.htm.

[153] Id. art. 240(§2)(I).

[154] Id. (II).

[155] Id. (III).

[156] Id. art. 241(§1)(I).

[157] Id. (II).

[158] Id. (III).

[159] Id. art. 241-A.

[160] Id. art. 241-C.

[161] Id. art. 241-D.

[162] Id. (I).

[163] Id. (II).

In: Children's Rights
Editors: Brooke Dabney and Michael Eldridge

ISBN: 978-1-62948-252-1
© 2013 Nova Science Publishers, Inc.

Chapter 6

CANADA: CHILDREN'S RIGHTS[*]

Stephen Clarke

EXECUTIVE SUMMARY

Canada has ratified the Convention on the Rights of the Child and the two optional protocols to it. Responsibility for implementation is split between the federal government and the provinces. Canada's ten provinces have nearly universal health insurance plans that cover virtually all children and maintain most social welfare agencies. Another provincial responsibility is education. Children receive tax-supported elementary and secondary education. Universities charge subsidized tuition. Minimum ages for employment are yet another provincial responsibility. On the federal level, there are many criminal laws designed to prevent child abuse. The number of related offenses and the maximum punishments for them have been greatly increased in recent years. In its national defense laws, the federal government now prohibits Canadian soldiers under the age of eighteen from being deployed in armed conflict. The federal government also created a new juvenile justice system in 2002 that gives the police and judges more options in handling cases of juveniles charged with criminal offenses than the previous law.

I. INTRODUCTION

Canada is a constitutional monarchy which has a Parliament, composed of a Senate and House of Representatives, and ten provinces which have legislative assemblies. Since Canada's various Constitution Acts do not assign the subject of children to either level of government, it is essentially split, with each level covering children as part of the jurisdictions conferred upon them. Thus, for example, the provinces have enacted child labor laws in exercising their powers over most private sector employment within a province, and

---

[*] This document was released by the Law Library of Congress August 2007.

Parliament has prohibited child pornography in exercising its exclusive jurisdiction to enact criminal laws for the country.

In Canada, the provinces have established ages of majority for such purposes as determining when a child has the legal capacity to enter into contracts, is able to purchase restricted products, is free of parental control, and can exercise full civil rights. In Alberta, Ontario, Saskatchewan, Manitoba, Quebec, and Prince Edward Island the age of majority is eighteen, and in British Columbia, New Brunswick, Nunavut, Nova Scotia, and Newfoundland and Labrador the age of majority is nineteen.[1] Quebec's age of majority is set out in its Civil Code.[2] However, under federal laws, all persons eighteen and older are eligible to vote in federal elections and may be tried as adults regardless of which province or territory they live in. Thus, there is no one age of majority for all purposes of Canadian law.

II. IMPLEMENTATION OF INTERNATIONAL RIGHTS OF THE CHILD

Canada has ratified the Convention on the Rights of the Child,[3] the Optional Protocol to the Convention of the Rights of the Child on the Involvement of Children in Armed Conflict,[4] and the Optional Protocol to the Convention on the Rights of the Child on the Sale of Children, Child Prostitution, and Child Pornography.[5] Since Canadian constitutional law does not generally permit the federal government to legislate over matters that fall under provincial jurisdiction even for the purpose of implementing an international agreement, Canada makes reservations to this effect if implementation would require provincial cooperation. The federal government has had to work with the provinces in implementing aspects of the original convention dealing with such matters as education and health care. On the other hand, the conduct of war and criminal law are matters under federal jurisdiction. Thus, the federal government has been able to implement the Optional Protocols by amending its statutes that regulate national defense and create a national criminal code.

III. CHILD HEALTH AND SOCIAL WELFARE

In Canada, each province operates its own health insurance program. Virtually all residents are enrolled in these programs. Most of the programs are funded through tax revenues, but some provinces also place a special tax on employers. The federal government gives financial assistance to the provinces to help defray health care costs. When the single-payer systems were created in the 1960's, the federal government paid approximately fifty percent of the programs' costs. However, this percentage has declined to around twenty percent. The decrease has placed a strain on the provincial health care systems, which has resulted in longer waiting times for medical services. The current government has increased the federal contributions in an effort to preserve and improve the universal health care system. Under this system, patients can choose their own physicians. The vast majority of physicians bill the health insurance programs for their services and are reimbursed in accordance with schedules of fees. These physicians cannot engage in the practice of extra-billing or charging their patients separate additional fees for expedited services, but physicians can opt out of the system.

Because Canada has provincial health care plans, virtually all children have health insurance. Hospitals are mostly operated by municipalities and charitable organizations. The major cities have hospitals that are devoted to treating sick children. Canadians do not have to pay special fees to have their children treated at these hospitals.

Statistics Canada reports that the infant mortality rate for children under the age of one year was 5.3 per 1,000 live births in 2004.[6]

IV. EDUCATION

Education in Canada is a provincial responsibility. The federal government does not have a federal department of education, but it does operate a limited number of schools on military bases and on Indian reservations.

Under Canada's original Constitution Act, 1867, the rights that previously existed respecting separate denominational schools were preserved.[7] Some of these rights differ from province to province and some of them have been expanded by subsequent legislation. At present, separate denominational and linguistic schools exist throughout much of Canada. In the largest cities and many other localities, there are separate Protestant and Catholic school boards. In practice, most non-Christians attend schools run by Protestant school boards in which religion is not taught. Because the Constitution Act guaranteed existing denominational rights, it does not confer on members of other religions the right to establish a tax-funded school board. However, provincial laws do allow for the establishment of private schools. Unlike the Protestant and Catholic school boards, these schools are not supported by taxes in proportion to the number of students enrolled in their elementary and secondary school programs. Many provinces also have separate English and French school boards. Thus, a bilingual city can have four separate school boards. Separate language schools generally exist where the numbers of students who wish to be enrolled in a minority language program are sufficient to sustain a separate school system.

Universities are also operated by the provinces. Canada does not have as extensive a system of private universities as in the United States. Tuition at universities within each province varies only slightly. Provinces have grant programs to assist university students. Most universities have a primary language of instruction, but a number offer courses in both official languages, including McGill University, the University of Ottawa, and the University of New Brunswick.

All students are entitled to virtually free elementary and secondary education in Canada. In fact, the Province of Ontario has recently enacted legislation to require students to remain in school until the age of eighteen.[8] Previously, children had been allowed to legally drop out of school upon reaching the age of sixteen. This initiative is part of a larger program that includes a Can$1.3 billion (about US$1.23 billion) Student Success Strategy to expand available programs. Ontario has also created 1,000 new skilled trades training spaces for vocational training.[9] The new requirement that children remain in school until the age of eighteen is enforceable with fines against parents who do not enroll their children in school. However, critics question whether the province will be able to force students to return to school if they decide to quit after reaching the age of sixteen.

Canada does not have an extensive system of vocational schools, but there are several institutes of higher education that emphasize job-related skills in major cities.

Some provincial laws respecting local secondary schools contain general language requiring school boards to address special needs. In Ontario, school boards are required to address the needs of "exceptional pupils."[10] More specific provisions are contained in the Ontarians with Disabilities Act.

This statute applies to schools, universities, and government and requires them to comply with barrier-free guidelines. The government is specifically required to consider as a barrier anything that prevents a person with a disability from fully participating in all aspects of society because of his or her disability, including a physical barrier, an architectural barrier, an information or communications barrier, an attitudinal barrier, a technological barrier, a policy, or a practice.[11] Schools and universities are not subject to this requirement, but as "scheduled organizations" they are required to consult with persons with disabilities and prepare annual accessibility plans. These plans must "address the identification, removal and prevention of barriers to persons with disabilities in the organization's by-laws, if any, and in its policies, programs, practices and services."[12] Accessibility plans must include a report on measures taken; the measures in place; a list of bylaws, policies, programs, practices, and services to be reviewed; and measures the organization intends to take in the coming year. Accessibility plans must be made available to the public. To help organizations in the preparation of their plans, the government is assigned the responsibility of preparing more detailed guidelines. In some cases, two or more organizations are allowed to prepare joint accessibility plans.

Ontario has passed a new law to replace the Ontarians with Disabilities Act which has not yet been brought into force.[13] This law will essentially extend many of the extant rules to the private sector.

Canada's Constitution prohibits "cruel and unusual punishment."[14] Whether this would apply to corporal punishment by teachers is not clear.[15] However, provincial school district associations have clearly banned corporal punishment. In Ontario, the guide to school district policies states as follows:

> The use of corporal punishment in any form is strictly prohibited in the district. No student will be subject to the infliction of corporal punishment.
>
> Corporal punishment is defined as the willful infliction of, or willfully causing the infliction of physical pain.
>
> No teacher, administrator, other school personnel or school volunteer will subject a student to corporal punishment or condone the use of corporal punishment by any person under his/her supervision or control. Permission to administer corporal punishment will not be sought or accepted from any guardian/parent ... .
>
> A staff member is authorized to employ physical force when, in his/her professional judgment, the physical force is necessary to prevent a student from harming self, others or doing harm to district property. Physical force shall not be used to discipline or punish a student. The superintendent shall inform all staff members and volunteers of this policy.[16]

V. Child Labor and Exploitation

In Canada, most contracts of employment in the public sector are covered by provincial labor laws. Each province has its own restrictions on child labor. The federal government also has enacted prohibitions on child labor, but these prohibitions only apply to work conducted in federal undertakings or in field that are governed by federal legislation such as aviation, broadcasting, and banking. Federal law does not generally supersede provincial law. Instead, each level of government regulates employment in fields within its jurisdiction. At the present time, the minimum age for employment extends from fourteen in Nova Scotia, Ontario, and Quebec to seventeen at the federal level and in the territories of the Northwest, Nunavut, and the Yukon.[17] Parliament and the provinces have also placed limitations on the type of work and the number of hours young people can be hired to perform. For example, the federal government has excluded certain categories of dangerous work, providing that any work performed must be unlikely to endanger health and safety; required all work to be outside school hours; and prohibited work between the hours of 11:00 p.m. and 6:00 a.m. for minors.[18] In the largest province of Ontario, minors may not be employed in logging operations until they are fifteen and may not be employed in factories until they are sixteen.[19] Employment in mines and on construction sites are also generally limited to sixteen and older, but employment in underground mines is generally limited to those at least eighteen years old.[20]

Parliament and the provinces also share responsibility for establishing minimum wages within their spheres of competence, but in this case, the federal government has aligned its rates with each province and territory in which a person subject to federal regulation is employed. The federal government does not have a special minimum wage for persons under the age of eighteen. Registered apprentices are exempt from the minimum wage provisions if they are paid in accordance with a schedule established for apprentices by their provincial government. Certain trainees may also be paid less than the prevailing minimum wage in their province of employment.[21] Ontario currently has a provincial minimum wage of Can$8.00 per hour (about US$7.60).[22] As of February 1, 2007, there is a special rate of $Can7.50 per hour for students whose weekly hours do not exceed twenty-eight or who are employed during a school holiday.[23] Other exemptions for trainees are not limited to persons within a certain age group.

Throughout Canada, employees under the age of eighteen generally have the same rights as other workers to holidays, union representation, and overtime pay. Other labor standards also generally apply to all employees equally.

Canada has a Cadet Corps for persons between the ages of twelve and nineteen. Persons in the Cadet Corps are involved in physical training and community service.[24] Cadets are not eligible for deployment. Canada permits persons between the ages of sixteen and eighteen to enlist in the armed forces with the consent of a parent.[25] However, persons under the age of eighteen cannot be deployed to a theater of armed hostilities by the Canadian Forces.[26]

VI. Sex and Trafficking of Children

Canada's Criminal Code contains a number of offenses related to the sexual exploitation of or the trafficking in children. The most important of these offenses can be summarized as follows:

1) *Sexual interference.* Touching a child under the age of fourteen for a sexual purpose is punishable with a maximum sentence of ten years' imprisonment and a minimum sentence of fourteen days.[27]

2) *Invitation to sexual touching.* Inviting a child under the age of fourteen to engage in sexual touching carries the same penalties as sexual interference.[28]

3) *Sexual exploitation.* The offense of sexual exploitation extends the offenses of sexual interference and invitation to sexual touching to persons who are in a position of trust or authority over a child between the ages of fourteen and eighteen. The maximum and minimum sentences for sexual exploitation are the same as for sexual interference and sexual touching.[29]

4) *Child pornography.* Any person who makes, prints, publishes, or possesses child pornography for publication is liable to a maximum sentence of ten years' imprisonment and a minimum sentence of ninety days' imprisonment. Any person who transmits, distributes, sells, imports, or advertises child pornography or possesses child pornography for one of those purposes is liable to the same maximum and minimum punishments. Any person who possesses child pornography is liable to a maximum sentence of five years' imprisonment and a minimum of fourteen days' imprisonment. Any person who knowingly accesses child pornography is liable to the same maximum and minimum punishments.

The term "child pornography" includes not only pictures, films, and other visual representations, but also written material which counsels sexual activity with a person under the age of eighteen and audio recordings that describe sexual activity with a person under the age of eighteen. It is not a defense to a child pornography charge that the person believed the person depicted was eighteen or older, unless the accused took all reasonable steps to ensure the persons was of legal age and that he or she was not depicted as being under the age of eighteen.

In a controversial 2001 decision, the Supreme Court of Canada ruled that the country's child pornography laws were mostly constitutional, but they could not support the conviction of a person who had been found to have created visual and written material for his own private use.[30] Parliament later responded to this decision by enacting a law that states that no person can be convicted of child pornography if the act that is alleged to constitute the offense "does not pose an undue risk of harm to persons under the age of eighteen years."[31] The law also now provides that it is a question of law whether any written material or visual representation advocates or counsels sexual activity with a person under the age of eighteen that would be an offense under the Criminal Code.[32] These exceptions only apply to material that is not distributed.

5) *Parent or Guardian Procuring Sexual Activity.* Any parent or guardian who procures a person under the age of eighteen for prohibited sexual activity with another person is liable to a maximum sentence of five years' imprisonment and a minimum sentence of six months' imprisonment if the child is under the age of fourteen and a maximum sentence of two years' imprisonment and a minimum sentence of forty-five days' imprisonment if the child is between the ages of fourteen and eighteen.[33]

6) *Householder Permitting Sexual Activity.* A householder who knowingly permits his or her premises to be used by a minor for illegal sexual activities is liable to the same ranges of punishment as a parent or guardian who procures sexual activity for a child.[34]

7) *Corrupting Children.* The offense of corrupting children is very broadly defined. Under it, a person who "participates in adultery or sexual immorality or indulges in habitual drunkenness or any other form of vice, and thereby endangers the morals of [a] child or renders the home an unfit place for the child to be in" is liable to two years' imprisonment.[35]

8) *Luring a child.* Using a computer to lure a child or a person he or she believes is a child for an unlawful sexual activity is a relatively new offense that is punishable with up to five years' imprisonment. In order to be able to raise mistake as to age as a valid defense, a defendant must prove that he or she took reasonable steps to ascertain the age of the person communicated with.[36]

9) *Abduction of person under fourteen.* Abducting a child with the intent to deprive a parent or guardian of possession of that child is punishable with up to ten years imprisonment.[37]

10) *Abduction in contravention of a custody order.* Abduction of a child under the age of fourteen in contravention of a custody order is also punishable with a maximum sentence of ten years imprisonment.

11) *Abduction.* A parent who abducts a child to prevent a parent or guardian to have possession of him or her is punishable with a maximum sentence of ten years imprisonment even if the child is not the subject of a custody order.[38]

12) *Procuring.* Any person who lives wholly or in part on the avails of a prostitute under the age of eighteen is liable to a maximum sentence of fourteen years imprisonment and a minimum sentence of two years imprisonment. Any person who uses violence, intimidation, or coercion for that purpose is liable to a minimum sentence of five years imprisonment. Any person who attempts to procure a prostitute under the age of eighteen is liable to a maximum sentence of five years imprisonment and a minimum sentence of six months imprisonment.[39]

13) *Removing a Child from Canada.* Removing children from Canada for certain illegal sexual purposes is an offense that is punishable with up to five years imprisonment.[40]

14) *Trafficking.* Canada has strict laws prohibiting the trafficking in persons of all ages. Under the Criminal Code, any person who "recruits, transports, transfers, receives, holds, conceals or habours a person...for the purpose of exploiting them or facilitating their exploitation is guilty of an indictable offense and is liable to imprisonment for life if they kidnap, commit an aggravated assault, or aggravated sexual assault against, or cause death to, the victim during the commission of the offense [and] to imprisonment for up to fourteen years in any other case."[41] Judges may exclude members of the public from the courtroom where it is in the proper

administration of justice, which includes ensuring that witnesses under the age of eighteen are safeguarded.[42]

In Canada, minimum sentences are fairly rare. The fact that so many of the offenses described above do carry minimum sentences indicates that Parliament has taken extraordinary steps to protect children. In addition to creating a number of offenses that are designed specifically to punish persons who exploit or abuse minors, Parliament has also provided that abusing a person under the age of eighteen is to be viewed as an aggravating factor by judges in sentencing persons convicted of offenses against children.[43]

VII. JUVENILE JUSTICE

In 2002, Parliament enacted a Youth Criminal Justice Act[44] to replace the Young Offenders Act.[45] The Preamble to this statute signals that it was intended to create a far more lenient system for juvenile justice by declaring that

> Canadian society should have a youth criminal justice system that commands respect, takes into account the interests of victims, fosters responsibility and ensures accountability through meaningful consequences and effective rehabilitation and reintegration, and that reserves its most serious intervention for the most serious crimes and reduces the over-reliance on incarceration for non-violent young persons.[46]

The Preamble also notes that Canada is a party to the United Nations Convention on the Rights of the Child and that young persons have rights and freedoms, including those set out in the Canadian Charter of Rights and Freedoms and have "special guarantees of their rights and freedoms. The Declaration of Principle then contains the following statements:

> The criminal justice system for young persons must be separate and apart from that of adults and emphasize: 1) rehabilitation and reintegration: 2) fair and proportionate accountability; 3) enhanced personal protection to ensure that young persons are treated fairly and that their rights, including their rights to privacy, are protected.[47]
>
> Special considerations apply in respect of proceedings against young persons and in particular ... young persons have rights and freedoms in their own right, such as a right to be heard in the course of and to participate in the process, other than the decision to prosecute, that lead to decisions that affect them, and young persons have special guarantees of their rights and freedoms.[48]

Young persons are thus guaranteed the right to be presumed innocent and to prompt notification of charges brought against them. The Act also has provisions for prompt trials and, in this connection, recognizes that young persons have a different perception of time.[49] The applicability of the Charter of Rights and Freedoms to youth criminal justice means that they are guaranteed the right against self-incrimination and the right to use French or English in legal proceedings.[50] The right to a fair trail also guarantees young persons the right to have an interpreter.[51]

The Youth Criminal Justice Act encourages the use of extrajudicial measures by the police and the courts to address youth crime. Extrajudicial measures are designed to be timely, to repair harm, to encourage families to become involved, to give victims an opportunity to participate, and to respect the right and freedoms of young persons.[52] The Act also provides for the imposition of extrajudicial sanctions such as placing young offenders in special programs.[53]

In Canada's youth courts, defendants have the right to counsel. Defendants found guilty of an offense are liable to a youth sentence if the judge finds that all the alternatives allowed for by the Youth Criminal Justice Act are inappropriate. Judges must consider pre-sentence reports. The maximum sentence a juvenile under the age of eighteen can receive for one crime is two years and the maximum sentence for multiple crimes is three years.[54] However, for first degree murder, a juvenile can be sentenced to up to ten years in custody, and for second degree murder, he or she may be sentenced to up to seven years in custody.[55] Also, for certain violent offenses, a youth can be sentenced to an adult sentence of more than two years in custody if the judge in the case finds that a youth sentence would not be sufficient to hold a young person accountable for his or her behavior.[56]

The Youth Criminal Justice Act contains protections for the privacy of young persons. Section 110 of the Act generally prohibits the publication of the names of young persons or information respecting them, except where they have been convicted of certain very serious offenses or have been given an adult sentence.[57] Exceptions are allowed to identify young persons who may be a danger to others or for the purpose of apprehending a young person.[58]

CONCLUSION

In 2003, the United Nations Committee on the Rights of the Child concluded its Thirty-Fourth Session by adopting reports on Canada and several other countries. The Committee stated that it "was encouraged by the numerous initiatives undertaken by" Canada. The Committee praised Canada's National Action Plan for Children and made only a few recommendations. Among these were that the federal government work more closely with the provinces on legislation and policy, prohibit reasonable force in the disciplining of children, and offer more assistance for child care. The Committee was also concerned with the relatively high rate of suicide among Canadian youths, particularly in aboriginal communities. To address this problem, the Committee recommended improvements in the quality of education. The fact that Canadian law did not come under more extensive scrutiny attests to the high level of regard for and adherence to the rights of children in Canada.[59]

Prepared by Stephen Clarke
Senior Foreign Law Specialist
August 2007

End Notes

[1] Government of Canada, Canadian Embassy in France, Age of Majority by Province or Territory (2007), http://www.dfait-maeci.gc.ca/canada-europa/france/canadaaz/agemajorite-en.asp (last visited Aug. 10, 2007).

[2] C.C.Q. 153 (2007).

[3] The Convention on the Rights of the Child, with a Preamble and fifty-four articles, was adopted by the U.N. General Assembly Nov. 20, 1989, and entered into force Sept. 2, 1990. G.A. Res. 44/25, annex, 44 U.N. GAOR Supp. (No. 49) at 167, U.N. Doc. A/44/49 (1989); 28 I.L.M. 1448 (1989). For an online text, see the OHCHR Web site, http://www.ohchr.org/english/law/crc.htm (last visited July 23, 2007); it includes the 1995 amendment to art. 43, para. 2 (G.A. Res. 50/155 (Dec. 21, 1995)), which entered into force Nov. 18, 2002. For an in-depth analysis of Part I of the Convention (articles 1-41), see SHARON DETRICK, A COMMENTARY ON THE UNITED NATIONS CONVENTION ON THE RIGHTS OF THE CHILD (1999); see also Convention on the Rights of the Child, AMNESTY INTERNATIONAL USA, http://www.amnestyusa.org/Children/Convention_on_the_Rights_of_the_Child/page.do?id=1101777&n1=3&n2=78&n3=1272 (last visited July 24, 2007).

[4] The Child Soldiers Protocol, comprising a Preamble and thirteen articles, entered into force Feb. 12, 2002. G.A. Res. A/RES/54/263 of 25 May 2000. For an online text, see the UNHCHR Web site, http://www.unhchr.ch/html/menu2/6/protocolchild.htm (last visited July 23, 2007).

[5] The Sex Trafficking Protocol comprises a preamble and seventeen articles. G.A. Res. A/RES/54/263, May 25, 2000. It entered into force Jan. 18, 2002. For an online text, see the UNHCHR Web site, http://www.unhchr.ch/html/menu2/ dopchild.htm (last visited July 23, 2007).

[6] Statistics Canada, Infant Mortality, by Province and Territory, http://www40.statcan.ca/l01/cst01/health21a.htm (last visited August 7, 2007).

[7] Constitution Act, 1867, R.S.C. No. 5, s. 93 (Appendix 1985).

[8] Education Act, c. E-2, s. 21 (1990), as amended by 2006 S.O. c. 28, s. 5(1).

[9] Ontario, Ministry of Government Services, McGinty Government Helps, Students Stay in School, http://ogov.newswire.ca/ontario/GPOE/2007/01/16/c6146.html?lmatch=%E2%8C%A9=_e.html (last visited Aug. 6, 2007).

[10] Education Act, R.S.O. c. E-2, s. 2 (1990).

[11] Ontarians With Disabilities Act, S.O. c. 32, s. 2.

[12] Id. S. 15.

[13] Accessibility for Ontarians with Disabilities Act, 2005 S.O. c. 11.

[14] Canadian Charter of Rights and Freedoms, Part I of the Constitution Act, 1982, being Sched. B. s. 12 to the Canada Act, 1982, c. 11 (U.K.).

[15] Peter Hogg, Constitutional Law of Canada, 50-2 (1997).

[16] Ontario, School District Policies, Code JGA, http://www.ontario.k12.or.us/District/NewDistrictPolicies/Section_J.html (last visited Aug. 7, 2007).

[17] CANADIAN LABOUR LAW REPORTER, para. 5112 (C.C.H. Can 2007).

[18] Canada Labour Standards Regulations, C.R.C. c. 986, s. 10, as amended (1985).

[19] Industrial Establishments Regulation. R.R.O. No. 851 (1990).

[20] Mines and Mining Plants Regulation, R.R.O. No. 854, s. 8 (1990).

[21] Canada Labour Standards Regulations, C.R.C., c. 986 , s. 20 (1978), as amended.

[22] Canadian Labour Law Reports, para. 6771 (C.C.H. Can. Para. 6771).

[23] Id.

[24] Frequently Asked Questions (FAQs) - Cadest, CADETS CANADA, Apr. 10, 2007, available at http://www.cadets. dnd.ca/recruit/faq-cadet e.asp.

[25] United Nations Office of the High Commissioner for Human Rights, Declarations and Reservations to the Optional Protocol to the Convention on the Rights of the Child on the Involvement of Children in Armed Conflict; http://www.unhchr.ch/html/menu2/6/crc/treaties/declare-opac.htm (last visited Aug. 9, 2007).

[26] National Defence Act, R.S.C. c. N-5, s. 34, as amended by 2000 S.C., c. 13, s. 1.

[27] Criminal Code, R.S.C. c. C-46 (1985) and c. 19, s. 1 (3d Supp. 1988), as amended by 2005 S.C. c. 32, s. 3.

[28] Id. S. 152.

[29] Id. S. 153.

[30] R. v. Sharp, {2001] 1 S.C.R. 45.

[31] Criminal Code, R.S.C. c. C-46, s. 163.1(6), as amended by 1993 S.C. c. 46, s. 2, c. 13, s. 5, and 2005 S.C. c. 32, s. 7.

[32] Id. S. 163.1(7).

[33] Id. S. 170.

[34] Id. S. 171.

[35] Id. S. 172

[36] 2002 S.C. c. 13, s. 8.

[37] Criminal Code, R.S.C. c. C-46, s. 281 (1985).

[38] Id. S. 283.

[39] Id. S. 212.

[40] Id. S. 273.3

[41] Id. S. 279.01.

[42] Id. S. 486.

[43] Id. S. 718.2(a)(ii.1).

[44] Youth Criminal Justice Act, S.C. 2002, c. 1.

[45] Young Offenders Act, R.S.C. c. Y-1 (1985).

[46] Youth Criminal Justice Act, S.C. 2000, c. 1, Preamble.

[47] Id. S. 3.

[48] Id.

[49] Id.

[50] Canadian Charter of Rights and Freedoms, Part I of the Constitution Act, 1982, being Sched. B. s. 12 to the Canada Act, 1982, c. 11, §§ 11(c) & 19 (U.K.).

[51] Id.

[52] Youth Criminal Justice Act, S.C. 2000, S. 5.

[53] Id. S. 6.

[54] Id. S. 42(14).

[55] Id.

[56] Id. S. 72

[57] Id. S. 110.

[58] Id.

[59] Press Release, United Nations, Committee on Rights of Child Concludes Thirty-Fourth Session (Mar. 10, 2003), available at http://www.un.org/News/Press/docs/2003/hr4698.doc.htm.

In: Children's Rights
Editors: Brooke Dabney and Michael Eldridge

ISBN: 978-1-62948-252-1
© 2013 Nova Science Publishers, Inc.

Chapter 7

CHINA: CHILDREN'S RIGHTS[*]

Laney Zang

EXECUTIVE SUMMARY

China has ratified major international documents with regard to children's rights protection. China's domestic legislation also provides protection for a wide range of children's rights. The reality, however, is disputable. Few accurate statistics could be obtained directly from the official source. In practice, enforcement of the treaty obligations and the legislative declarations remains a huge problem.

I. INTRODUCTION

The People's Republic of China (PRC)[1] declares to protect a wide range of children's rights through domestic legislation and by ratifying and joining the relevant international treaties. The PRC Constitution provides for the state protection of children, and prohibits maltreatment of children. [2] Among many laws and regulations providing children's rights protection, the primary law in this field is *The PRC Law on the Protection of Minors* (first passed in 1991, revised in 2006) (Minors Protection Law).[3] The newly revised Minors Protection Law entered into force on June 1, 2007.[4] This law sets up responsibilities of the families, the schools, and the government with regard to the protection of children's rights, and judicial protection, as well.[5]

Children under Chinese Law

Eighteen is the age of majority in China. Under the Minors Protection Law, "minors" are defined as citizens less than eighteen years old.[6] The civil law of China provides that people

---

[*] This document was released by the Law Library of Congress August 2007.

above eighteen years old and those from sixteen to eighteen who make a living on their own have full civil conduct capacity. [7] People aged from ten to eighteen have limited capacity of civil conduct, and may only engage in civil activities appropriate to the age range and intellect. People under ten years old have no civil conduct capacity.[8] Unless otherwise indicated, "children" or "minors" hereinafter refers to people under the age of eighteen.

II. IMPLEMENTATION OF INTERNATIONAL RIGHTS OF THE CHILD

Major international documents relating to children's rights that the PRC government has signed and ratified are as follows:

(i) U.N. Convention on Rights of the Child 1989 (CRC) (Entry into force for China: April 1, 1992); [9]

(ii) Optional Protocol to the Convention on Rights of Child on the Sale of Children, Child Prostitution, and Child Pornography 2000 (Entry into force for China: January 3, 2003);[10]

(iii) International Covenant on Economic, Social and Cultural Rights 1966 (Entry into force for China: June 27, 2001);[11]

(iv) The Convention on the Elimination of All Forms of Discrimination Against Women 1979 (Entry into force for China: December 3, 1981);[12]

(v) Worst Forms of Child Labor Convention 1999 (Entry into force for China: August 8, 2003);[13]

(vi) The Hague Convention on the Protection of Children and Cooperation in Respect of Intercountry Adoption 1993 (Receipt of Instrument: September 16, 2005).[14]

It is worth noting that when deciding on ratification of the CRC, the PRC Standing Committee of the National People's Congress (NPC, China's top legislative body) made a reservation to Article 6 of the CRC on the inherent right to life, stating that China shall fulfill its obligation provided by this article under the prerequisite of planned birth provided by Article 25 of the PRC Constitution.[15]

In addition, China signed but did not ratify the International Covenant on Civil and Political Rights 1966 on October 5, 1998, which, up to now, has not taken effect in China.[16]

With regard to the implementation of its promises for international cooperation, the Chinese government reported in its 2004 human rights white paper that it "conscientiously wrote its first reports on the implementation of the "International Covenant on Economic, Social and Cultural Rights" and the "Optional Protocol to the Convention on the Rights of the Child on the Sale of Children, Child Prostitution and Child Pornography."[17] It also claimed to have held a seminar on the questionnaire of the UN Independent Expert on Violence against Children, "given an honest, detailed answer to it, and submitted it to the United Nations."[18] In addition, "in December 2004, China submitted to the United Nations its answer to the questionnaire on child pornography on the Internet based on careful study."[19]

III. Child Health and Social Welfare

The PRC Law on Maternal and Infant Health Care

The primary law governing child health in China is *The PRC Law on Maternal and Infant Health* (promulgated by the NPC Standing Committee, effective June 1, 1995) (Maternal and Infant Health Law).[20] According to Article 2 of the Maternal and Infant Health Law, "[t]he State shall develop maternal and infant health care projects and provide the necessary environments and material aids so as to ensure that mothers and infants receive medical and health care services." As the body authorized to implement the law, the PRC State Council (China's cabinet) issued an *Implementation Rules of the Maternal and Infant Health Law* in 2001.[21]

The 135-article law covers pre-marital healthcare, pre-natal and post-natal healthcare, administrative provisions for medical assistance and facilities for treatment and health. The law requires medical institutions to offer pre-marital healthcare service, including health instruction, consultation, and medical examination.[22] In cases of certain serious genetic disease found through the examination, longterm contraceptive measures or performance of tubal ligation operations shall be taken upon the agreement of the marrying couple.[23] Medical institutions are also required to provide pre-natal and post-natal healthcare, including instructions, healthcare services for pregnant women, lying-in women, fetuses, and newborns.[24]

It is worth noting that although the law sets up the duties for medical institutions and local governments in offering and assisting maternal and infant healthcare, the services are not always free. The only service clearly provided by this law to be free is in Article 19: "The operations of terminating gestation or ligation operations in accordance with the law are free of any charge."[25]

Medical Insurance

China has been in the process of reforming the health care system for more than one decade. Under the old system implemented in the planned economy, "the labor insurance system" provided that all the "socialist workers" get healthcare from the state for free, with children's healthcare covered through their parents' labor insurance. According to article 13 of *The 1950 PRC Regulation on the Labor Insurance*, a worker's medical bill shall be paid by the state-owned enterprises for which he or she works, and their children get fifty percent of their medical costs reimbursed.[26]

The labor insurance was replaced by "the employee's basic medical insurance" in 1998. The State Council of China issued *The Decision on Establishing the Urban Employees' Basic Medical Insurance System* at the end of that year.[27] Children's health care is not covered in this decision, which actually pushes them out of the state's medical insurance system.[28] The State Council is now considering a new medical insurance system, aiming to cover children and other citizens who are not eligible to join the employees' basic medical insurance. Local governments, especially those in developed areas, are establishing local medical insurance systems for the children residing in those areas.[29]

Birth Control

Birth control is established by the Chinese Constitution as a fundamental policy of the nation.[30] Citizens bear the statutory obligation to practice birth control under the law.[31] *The PRC Law on the Population and Family Planning* "advocates" one couple to have only one child, with exceptions provided by provincial-level population control regulations when a couple "may apply" to have two children (most likely to couples in rural areas whose first child is female).[32]

The government, however, implements the "advocated" policy strongly, which is widely criticized to be to be violating international human rights standards set up in the international children's right documents mentioned in above part II. The Congressional-Executive Commission on China (CECC) detailed the coerced compliance with the policy performed by the officials to be "through a system marked by pervasive propaganda, mandatory monitoring of women's reproductive cycles, mandatory contraception, mandatory birth permits, coercive fines for failure to comply, and in some cases, forced sterilization and abortion."[33] In its 2007 Annual Report, the CECC concludes that in 2007:

> China continues to implement population planning policies that violate international human rights standards. These policies impose government control over women's reproductive lives, result in punitive actions against citizens not in compliance with the population planning policies, and engender additional abuses by officials who implement the policies at local levels. In 1007, the Party and government leadership reaffirmed its commitment to its population planning policies, and continues to implement such actions as charging large "social compensation fees" to families that bear children "out of plan."[34]

IV. Education, including Special Needs

Compulsory Education

The PRC Law on Compulsory Education (Compulsory Education Law) codifies school-age children the right to receive nine years of compulsory education (a six-year primary school and a three-year middle school).[35] The law lays down the principle that the state shall establish a funding system to guarantee implementation of compulsory education.[36] Under the Compulsory Education Law, children shall be sent to school at the age of six (or seven in the undeveloped areas) to receive education, and no tuition fees and miscellaneous fees shall be charged during the nine years of compulsory education.[37] In order to promote balanced development of all the schools, the local government educational authorities are prohibited from dividing schools into key schools and ordinary schools, and the schools are prohibited from dividing classes into elite classes and non-elite classes, which were actually the common situation before implementation of the law.[38] The law also bans any entrance examinations for basic education.[39]

The curriculum in all Chinese schools is decided by the governmental educational authority, namely the Ministry of Education.[40] Text books will be reviewed and may be censored by the government and may not be used without pre-approval of the state.[41]

The local-level government implementation of their statutory obligations of compulsory education varies from the economically developed east to the undeveloped west, from urban areas to the rural areas. According to a report by an official news agency in 2006, China "will exempt primary and junior high school students in its rural west from tuition and other education expenses this year, pledging to implement similar policies in other areas starting 2007,"[42] evidencing that at least in the western rural areas, compulsory education has not been fully established. The government published a national net enrollment statistic ratio to primary schools, which is 99.2% in 2005.[43] This number may have excluded the children of the migrant workers in the cities, who are not present at their household registration addresses and therefore hard to be calculated in the statistics. Their education resources are so insufficient that in 2003, the State Council circulated an official notice urging the local-level governments to improve equal education rights of the migrant children, in which it admits that the education of the migrant children has been an increasingly difficult problem of the county.[44] Approximately 9.3% of the migrant children do not get access to schools in the cities, according to a report of the China Youth Daily, a government related newspaper.[45]

Special Education for Disabled Children

The local government at or above county level is required to set up special schools to provide compulsory education for school-age children who have disabilities in vision, hearing, and intelligence.[46] These special schools are to be equipped with sites and facilities which adapt to the study, recovery, and living needs of the disabled children.[47] For those special-needs children who are capable of studying in the ordinary school, the schools must accept them without discrimination and provide aids for their study and recovery, according to the law.[48]

Correctional Education and Work-Study Schools

The local government is also required to set up special schools for children "who perpetrate serious misbehaviors" as specified in *The Law on Prevention of Juvenile Delinquency* (Prevention Law) as a part of the compulsory education.[49]

The Prevention Law took effect from 1999, aiming to prevent juveniles from committing criminal offenses and assisting in rehabilitation.[50] The law prohibits parents and other guardians from leaving children under the age of sixteen to live alone.[51] Violation of this provision may result in a reprimand from the public security authorities.[52]

The Prevention Law spells out a list of "serious misbehaviors," which refers to certain offenses that "seriously harm the society but are not enough for criminal punishment."[53] For a juvenile who has committed such offenses, his parents or other guardians may apply, through approval of the government educational authorities, to send him to one of the special correctional work-study schools.[54] It is worth noting that before the law took effect in 1999, it was not necessary that the parents or guardians agree to special placement; it could simply be enforced by the public security authorities. It is reported that the first work-study school was established in Beijing in 1955; the highest number of such schools around the country was 180; by 2004, however, only eighty-three were left.[55] The curriculum provided in such work-study schools is to be consistent with the ordinary schools, with additional "education on legality."[56]

V. CHILD LABOR AND EXPLOITATION

The minimum age for working in China is sixteen. Before *The PRC Labor Law* (Labor Law) was passed in 1994, the State Council issued *The Provisions on the Prohibition of Using Child Labor* (Child Labor Provisions) in 1991, which were amended in 2002.[57] In 2003, eight central government authorities including the Ministry of Labor, the Ministry of Public Security, and the Ministry of Education jointly issued a notice to reinforce implementation of Child Labor Provisions.[58]

Article 15 of the Labor Law prohibits an employer to recruit minors under the age of sixteen, with exception made for institutions of literature, art, physical culture, and special crafts which may recruit minors through investigation and approval of the government authorities, and must guarantee the minors' rights to compulsory education.[59] Using child labor without government approval may result in RMB5,000 (equivalent to about USD $660) fine per child worker per month.[60]

Despite the legislative requirements, the practice of child labor is believed to be "a persistent problem within China" by some China watchers.[61] Though the CECC agrees that "the overall extent of child labor in China is unclear due to the government categorizing data on the matter as 'highly secret,'"[62] it cited a report on child labor in China finding that "child labors generally work in low-skill service sectors as well as small workshops and businesses, including textile, toy, and shoe manufacturing enterprises."[63]

VI. SALE AND TRAFFICKING OF CHILDREN

China is on the "Tier 2 Watch List" in the U.S. State Department Trafficking in Persons Report. According to this report, "The People's Republic of China is a source, transit, and destination country for men, women, and children trafficked for the purposes of forced labor and sexual exploitation. A significant number of Chinese women and children are trafficked internally for forced marriage and forced labor." The report admits the PRC government is making significant efforts to comply with the minimum standards for the elimination of trafficking. Its placement on the Tier 2 Watch List is due to its failure to provide evidence of increasing efforts to combat trafficking, specifically its inadequate protection for trafficking victims, particularly foreign women and P.R.C. women identified from Taiwan.[64]

The Chinese government claims that it has taken effective measures to prevent and severely punish crimes in the trafficking of women and children, in the national report on child development mentioned above.[65]

Crime of Abducting and Trafficking a Woman or Child

To commit the crime of abducting and trafficking a woman or child in China may result in a range of punishments from five years imprisonment to the death penalty, according to *The PRC Criminal Law*.[66] One of the circumstances the judge may consider in imposing a heavier sentence is whether the abducted child has been sold abroad.[67] Buying an abducted child may result in up to three years imprisonment.[68]

Age of Consent for Marriage

The PRC Marriage Law sets the minimum age of marriage at twenty-two for a male and twenty for a female.[69]

Statutory Rape

Having sexual intercourse with a girl under fourteen years of age is statutory rape, with a sentence of heavier punishment within the range of punishments for rape.[70] Committing rape in China may result in sentencing of a fixed-term imprisonment from three years to ten years, and if one of a list of "serious circumstances" spelled out in The PRC Criminal Law happens, a fixed-term imprisonment from ten years up to the death penalty may be imposed. The "serous circumstances" include (i) raping women or minors; (ii) raping a number of women or girls under the age of fourteen; (iii) raping a woman in public; (iv) raping in rotation by more than two offenders; and (v) causing serious injury or death to the victim or any other serious consequences.[71]

Indecent Assault

Indecent assault against a woman's will, or by force, may result in up to five years imprisonment. If the offence happens in public, the sentence may be over five years.[72] Fingering or sodomy committed against minors under fourteen years old may result in heavier punishment in the abovementioned range of punishments.[73]

Child Prostitution

Promiscuity may result in imprisonment for up to five years or forced labor under the PRC Criminal Law. Those who lure minors into promiscuity will be punished by a heavier penalty.[74]

Organizing or compelling others to prostitution may result in fixed-term imprisonment from five years to ten years and a fine. Organizing or compelling girls under the age of fourteen to prostitution, however, may result in a fixed-term imprisonment from ten years to life imprisonment or even the death penalty and confiscation of property.[75]

Inducing girls under the age of fourteen into prostitution may result in fixed-term imprisonment of five years and fine.[76]

Having sex with girls under the age of fourteen who are acting as prostitutes may result in a fixed-term imprisonment of five years and fine.[77]

Child Pornography

The PRC Criminal Law does not specifically regulate child pornography. Distributing pornography to minors under age eighteen is punishable by a heavier penalty within the punishments for distributing pornography.[78]

VII. JUVENILE JUSTICE

Age Requirement for Bearing Criminal Responsibility

The general age requirement for bearing criminal responsibility under Chinese law is sixteen. A person aged from fourteen to sixteen bears criminal responsibility in intentionally committing serious criminal offenses spelled out in the Criminal Law, including homicide, rape, and robbery. An offender aged from fourteen to eighteen shall be given a lighter or mitigated punishment.[79] An offender under the age of fourteen does not result in criminal punishments under Chinese law.

Judicial Protection of the Juvenile

The Minors Protection Law requires the judiciary to protect minors' legal rights during judicial proceedings. [80] There are ten articles in this law specifically dealing with judicial protection.

Unfortunately, most of these p legislative declarations are not enforced effectively in practice.[81]

Article 51 of the Minors Protection Law provides prompt trial of cases brought by minors whose lawful rights and interests are injured. However, no specific time line is found in this law to decide how prompt the case shall be brought to trial.[82] This article also requires the legal aid institutions or the courts to provide legal aid to the minors, which in practice is yet not fulfilled.[83] Article 52 requires the court to protect the property rights of the minors, and respect the minors' wishes in handling the disputes over foster care.[84] This article just repeats existing laws. Article 57 provides separate custody or imprisonment of minors from an adult jail or prison population, and provides for compulsory education for minors in prison.[85] Article 55 requires the judiciary to appoint a special institution or personnel to handle juvenile cases. Up to 2007, China is reported to have organized 2420 juvenile tribunals in the courts around the country.[86] Broadcasting of any information on minor criminal offenders is prohibited.[87]

Prepared by Laney Zhang
Foreign Law Specialist
August 2007

End Notes

1 For purposes of this report only, the "PRC" and "China" used hereafter refers to the mainland of the People's Republic of China, with the exclusion of the Hong Kong Special Administrative Region, the Macau Special Administrative Region, and Taiwan.

2 XIAN FA [CONSTITUTION] art. 49 (1982) (P.R.C).

3 The PRC Law on the Protection of Minors, 2007 GAZETTE OF THE STANDING COMMITTEE OF THE NATIONAL PEOPLE'S CONGRESS 5 (P.R.C) (official source).

4 Id.

5 The Minors Protection Law has seven chapters as follows: Chapter 1, General Principles; Chapter 2, Family Protection; Chapter 3, School Protection; Chapter 4, Society Protection; Chapter 5, Judicial Protection; Chapter 6, Legal Penalties; and Chapter 7, Miscellaneous.

6 The Minors Protection Law, art. 2.

7 Minfa Tongze [General Principle of Civil Law] (promulgated by the NPC, effective Jan. 1, 1987), art 11, 1986 FAGUI HUIBIAN 1, 4 (official source).

8 Id., art. 12.

9 G.A. Res. 44/25, annex, 44 U.N. GAOR Supp. (No. 49) at 167, U.N. Doc. A/44/49 (1989); 28 I.L.M. 1448 (1989). Available online at the Office of the U.N. High Commissioner for Human Rights (UNHCHR) Web site,: http://www.ohchr.org/english/law/crc.htm (last visited Aug. 7, 2007). For the status of signatures, ratifications, and accessions, see the OHCHR Web site, http://www.ohchr.org/english/ countries/ ratification/ 11.htm (last visited July 27, 2007).

10 G.A. Res. A/RES/54/263 of 25 May 2000. For an online text, see the UNHCHR Web site, http://www. unhchr. ch/html/menu2/dopchild.htm (last visited Aug. 7, 2007). For the status of ratifications and reservations, see the OHCHR Web site, http://www.ohchr.org/english/countries/ratification/11_c.htm (last updated July 13, 2007) (last visited Aug. 3, 2007).

11 G.A. Res. 2200A (XXI), 21 U.N.GAOR, 21st Sess., Supp. (No. 16) at 49, U.N. Doc. A/6316 (Dec. 16, 1966), 993 U.N.T.S. 3. For an online text, see the OHCHR Web site, http://www.ohchr.org/english/law/cescr.htm (last visited Aug. 7, 2007). For the status of ratifications and reservations, see the OHCHR Web site, http://www.ohchr.org/english/countries/ratification/3.htm#ratifications (last visited Aug. 7, 2007).

12 G.A. Res. 34/180, 34 U.N. GAOR Supp. (No. 46) at 193, U.N. Doc. A/34/46. For an online text, see the U.N. Division of the Advancement of Women Web site, http://www.un.org/womenwatch/ daw/cedaw/text /econvention.htm#article1 (last visited Aug. 7, 2007). A list of the status of signatures, ratifications, and accessions is available on the same Web site, at http://www.un.org/womenwatch/daw/cedaw/states.htm (last visited Aug. 7, 2007). China made a reservation to paragraph 1 of article 29 with regard to dispute resolution.

13 2002 GAZETTE OF THE STANDING COMMITTEE OF THE NATIONAL PEOPLE'S CONGRESS 308 (P.R.C.) (official source). See also 2003 ZHONGGUO FALV NIANJIAN [2003 CHINA LAW YEARBOOK] 701 (official source). For an online text for the convention, see the OHCHR Web site, http://www.ohchr.org/ english/law/childlabour.htm (last visited Aug. 7, 2007).

14 2005 GAZETTE OF THE STANDING COMMITTEE OF THE NATIONAL PEOPLE'S CONGRESS 371 (P.R.C.) (official source). See also, 2006 ZHONGGUO FALV NIANJIAN [2006 CHINA LAW YEARBOOK] 491 (official source). For an online text, see the HCCH Web site, http://www.hcch. net/index_ en.php?act=conventions.text&cid=69 (last visited Aug. 7, 2007).

15 G.A. Res. 44/25, annex, 44 U.N. GAOR Supp. (No. 49) at 167, U.N. Doc. A/44/49 (1989); 28 I.L.M. 1448 (1989). See also 1991 GAZETTE OF THE STANDING COMMITTEE OF THE NATIONAL PEOPLE'S CONGRESS 662 (P.R.C.) (official source).

16 G.A. Res. 2200A (XXI), 21 U.N. GAOR, 21st Sess. Supp. (No. 16) at 52, U.N. Doc. A/6316 (Dec. 16, 1966), 999 U.N.T.S. 171. For an online text, see the OHCHR Web site, http://www.ohchr.org/english/law/ccpr.htm (last visited Aug. 7, 2007). For the status of ratifications, see the OHCHR Web site, http://www.ohchr.org/ english/countries/ratification/4.htm (last visited Aug. 7, 2007).

[17] The Information Office of the PRC State Council, China's Progress in Human Rights in 2004, available at the official news Web site, http://news.xinhuanet.com/english/2005-04/13/content_2822511.htm.

[18] Id.

[19] Id.

[20] Muying Baojian Fa [Law on Maternal and Infant Health] (promulgated by the NPC Standing Committee, effective June 1, 1995), 1994 FAGUI HUIBIAN 158 (official source).

[21] Muying Baojian Fa Shishi Banfa [Implementation Rules of the Maternal and Infant Health Law] (promulgated by the State Council, effective June 20, 2001). ChinaLawInfo (Chinalawinfor ID No. 35752) (unofficial source).

[22] Id., art. 7.

[23] Id., art. 10.

[24] Id., art. 14.

[25] Id., art. 19 § 2.

[26] Laodong Baoxian Tiaoli [Regulation on the Labor Insurance] (promulgated by Zhengwu Yuan (then China's cabinet), effective Feb. 26, 1951). ChinaLawInfo (Chinalawinfo ID No. 44332) (unofficial source).

[27] Guowuyuan Guanyu Jianli Chengzhen Zhigong Jiben Yiliao Baoxian Zhidu de Jueding [The Decision on Establishing the Urban Employees' Basic Medical Insurance System] (issued by the State Council on Dec. 14, 1998). ChinaLawInfo (Chinalawinfo ID No. 21638) (unofficial source).

[28] The State Council Instructive Opinions on Launching Testing of Urban Residents Basic Insurance (July 10, 2007), available at the central government official Web site: http://www.gov.cn/zwgk/2007-07/24/content_695118.htm.

[29] E.g., Suzhou, a rich city of Jiangsu Province in east China, implemented the Children's In-Hospital Medical Insurance System. Ertong Dabing Yiliao Baozhang Xu Jinkuai Quanguo Tongyi [Children's Major Medical Insurance Needs to be Uniformed throughout the Country], http://news.xinhuanet.com/comments/2007-03/05/content_5800253.htm (last visited Aug. 7, 2007).

[30] Article 25 of the PRC Constitution reads: "The state promotes family planning so that population growth may fit the plans for economic and social development." XIAN FA art. 25 (1982) (P.R.C).

[31] Renkou Yu Jihua Shengyu Fa [Law on the Population and Family Planning] (promulgated by the NPC Standing Committee, effective Sept. 1, 2002), art. 17, 2001 FALÜ HUIBIAN 316, 320 (official source).

[32] Id., art. 18, 2001 FALÜ HUIBIAN 316, 320 (official source).

[33] CONGRESSIONAL EXECUTIVE COMMISSION ON CHINA, 2007 ANNUAL REPORT 108, available at http://frwebgate.access.gpo.gov/cgi-bin/getdoc.cgi?dbname=110 house hearings&docid=f:38026.pdf (last visited Aug. 7, 2007).

[34] Id., at 16.

[35] Yiwu Jiaoyu Fa [The PRC Law on Compulsory Education](promulgated by the NPC Standing Committee on April 12, 1986, amended June 29, 2006, effective Sept. 1, 2006), art 2, VII 2006 XIN FAGUI HUIBIAN 6 (official source).

[36] Id., art. 2 § 4.

[37] Id., arts. 2 and 11.

[38] Before the middle 1980s, because educational resources were scarce, selected "key schools" — usually those with records of past educational accomplishment — were given priority in the assignment of teachers, equipment, and funds. They were also allowed to recruit the best students for special training to compete for admission to top schools at the next level.

[39] Id., art. 12.

[40] Id., art. 35.

[41] Id., art. 39.

[42] China Pledges Free 9-year Education for Students in Rural West, XINHUA NEWS AGENCY (Feb. 21, 2006), available at http://english.peopledaily.com.cn/200602/21/eng20060221_244658.html.

[43] China Education Statistics, available at http://www.stats.edu.cn/sjcx.aspx# (last visited Aug. 7, 2007).

[44] Guowuyuan Bangongting Zhuanfa Jiaoyubu Deng Bumen Guanyu Jinyibu Zuohao Jincheng Wugong Jiuye Nongmin Zinv Yiwu Jiaoyu Gongzuo Yijian De Tongzhi [State Council Circular Transmitting the Opinion of the Education and Other Ministries Relating to Further Work on Migrant Children's Compulsory Education] (Sept. 17, 2003), available at the online subscription Chinese law database Chinalawinfo (Chinalawinfo ID no. 52706).

[45] Woguo Liudong Ertong Shixuelv Gaoda 9.3% [The Dropout Rate from School of Floating Children in China Is as High as 9.3%], CHINA YOUTH DAILY (May 14, 2004), available at http://news.sina.com.cn/c/2004-05-14/16023231841.shtml.

[46] Compulsory Education Law, art. 19.

[47] Id.

[48] Id.

[49] Id., art. 20.

[50] Y ufang Wei Chengnian Ren Fanzui Fa [The Law on Prevention of Juvenile Delinquency] (promulgated by the NPC Standing Committee, effective Nov. 1, 1999). 1999 GAZETTE OF THE STANDING COMMITTEE OF THE NATIONAL PEOPLE'S CONGRESS 276 (P.R.C.) (official source).

[51] Id., art. 19.

[52] Id., art. 50.

[53] Id., art. 34.

[54] Id., art. 35.

[55] Guanzhu Weichengnian Ren: Shenmeyang de Haizi Song Gongdu Xuexiao? [Focus on Minors: To Send What Kind of Children to the Work-Study School?], an official Xinhua News Agency report, available at http://news.xinhuanet.com/newscenter/2004-05/26/content_1491207.htm (last visited Aug. 7, 2007).

[56] Id., art. 36.

[57] Jinzhi Shiyong Tonggong Guiding [The Provisions on the Prohibition of Using Child Labor](promulgated by the State Council, effective April 15, 1991, amended Oct. 1, 2002, effective Dec. 1, 2002). 2002 FAGUI HUIBIAN 1210 (official source).

[58] Guayun Guanche Luoshi Jinzhi Shiyong Tonggong Guiding de Tongzhi [Notice on Implementation of the Child Labor Provisions] (April 18, 2003), iSinoLaw (iSinoLaw ID No. 10063 -2004579) (last visited Aut. 7, 2007).

[59] Lao Dong Fa [Labor Law] (promulgated by the NPC Standing Committee, effective Jan. 1, 1995), art. 15. 1994 FAGUI HUIBIAN 91, 94 (official source).

[60] Child Labor Provisions, art. 6.

[61] E.g., The CECC 2007 Annual Report, supra note 33, at 70).

[62] Id.

[63] Id.

[64] THE U.S. DEPARTMENT OF STATE, 2005 REPORT VICTIMS OF TRAFFICKING AND VIOLENCE PROTECTION ACT OF 2000: TRAFFICKING IN PERSONS REPORT, available at http://www.state.gov/g/tip/rls/tiprpt/2005/ (last visited Aug. 7, 2007).

[65] The National Working Committee report, supra note 34.

[66] Xing Fa [Criminal Law], art. 240. 1997 FAGUI HUIBIAN, 18, 83 (official source).

[67] Id., art. 240 §8.

[68] Id., art. 241.

[69] Hun Yin Fa [Marriage Law] (promulgated by the NPC, amended and effective April 28, 2001), art. 6. 2001 GAZETTE OF THE STANDING COMMITTEE OF THE NATIONAL PEOPLE'S CONGRESS 40 (P.R.C.) (official source).

[70] Criminal Law, art. 236.

[71] Id.

[72] Id., art. 237.

[73] Id.

[74] Criminal Law, art. 301.

[75] Criminal Law, art. 358.

[76] Criminal Law, art. 359.

[77] Criminal Law, art. 360 §2.

[78] Criminal Law, art. 364 §4.

[79] Criminal Law, art. 17.

[80] The Minors Protection Law, art. 50.

[81] See Fan Rongqing, Weichegnian Ren Sifa Baohu de Kunjing Yu Sikao [Difficulties of and Thoughts on Judicial Protection of Minors], 2 QINGSHAONIAN FAZUI WENTI [ISSUES ON JUVENILE CRIMES AND DELIQUENCY] 42-45 (2005). According to the author, a prosecutor in the People's Procuratorate in Shanghai, the Minors Protections Law has never been cited by the court when trying cases with minors as defendants. Id. at 43.

[82] Id., art. 51 §1.

[83] Id., art. 51 §2.

[84] Id., art. 52.

[85] Id., art. 57.

[86] Tian Yu, Zhongguo Shaonian Fating Goujian Shiying Wei Chengnian Ren Tedian Shenpan Zhidu [China Juvenile Tribunals Forming Judicial Systems Adapted to the Minors Characteristics], CHINA COURT NET (June 1, 2007), http://www.chinacourt.org/public/detail.php?id=249471 (last visited Aug. 7, 2007).

[87] The Minors Protection Law, art. 58.

In: Children's Rights
Editors: Brooke Dabney and Michael Eldridge

ISBN: 978-1-62948-252-1
© 2013 Nova Science Publishers, Inc.

Chapter 8

FRANCE: CHILDREN'S RIGHTS[*]

Nicole Atwill

EXECUTIVE SUMMARY

France is a signatory to all the significant treaties dealing with children rights.

It has in place several mechanisms to monitor the implementation of the 1989 Convention on the Rights of the Child, in particular, an ombudsman for children.

Pregnant women are entitled to paid maternity leave. To offset the loss of salary, they receive benefits via the public maternity insurance, often supplemented by a complementary sum payable by the employer as per a collective bargaining agreement. Several categories of family allowances are provided without any condition of employment.

Children under six receive free and mandatory preventive health services in a widespread network of thousands of health-care facilities. After the age of six, children's health is monitored by school health services. Mandatory physical and psychological checkups take place when the children are ages six, nine, twelve, and fifteen. When they are of sufficient maturity, children must be informed of their medical treatment and participate in the decision-making process.

School is mandatory from ages six to sixteen. Although not compulsory, preschool for children under six is widely available and strongly encouraged. Children with special educational needs are educated in mainstream classes alongside their peers wherever possible, to better incorporate them into society.

There is no specific legal age under which a juvenile cannot be prosecuted. The sole criterion is that of moral discernment. Penalties, however, are adapted to the age of the child.

---

[*] This document was released by the Law Library of Congress August 2007.

I. INTRODUCTION

In the past twenty-five years, laws concerning children have multiplied in France. These laws generally use the term "minor" instead of "child"; the Civil Code defines "minor" as "an individual of either sex who has not yet reach eighteen years of age." The recent changes aim at developing a greater legal status for minors, to reflect their place in today's society. The new legislation has also been geared towards the implementation of the fundamental rights and obligations enshrined in the 1989 UN Convention on the Rights of the Child. The government and Parliament have tried to strike a balance between children's rights, the protection of children, and the parents' rights and duties.

II. IMPLEMENTATION OF INTERNATIONAL RIGHTS OF THE CHILD

Among others, France has ratified the following treaties addressing or having an impact on children rights:

- International Covenant on Economic, Social and Cultural rights 1966. Entry into force for France: February 4, 1981;[1]
- International Covenant on Civil and Political Rights 1966. Entry into force for France: February 4, 1981;[2]
- Minimum Age Convention 1973. Entry into force for France: July 13, 1991;[3]
- Convention on the Recognition and Enforcement of Decisions relative to Maintenance Obligations 1973. Entry into force for France: October 1, 1977;[4]
- International Convention on the Elimination of all Forms of Discrimination against Women 1979. Entry into force for France: April 25, 1984; [5]
- Optional Protocol to the Convention on the Elimination of all Forms of Discrimination against Women 1999. Entry into force for France: December 22, 2000;[6]
- Convention on the Rights of the Child 1989. Entry into force for France: September 6, 1990;[7]
- Optional Protocol to the Convention on the Rights of the Child on the Involvement of Children in Armed Conflict 2000. Entry into force in France: March 5, 2003;[8]
- Optional Protocol to the Convention on the Rights of the Child, on the Sale of Children, Child Prostitution and Child Pornography 2000. Entry into force in France: March 5, 2003;[9]
- European Convention on Human Rights 1950. Entry into force in France: May 3, 1974; [10]
- Hague Convention on the Civil Aspects of International Child Abduction 1980. Entry into force December 1, 1983;[11]
- European Convention on Recognition and Enforcement of Decisions concerning Custody of Children and on Restoration of Custody of Children 1980. Entry into force for France September 1, 1983;[12]
- Hague Convention on Protection of Children and Cooperation in respect of Inter-Country Adoption 1993. Entry into force for France : October 1, 1998;[13] and

- Hague Convention on Jurisdiction, Applicable Law, Recognition, Enforcement and Cooperation in Respect of Parental Responsibility and Measures for the Protection of Children 1996. Entry into force for France: no date was specified in the law authorizing ratification. An additional decree should be published at a later date.[14]

France entered a reservation to the 1989 Convention on the Rights of the Child concerning article 30, which provides:

In those States in which ethnic, religious, or linguistic minorities or persons of indigenous origin exist, a child belonging to such a minority or who is indigenous shall not be denied the right, in community with other members of his or her group, to enjoy his or her own culture, to profess and practice his or her own religion, or to use his or her own language.

The French government declined to apply article 30, as article 2 of the 1958 Constitution reads that "France is a republic, indivisible, secular democratic and social. It shall ensure the equality of all citizens before the law without distinction of origin, race or religion. It shall respect all beliefs." The Constitution, therefore, excludes recognition of groups enjoying a special status.

France has in place several mechanisms to supervise the implementation of the Convention. The government, for example, must submit each year a report to Parliament on the implementation of the Convention. Since 2000, France also has an ombudsman for children whose mission is to defend and promote children's rights in France.

III. CHILD HEALTH AND SOCIAL WELFARE

General Access to Healthcare

All legal residents of France are covered by public health insurance (*Assurance maladie*), a branch of the social security system. Workers and their families are affiliated with public health insurance funds determined by their social and/or professional category, while the neediest members of society are covered under Law 1999-641[15] on Universal Health Insurance. The universal health coverage provides basic coverage to all those residing lawfully in France, irrespective of their employment situation or insurance contribution record. It also provides free supplementary coverage to people whose income is less than €7,178.79 (about US$9,900) per year per person.[16] The benefits of the public health insurance include the full range of health services.

Children under sixteen, under seventeen if they are looking for work and registered at the National Employment Agency, under eighteen if in an apprenticeship, and under twenty if they are students or are disabled, are covered by their parents' health insurance.[17]

Health and Social Protection of Pregnant Women

The Public Health Code guarantees the health and social protection of pregnant women. Prenatal and post natal examinations are mandatory.[18] There is a widespread network of thousands of health-care facilities, called *Centres de Protection Maternelle et Infantile,* to ensure that every mother and child receives basic preventive care. Each pregnant woman receives a booklet (*carnet de grossesse*) where every visit and all test results are recorded.[19] Some of the family allowances are tied to the attendance at the mandatory pre- and post-natal visits. The maternity insurance, a branch of the public health insurance, covers the cost of the mandatory natal visits, of the delivery, of all prescribed medicines and tests, and of home care, if the condition of the woman requires it.[20]

Pregnant women are entitled to maternity leave as follows: six weeks before and ten weeks after birth for the two first children; eight weeks before and eighteen weeks after birth for the third child; thirty-four weeks (twelve before birth) for twins; and forty-six weeks (twenty-four before birth) for triplets or more. Their right to return to the same position is guaranteed. To offset the loss of salary during their maternity leave, pregnant women receive benefits paid via maternity insurance known as *indemnités journalières de repos* (per diem rest allowances).[21] The payments often are supplemented by a complementary sum payable by the employer, as per a collective bargaining agreement. Women who breastfeed their children are entitled to take one hour every day (two thirty-minute breaks) at work. Employers who employ more than one hundred women must have at their disposal a breastfeeding bedroom.[22]

Preventive Health Services for Children

Children under the age of six are evaluated by team of pediatricians, nurses, psychologists, and social workers in the *Centres de Protection Maternelle et Infantile.*[23] A decree provides for a number of mandatory medical visits: nine during the first year, one of them to take place within eight days of birth, one during the ninth or tenth month, three between the thirteenth month and the twenty-fifth month, and finally two for each of the next four years.[24] When parents fail to bring their children in for regular checkups, social workers are dispatched to the family home. After the age of six, children's health is monitored by school health services. Mandatory physical and psychological checkups take place when the children are ages six, nine, twelve, and fifteen.[25] In addition to monitoring children's health, schools also have the responsibility to educate children on health issues including, for example, nutrition, sexual education, and addictions (drugs, alcohol, & tobacco).[26]

Consent to Medical Treatment

The Public Health Code provides that minors, where they are of sufficient maturity, must be informed of their medical treatment and participate in the decision-making process.[27] The consent of the parents or legal guardian is also necessary.[28] When a minor refuses a medical treatment that would save his life, however, the juvenile justice judge may enter an order to force him to undergo the treatment.[29]

Minors have access to contraceptives without the consent of their parents.[30] Family planning centers are authorized to deliver to minors anonymously and at no cost certain medicines or contraceptives.[31] A minor may request an abortion without parental consent. In such a case, she must be accompanied by an adult of her choice.[32]

Family Benefits

The Social Security Code provides that "every French citizen or foreign national residing in France, having one or several dependent children residing in France, will receive for these children family benefits."[33] These benefits are supplementary income designed to offset some of the costs of bringing up children. There is no condition of employment. Benefits are paid for dependent child until the age of sixteen, when the period of compulsory schooling ends. They are extended until the age of twenty for children who do not work or whose income does not exceed fifty-five percent of the statutory minimum wage. They include: [34]

- A family allowance due with the second child and varying in amount depending on the number of children;
- A supplementary family allowance payable to any family with at least three children, all aged three and above. It is subject to a means-test;
- An allowance for young children to assist the family before and upon the birth of a child;
- A back to school allowance to help low income families to meet part of the expenses incurred at the beginning of each school year;
- A single parent allowance to help parents with the sole responsibility for raising one or more children. Recipients must earn less than the official minimum family income; and
- A family support allowance granted to a parent or family with dependent orphan children or when one of the parents refuses to pay maintenance or alimony for that child.

When a child is being raised under harsh conditions or the amount of the allowances is not used for his welfare, a juvenile justice judge may order that these allowances be paid to an allowance guardian. This guardian will use the funds to improve the life conditions of the child.

Access to Social Assistance

France has a dual system of child welfare. Social welfare is the responsibility of the local authorities (social services, early childhood health services, and child protection services), while judicial juvenile protection is the responsibility of the central government. Social services provide material and pschological support to minors and families facing social problems that are likely to have an impact on family stability. These types of services usually require the family's approval with respect to the proposed measures concerning child protection. If the family means are insufficient, additional financial aid may be granted. In case of danger or if it is impossible to obtain the family's approval, the youth judicial protection service will intervene. A juvenile justice judge may order family counseling or placement. The danger to a child and the child's best interest are the two fundamental concepts which must guide social welfare workers and judges in choosing the best possible protection measures.[35]

Infant and Child Mortality

According to the 2007 World Health Statistics published by the World Health Organization, the infant mortality rate (per 1000 live births) is four, the neonatal mortality rate is two, and the under five-year old mortality rate is five.[36]

IV. EDUCATION

General Principles and Statistics

The Constitution proclaims that, "The nation guarantees equal access of children and adults to education, vocational training, and culture. The organization of a free and secular public education system at all levels is a duty of the state."[37] The Education Code further provides that "the right to education is guaranteed to every one to enable [pupils] to develop their personality, to rise above their level of initial education, to integrate into social and professional life, and to exercise their citizenship.[38] Public schooling is provided free through the age of eighteen, and education is compulsory for children between the ages of six and sixteen.[39]

There were approximately twelve million students in primary and secondary public and private schools for 2005-2006, in a population of sixty million. One primary student out of seven and one secondary student out of five attended a private school. The majority of private schools are Catholic schools that have signed a contract with the state. This entitles them to receive public funding. In return, they must adhere to the public school curricula and are subject to state supervision. Two million, three hundred thousand students attended universities or other institutions of higher education. The national education budget was €66 billion (about US$90.8 billion) or 23.31 percent of the overall national budget and represented 3.91 percent of the GNP. The French government spends an average of €6,970 per student per year (about US$9,600).[40]

General Organization Pre-School

Although not compulsory, pre-school (*école maternelle*) for children under six is widely available, as the Education Code further provides that "any children over three must be able to attend the nearest pre-school to their domicile."[41] In addition, the option to attend is offered to children over two who are socially disadvantaged. Attendance is strongly encouraged. Preschools follow an established curriculum; psychomotor, developmental, academic, and social aims have been set forth nationwide. The children are generally divided into three sections: lower, middle, and upper, to take into account their different learning rates, degrees of maturity, and skills. Teachers are well-trained professionals, as highly paid and respected as teachers in the later grades. The percentage of children attending pre-school ranges from thirty-three percent for two-year olds to about one hundred percent for five-year olds.[42]

Primary Education

Primary education lasts five years, from the age of six to eleven. It is divided into two cycles, a two-year basic cycle focusing on mathematics, reading, writing, and the introduction of foreign languages and a three year advanced cycle focusing on literature, history, geography, social sciences, sciences, and technology.[43]

Secondary Education

Secondary education extends over seven years, divided into two cycles. The first cycle lasts four years, from age eleven to fifteen. It is offered in a *collège*. Children study the same core curriculum. A diploma is awarded upon the successful completion of a national examination at the end of the fourth year. The second cycle last three years, for children aged fifteen to eighteen.[44] It is offered in a *lycée,* which offers a wide variety of courses. There are two types of *lycées,* vocational ones and the general and technical education *lycées* that prepare students for the *baccalauréat* examination, which they usually take at eighteen. This exam opens access to higher education. Vocational *lycées* prepare for various types of vocational degrees or certificates or for a vocational *baccalauréat.*[45]

Higher Education

Higher education is provided through universities or other prestigious establishments where admission is by competitive examination, entrance examination, or applications accompanied by interviews. All *baccalauréat* holders have the right to enter universities without any prior selection procedure. These universities offer an extremely wide range of studies.[46]

Special Needs Education

Law 2005-102 of February 11, 2005, on Promoting Equal Rights and Opportunities, Participation, and Citizenship for Disabled Persons, proclaims the right to education of disabled children and the responsibility of the state to ensure them an uninterrupted education.[47] Children with special educational needs are educated in mainstream classes alongside with their peers wherever possible, to better prepare them to participate in society.

They are schooled in special classes within mainstream schools or part-time or full-time in special schools when it is not possible to educate them in mainstream schools. Learning assistance at home may also be arranged.[48]

V. CHILD LABOR AND EXPLOITATION

Employment of children

With a few exceptions for those enrolled in certain apprenticeship programs, doing light work during school holidays from the age of fourteen within the limits set forth by the law or working in the entertainment industry, children under the age sixteen may not be employed.[49]

It is expressly prohibited to employ minors under the age of eighteen in the preparation, handling, or sale of written material, posters, drawings, and other materials whose sale, supply, exhibit, display, or distribution are contrary to public morality and constitute a criminal offense.[50] Employing young people under the age of eighteen in certain dangerous jobs is also prohibited.[51]

As for the employment of children under school-leaving age in the entertainment industry, they may not be employed by fixed or itinerant entertainment companies or in radio or television unless they have received an authorization in advance from the competent administrative authority. Written authorization from the child's legal representative must be attached to the employer's application for authorization.[52] Agencies wishing to employ child models must also apply in advance for an authorization from the competent administrative authority, unless the agency has been approved and granted a general license for hiring child models. A decree has set forth the conditions under which approval is granted and the maximum amount of time the child may work per day and per week.[53]

As a general rule, minors under eighteen cannot work more than seven hours a day and thirty-five hours a week. In addition, those over the age of sixteen may not work between the hours of 10:00 pm and 6:00 am; minors under sixteen may not work between 8:00 pm and 6:00 am. Laws prohibiting child employment are strictly enforced through periodic checks by labor inspectors who have the authority to take employers to court for non-compliance with labor laws.[54]

Children and the Armed forces

The minimum recruitment age is seventeen, or sixteen for entrants to military schools.[55] Personnel wishing to join the French Armed Forces must provide evidence of their age and written consent from their parents or guardians. Upon ratification of the Optional Protocol to the Convention on the Rights of the Child on the Involvement of Children in Armed Conflict, France made the following declaration:

> France hereby declares that it recruits only volunteers aged at least 17 who have been informed of the rights and duties involved in military service and that the enlistment of recruits under the age of 18 is valid only with the consent of their legal representatives.

In addition, minors do not participate in military operations taking place abroad. The national service was suspended in 1997. If ever reinstated, minors would not be called, because the National Service Code provides that "French nationals, who are male, owe their national service between the ages of eighteen and fifty."[56]

VI. SALE AND TRAFFICKING OF CHILDREN

Sexual Exploitation and Abuse

Categories of Offenses

The Penal Code distinguishes several categories of sexual offenses according to their nature and their gravity. When committed on a minor, the law generally provides for stiffer penalties. They are as follows:

- Rape: The penalty is increased from fifteen years' imprisonment to twenty years in cases where the rape is committed on a minor under the age of fifteen; on a person who is particularly vulnerable due to age, sickness, infirmity, physical or mental deficiency, or pregnancy; or where it is committed by an ascendant relative or by any person having authority over the victim.[57]

- Sexual assault: It consists of any sexual infringement committed with violence, constraint, threat, or surprise. The penalty is increased from five years' imprisonment and a €75,000 (about U.S. $102,750) fine to seven years' imprisonment and a €100,000 (about U.S. $137,000) fine when committed on a minor less than fifteen years of age or on a person who is particularly vulnerable due to age, sickness, infirmity, physical or mental deficiency, or pregnancy. It is further raised to ten years' imprisonment and a €150,000 fine when it results in an injury or is committed by an ascendant relative or by any person having authority over the victim.[58]

- Indecent assault: Performing without violence, constraint, threat, or surprise, a sexual assault on the person of a minor less than fifteen years old is punishable by five years' imprisonment and a fine of €75,000. This offense is punishable by ten years' imprisonment and a €150,000 fine when committed by an ascendant relative, by any person having authority over the victim, or when the minor has been put in contact with the perpetrators of the act by the use of a telecommunication network for the dissemination of messages intended for the general public. Indecent assault performed on a minor over fifteen years old is punishable by two years' imprisonment and a €300,000 fine when committed by an ascendant relative or by any person having authority over the victim.[59]

- Corruption of a minor: Encouraging or attempting to encourage the corruption of a minor is punishable by five years of imprisonment and a €75,000 fine. These penalties are raised to seven years' imprisonment and a fine of €100,000 when the minor is less than fifteen years old; when the minor has been put in contact with the perpetrators of the act by the use of a telecommunication network for the dissemination of messages intended for the general public, or when the conduct occurs inside a scholastic or educational establishment or, at a time when students are entering or leaving, in the vicinity of such an establishment. The same penalties are applicable to the conduct of an adult who organizes meetings involving sexual exhibitions or relations in which a minor assists or participate.[60]

- Sex tourism: A French national or a person habitually residing in France who while abroad commits one of the following offenses may be prosecuted in France: sexual assault, indecent assault, child pornography, corruption of a minor, or sex with a minor against remuneration. French law applies even if the offense committed is not punishable under the legislation of the country where the offense took place, and prosecution is not conditioned on a complaint from the victim, next of kin, or official report from the authorities of the country where the offense was committed. The offense need only be brought to the attention of the French judicial authorities. These provisions apply even though the defendant acquired French nationality subsequent to the conduct imputed to him or her.[61]

1998 Law Increasing Protection for Minors against Sexual Predators

Law 98-468 of June 17, 1998, reinforcing the prevention and punishment of sexual offenses and increasing protections for minors against sexual predators, establishes a social and judicial follow-up of sexual offenders and strengthens the rights of minor victims of sexual offenses.[62]

The Law obliges a sexual convict to submit to surveillance and assistances measures and, in some cases, to mandatory medical treatment designed to prevent a relapse.[63] The trial court may impose some or all the measures listed in the Law for up to ten years when the offense is classified as a *délit* and twenty years when a *crime* was committed.[64] The follow-up period starts when the convict has served his sentence. Failure to carry out the obligations set by the court may result in an additional term of imprisonment, two years maximum in the case of a *délit* and five years in the case of a crime. The convict is informed of these consequences by the trial court at the time of his sentencing.[65]

In addition, several provisions of the Law aim at improving the reparation of the moral and physical injuries suffered by minors who have been the victims of sexual predators. They include:

- The public prosecutor may request a medical-psychological evaluation in the early stage of the investigation to better appreciate the extent of the damage inflicted on the minor and to establish whether treatment is necessary.[66] The costs of treatment are fully covered by national health insurance;
- Hearings are videotaped in order to limit their number, since such hearings are very trying for the minor;[67]
- The statute of limitations for civil actions resulting from torture, cruel acts, violence, or sexual violence was increased from ten years to twenty years;[68]
- The statute of limitations for sexual offenses starts to run from the time the victim reaches the age of eighteen, as opposed to the time of the commission of the offenses;[69]

- Hazing has become a criminal offense and is punishable by a six-month term of imprisonment and a €7,500 (about U.S. $10,280) fine. These penalties may be doubled in cases where the victim was particularly vulnerable.[70]

Sale, Trafficking, and Kidnapping of Children

The Penal Code contains provisions on trafficking of person,[71] kidnapping,[72] concealment and confinement of children,[73] and the substitution of one child for another.[74] Trafficking is defined as the recruitment, transport, accommodation, or reception of a person in exchange for remuneration or any other consideration, or for the promise of remuneration or other consideration, in order to place that person at the disposal of an identified or unidentified third party so as to allow the commission against that person of the offense of procuring, sexual assault, the exploitation of begging, or living or working conditions inconsistent with human dignity, or to compel that person to commit any such offense. Trafficking is punished by ten years' imprisonment and a €1,500,000 (about $U.S. $2,055,000) fine when committed against a minor.[75]

The Code also punishes anyone who encourages parents to abandon their children or who serves as an intermediary in the placement or adoption of children. When this conduct is committed habitually or for profit, the penalties are doubled.[76]

Procuring and Child Prostitution

Procuring is punished with ten years' imprisonment and a fine of €1,500,000 where it is committed with respect to a minor.[77] If the minor is under fifteen, the penalty is increased to fifteen years' imprisonment and a €3,000,000 (about U.S. $4,110,000) fine.[78] The prostitution of minors is prohibited. Any minor who prostitutes him/herself is considered in danger and falls under the protection of the competent juvenile justice judge.

In addition, soliciting; accepting; or obtaining, in exchange for remuneration or a promise of a remuneration, relations of a sexual nature with a minor who engages in prostitution, even if not habitually, is punished by three years' imprisonment and a fine of €45,000 (about U.S. $61,650).[79] The penalty is increased to five years' imprisonment and a €75,000 fine where the offense is committed habitually or against more than one person, the person was put in contact with the offender by the use of a public communications network, the offense was committed by a person abusing the authority conferred upon him by his position, or the offender involuntarily put the life of the person in danger or committed violence against this person.[80] The penalty is increased to seven years' imprisonment and a fine of €100,000 where the offense was committed against a minor under the age of fifteen.[81]

Child Pornography

Taking, recording, or transmitting a picture or representation of a minor with a view to circulating it, where that image or representation has a pornographic character, is punished with five years' imprisonment and a fine of €75,000. The same penalty applies to offering or distributing such a picture or representation by any means, and to importing or exporting it, or causing it to be imported or exported.[82] The penalties are increased to seven years' imprisonment and a fine of €100,000 where use was made of a public communications network in order to circulate the image or representation of a minor.[83] Possessing such an image or representation is punished by two years' imprisonment and a fine of €30,000 (about U.S. $41,100).[84]

The offenses described above are punished with ten years' imprisonment and a fine of €500,000 (about U.S. $685,000) where they are committed by an organized gang. These provisions also apply to the pornographic images of a person whose physical appearance is that of a minor, unless it is proved that the person was over eighteen on the day his picture was taken or recorded.[85]

VII. JUVENILE JUSTICE

Juvenile offenders are governed by an Ordinance of February 2, 1945, on Juvenile Offenders which has been amended several times. The Ordinance sets forth the principles applicable in this area, in particular, the priority of the educational approach over punishment and the necessity of special courts and procedures. [86]

Criminal Responsibility

There is no specific legal age under which a juvenile cannot be prosecuted. The sole criterion is that of moral discernment, which may vary depending upon the maturity of the child and the nature of the offense committed. The Penal Code provides:[87]

> Minors capable of discernment are criminally responsible for the crimes, délits and contraventions of which they have been found guilty, and are subject to measures of protection, assistance, supervision and education according to the conditions laid down by specific legislation.
>
> This legislation also determines the educational measures that may be imposed upon minors aged between ten and eighteen years of age, as well as the penalties which may be imposed upon minors aged between thirteen and eighteen years old, taking into account the attenuation in responsibility resulting from their age.

Penalties

Penalties, however, are adapted to the age of the child. The Penal Code distinguishes five categories:[88]

- Children without discernment: there is no criminal liability. The juvenile justice judge may, however, consider that the child is in danger or that the conditions of his education are gravely compromised and order an educational or assistance measure;
- Children under ten with discernment: the child may be found criminally responsible before a juvenile justice court. He/she cannot receive either a criminal penalty or an educational sanction. Educational sanctions are a new tool introduced in 2002. They fall between educational measures and criminal sanctions. The judge may only order an educational, protection, or assistance measure.
- Children from ten to thirteen: the judge may order the following educational sanctions: confiscation of the object used in the commission of the offense, ban on associating with the victim or the accomplices, ban on going to the place where the offense took place, compensation of the victim, and mandatory civic education. In the event of non-compliance with these sanctions, the judge may order placement in an institution. The sanctions will appear on the child's criminal record.
- Children from thirteen to sixteen: the criminal penalties incurred are half the ones stipulated for adult offenders. The juvenile justice court may combine criminal penalties with educational measures.
- Children from sixteen to eighteen: they may benefit from the same penalty reduction than children from thirteen to sixteen receive, but in their case, this reduction is optional.

Prosecution

When an offense committed by a minor is brought to the attention of the public prosecutor, he/she may decide to instigate criminal proceedings or use alternative procedures, in particular where the offense has limited consequences for both the victim and the society. They include admonition with compensation of the victim, conditional closure of the case with the obligation to compensate the victim, or instruction to undergo treatment or punitive mediation.[89]

Juvenile Justice Courts

The juvenile justice courts consist of the juvenile justice judge, the children's tribunal, and the *Cour d'assises des mineurs*. The juvenile justice judge deals with contraventions and *délits*. He may only order educational measures. The children's tribunal is comprised of one juvenile justice judge and two non-professional judges with an interest in the field of childhood. It has the same jurisdiction as the juvenile justice judge but, in addition, the tribunal deals with *crimes* perpetrated by minors under sixteen. It may decide to send the juvenile to a specialized institution or sentence him. The *Cour d'assises des mineurs* is comprised of three professional judges and nine jurors. It adjudicates the most serious offenses perpetrated by minors over sixteen.[90]

Recent Legislation

The French Parliament recently adopted Law 2007-297 of March 5, 2007, on Prevention of Delinquency, that primarily targets young offenders. It emphasizes the role of local authorities, in particular mayors, in the fight against crime. Security and Crime Prevention Councils will be created in cities with more than 10,000 inhabitants; each will be presided over by the mayor or his designated representative. In addition, Councils for the Rights and Duties of Families, also chaired by the mayor, will be established to give official admonitions to minors for any disorderliness, or impose "parental supervision" on parents the Councils consider are "failing in their duties." Mayors may notify the juvenile justice court of families and minors in difficult social and/or psychological situations.[91]

Finally, Parliament presently is debating a draft law on minor and adult repeat offenders. If passed, the law would set automatic minimum sentences for repeat offenders (minors and adults) higher than the minimum penalties already set forth for each offense. The courts, however, would still be able to sentence a repeat offender to a lesser sentence than the automatic minimum sentence where the circumstances of the offense, the personality of its author, or the rehabilitation guaranties justify it. Rehabilitation guarantees are guarantees that the offender gives to show that he will be able to be part of society again. The draft law also stipulates that minors sixteen and older would be treated as adults when repeating one of the gravest offenses listed in the law.[92]

CONCLUSION

As a general rule, children in France enjoy all the rights and liberties enshrined in the 1989 UN Convention on the Rights of the Child. The state plays an important role in the social welfare and protection of children, along with local authorities. The ombudsman for children and several governmental and non-governmental organizations and associations closely monitor the children's welfare. They regularly identify problem areas and make recommendations to the President of the Republic or to the government for improving the legislation in force.

Prepared by Nicole Atwill
Senior Foreign Law Specialist
August 2007

End Notes

[1] Decree 81-77, Jan. 29, 1981, JOURNAL OFFICIEL [Official Gazette of France, J.O.], Feb. 1, 1981, 405.
[2] Decree 81-76, Jan. 29, 1981, J.O., Feb. 1, 1981, at 398.
[3] Decree 91-1088, Oct. 16, 1991, J.O., Oct. 22, 1991, at 13826.
[4] Decree 77-1120, Sept. 22, 1977, J.O., Oct. 5, 1977, at 4835.
[5] Decree 84-193, Mar. 12, 1984, J.O., Mar. 20, 1984, at 875.
[6] Decree 2001-953, Oct. 15, 2001, J.O., Oct. 20, 2001, at 16578.
[7] Decree 90-917, Oct. 8, 1990, J.O., Oct 12, 1990, at 12363.
[8] Decree 2003-373, Apr. 15, 2003, J.O., Apr. 24, 2003, at 7306.

[9] Decree 2003-372, Apr. 5, 2003, J.O., Apr. 24, 2003, at 7303.

[10] Decree May 3, 1974, J.O., May 4, 1974, at 4750.

[11] Decree 83-1021, Nov. 29, 1983, J.O., Dec. 1, 1983, at 3466.

[12] Decree 83-724, July 27, 1983, J.O., Aug. 6, 1983, at 2567.

[13] Decree 98-815, Sept. 11, 1998, J.O., Sept. 13, 1998, at 13997.

[14] Law 2007-1161, Aug. 1, 2007, J.O., Aug 2, 2007, at 12988.

[15] Law 99-641, July 27, 1999, J.O., July 28, 1999, at 11229.

[16] CODE DE LA SECURITE SOCIALE, art. D.861-1 (Dalloz, 2007) (The Dalloz Codes are an unofficial source of law but are widely used by attorneys and judges).

[17] Id., art. L .313-3.

[18] CODE DE LA SANTE PUBLIQUE, art. L.2122-1 (Dalloz, 2007).

[19] Id., art. L.2122-2.

[20] CODE DE LA SECURITE SOCIALE, art.L.331-2.

[21] Id., arts. L.331-3 to L.331-8.

[22] CODE DU TRAVAIL, arts. R.224-1& R.224-4 to R., 224-23 (Dalloz, 2007).

[23] CODE DE LA SANTE PUBLIQUE, arts. L.2111-1 & subsequent.

[24] GUY RAYMOND, DROIT DE L'ENFANCE ET DE L'ADOLESCENCE 255 (Litec, 2006).

[25] CODE DE L'EDUCATION, art. L-541-1, LEGIFRANCE, http://www.legifrance.gouv.fr/ (Les Codes) (last visited Aug. 13, 2007).

[26] Id., arts. L312-16, L312-17.

[27] CODE DE LA SANTE PUBLIQUE, arts. L.111-2 & L.111-4.

[28] Id., art. L.111-7.

[29] CODE CIVIL, art. 375 (Dalloz, 2007).

[30] CODE DE LA SANTE PUBLIQUE, art. L.5134-1.

[31] Id. art. L.2311-4.

[32] Id., art. L. 2212-7.

[33] CODE DE LA SECURITE SOCIALE, art. L.512-1.

[34] Id. arts. R.521-1 to R-544-1.

[35] GUY RAYMOND, DROIT DE L'ENFANCE ET DE L'ADOLESCENCE 61- 67 (Litec, 2006).

[36] 2007 World Health Statistics Published, WORLD HEALTH ORGANIZATION, http://www.who.int/research/en/ (last visited Aug. 13, 2007).

[37] 1958 Constitution, Preamble, LEGIFRANCE, http://www.legifrance.gouv.fr/ (Constitution) (last visited Aug. 13, 2007).

[38] CODE DE L'ÉDUCATION, art. L.111-1, http://www.legifrance.gouv.fr/ (Les Codes) (last visited Aug. 13, 2007).

[39] Id., art. L.131-1.

[40] Ministère de l'Éducation Nationale, Les chiffres clés, http://www.education (last visited Aug. 13, 2007).

[41] CODE DE L'ÉDUCATION, art. L. 113-1, http://www.legifrance.gouv.fr/ (Les Codes) (last visited Aug. 13, 2007).

[42] Ministère de l'Éducation Nationale, L'école maternelle, http://www.education. (last visited Aug. 13, 2007).

[43] Ministère de l'Éducation Nationale, L'école élémentaire, http://www.education. (last visited Aug. 13, 2007).

[44] Ministère de l'Éducation Nationale, Le collège, http://www.education (last visited Aug. 13, 2007).

[45] Ministère de l'Éducation Nationale, Le lycée, http://www.education (last visited Aug. 13, 2007).

[46] Ministère de l'Éducation Nationale, L'enseignement supérieur, http://www.education. (last visited Aug. 13, 2007).

[47] Law 2005-102, Feb. 11, 2005, on Promoting Equal Rights and Opportunities, Participation and Citizenship for Disabled Persons, J. O., Feb. 12, 2005, at 2353.

[48] Ministère de l'Éducation Nationale, La scolarisation des enfants handicapés, http://www.education.gouv.fr/ cid207/ la-scolarisation-des-eleves-handicapes.html (last visited Aug. 13, 2007).

[49] CODE DU TRAVAIL, art. L. 211-1 (Dalloz, 2007).

[50] Id., art. R.234-1.

[51] Id., arts. R.234-5 & subsequent.

[52] Id., art. L.211-6.

[53] Id., arts. L 211-6, R. 211-6 & subsequent.

[54] Id., art. L.L.213-7.

[55] CODE DE LA DEFENSE, art. L 4132-1, LEGIFRANCE, http://www.legifrance.gouv.fr/ (Les Codes) (last visited Aug. 13, 2007).

[56] NATIONAL SERVICE CODE, art. L. 3, http://www.legifrance.gouv.fr/ (Les Codes) (last visited Aug. 13, 2007).

[57] CODE PENAL, art. 222-24, (Dalloz, 2007).

[58] Id., arts. 222-27, 222-29 & 222-30.

[59] Id., arts. 227-25, 227-26 & 222-27.

[60] Id., art. 227-22.

[61] Id., arts. 222-22 & 227-27-1.

[62] Law 98-468, June 17, 1998, J.O., June 18, 1998, at 9255.

[63] CODE PENAL, art. 131-36-1.

[64] There are three grades of criminal offenses under French law: crimes, délits, and contraventions. Crimes (the gravest offenses) include, for example murder, armed robbery, serious drug offenses, and rape. Délits are the largest group of offenses and include sexual violence, theft, fraud, and assaults among others. Contraventions are punishable only by a fine.

[65] CODE PENAL, art. 131-36-5

[66] CODE DE PROCEDURE PENALE, art. 706-48.

[67] Id., art. 706-52.

[68] CODE CIVIL, art. 2270-1

[69] CODE DE PROCEDURE PENALE, arts. 7 & 8.

[70] CODE PENAL, arts 225-16-1 & 225-16-2.

[71] Id., art. 225-4-1.

[72] Id., arts. 224-1 to 224-5.

[73] Id., arts. 227-5 to 227-11.

[74] Id., art. 227-13.

[75] Id., art. 225-4-2.

[76] Id., art. 227-12.

[77] Id., art. 225-7.

[78] Id., art. 225-7-1.

[79] Id., art. 225-12-1.

[80] Id., art. 225-12-2.

[81] Id.

[82] Id., art. 227-23.

[83] Id.

[84] Id.

[85] Id., art. 227-23.

[86] Ordinance, Feb. 2, 1945, on Juvenile Offenders, CODE PENAL, Appendice, at 1707.

[87] CODE PENAL, art. 122-8.

[88] GUY RAYMOND, DROIT DE L'ENFANCE ET DE L'ADOLESCENCE 381-385 (Litec, 2006).

[89] Id.

[90] Ordinance, Feb. 2, 1945, on Juvenile Offenders, CODE PENAL, Appendice, at 1707.

[91] Law 2007-297, Mar. 5, 2007, on Prevention of Delinquency, J.O., Mar. 7, 2002, at 4297.

[92] Projet de loi renforçant la lutte contre la récidive des majeurs et des mineurs, LEGIFRANCE, http://www.legifrance.gouv.fr/html/actualite/actualite_legislative/exp_lutte_recidive_majeurs_mineurs.htm (last visited Aug. 13, 2007).

In: Children's Rights
Editors: Brooke Dabney and Michael Eldridge

ISBN: 978-1-62948-252-1
© 2013 Nova Science Publishers, Inc.

Chapter 9

GERMANY: CHILDREN'S RIGHTS[*]

Edith Palmer

EXECUTIVE SUMMARY

Germany is a party to the global conventions that protect the rights of the child, yet Germany prefers to interpret these according to the precepts of European agreements, in particular the European Human Rights Convention, and also in accordance with German Constitutional guarantees. Germany has generous systems of health care and social welfare that benefit all citizens and long-term residents, while being less generous for new immigrants.

The education system differentiates between vocational and college-bound tracks, and that is sometimes criticized in international comparisons. Problems occur in particular with the children of immigrants. Stringent laws against child labor are fully enforced, as are criminal provisions against the sexual exploitation of children and human trafficking. The juvenile justice system was path-breaking in the 1920s, but more recently it has borrowed ideas from the United States, particularly on diversion.

I. INTRODUCTION

In Germany the parents are primarily responsible for raising their children, yet governmental policy protects and supports children and youth in various ways to promote their personal and social development and to assure that they will find their place in the world when they are adults.

These goals are accomplished through protective legislation and various forms of assistance. In these efforts, the Federal Government often takes the lead in cooperative programs with the states and non-profit organizations.

---

[*] This document was released by the Law Library of Congress August 2007.

II. Implementation of International Rights of the Child Global Conventions

Germany ratified the Convention on the Rights of the Child in February 1992,[1] and it became effective for Germany on April 5, 1992.[2] However, when Germany deposited the ratification documents, it made interpretative statements and reservations[3] that show that Germany views the Convention as a welcome development in international law that hopefully will improve the situation of children worldwide, and that Germany will play its part, in keeping with article 3 paragraph 2 of the Convention, by drafting legislation to live up to the spirit of the Convention and to ensure the well-being of the child. As an example of such legislation, Germany promised to reform parental custody law.[4] However, Germany makes it clear that the Convention is not considered as being self-executing by making the following sweeping statement:

> The Federal Republic of Germany also declares that domestically the Convention does not apply directly. It establishes state obligations under international law that the Federal Republic of Germany fulfills in accordance with its national laws, which conform with the Convention.

This statement may contain an implied reference to the fundamental rights guaranteed by the German Constitution,[5] in particular its article 6 guaranteeing the family and the welfare of children, as well as its article 1 and 2, guaranteeing human dignity and personal freedom.

In addition to denying any domestic effects of the Convention, Germany made specific reservations or interpretative statements to several articles of the Convention. For instance, concerning article 18 (1), dealing with the common responsibility of the parents to raise the child, Germany declared that parental custody has to be awarded on a case–by–case basis, taking into consideration the situation of the parents, and declared furthermore that this article does not derogate German law concerning legal representation of minors, custody for children born in wedlock, and family and inheritance law for children born out of wedlock. Moreover, Germany made exceptions to the Convention's guarantees of legal representation and appellate proceedings by stating that these guarantees might not be provided in some cases for minor infringements.

Germany made an even more serious reservation in favor of its immigration laws by stating that:

> Nothing in the Convention may be interpreted as implying that unlawful entry by an alien into the territory of the Federal Republic of Germany or his unlawful stay there is permitted; nor may any provision be interpreted to mean that it restricts the right of the Federal Republic of Germany to pass laws and regulations concerning the entry of aliens and the conditions of their stay or to make a distinction between nationals and aliens.

In several immigration cases, the German courts have upheld the German government's intent to deny any domestic effects to the Convention,[6] and this also appears to be the prevailing opinion in the legal literature, where it is often pointed out that article 6 of the German Constitution guarantees to children at least the same level of rights as the Convention.[7] However, there is a strong minority opinion in the legal literature arguing that

Germany is bound by the Convention and that its domestic applicability cannot be totally excluded.[8] Public interest groups, particularly those advocating a higher level of rights for child immigrants, want Germany to withdraw the reservations.[9]

In 2004, Germany ratified the Optional Protocol to the Convention on the Rights of the Child on the Involvement of Children in Armed Conflict,[10] without any reservations, and declared that seventeen is the minimum age for military service in Germany.[11] Germany did not ratify the Sex Traffic Protocol,[12] yet joint action is being contemplated within the European Union.[13]

Germany ratified the International Covenant on Civil and Political Rights of 1966 in 1973, and it became effective in the country in 1976.[14] Germany made a few reservations on matters relating to criminal law and procedure,[15] which Germany declared it would handle according to the guarantees of the European Convention on Human Rights [EHRC].[16] Generally, however, the Pact is applicable statutory law in Germany.[17] Germany is also a member of the International Covenant on Economic, Social and Cultural Rights[18] and of the Convention on the Elimination of All Forms of Discrimination against Women.[19]

UN Resolutions and Declarations

Germany is not in the habit of adopting U.N. declarations and resolutions;[20] instead, it is assumed that these are binding on the basis of article 25 of the U. N. Charter.[21] These principles undoubtedly apply to the UN Universal Declaration on Human Rights.[22] This instrument is highly respected in Germany and frequently relied upon for the interpretation of the fundamental rights guaranteed by the German Constitution.[23]

European Human Rights Convention

Germany is also a member of the European Convention on Human Rights [EHRC].[24] This Convention is fully applicable in Germany and theoretically it ranks at the level of statutory German law; [25] however, due to the possibility of every individual petitioning the Court in case of alleged violations of human rights, the human rights guarantees of this convention are taken very seriously in Germany. Yet its application causes few problems because many of its principles are mirrored in the German Constitution.[26]

Agreements on Jurisdiction, Applicable Law, and Child Protection

Germany is a member of the Convention on the Protection of Minors,[27] and in the past this Convention has been of great importance in the German legal practice. However, the influence of this Convention is waning. Within the European Union, it has been replaced by community legislation.[28] In 1996, some thirty-five states signed a replacement for this Convention, hoping that it might apply also to countries beyond the European civil law sphere. This replacement Convention, the Hague Convention on Jurisdiction, Applicable Law, Recognition, Enforcement and Co-operation in Respect of Parental Responsibility and Measures for the Protection of Children,[29] has already been ratified by five East European member states of the European Union [EU]. The other EU member states had agreed to ratify it jointly, possibly in 1996;[30] but this had not happened as yet.

In 1980, Germany ratified the European Convention on the Adoption of Children[31] that harmonizes substantive adoption law among the treaty members. In 2002, Germany ratified the Hague Convention on the Protection of Children and Cooperation in Respect of Intercountry Adoption.[32] In, addition, Germany ratified the European Convention on the Exercise of Children's Rights[33] in 2001, together with a statement specifying the matters of family law for which the Convention would be applied.[34] According to the German legal literature, the German level of compliance lives up to the mandatory portion of the Convention.[35]

III. CHILD HEALTH AND SOCIAL WELFARE HEALTH CARE

Germany has a universal health care system that provides coverage for virtually all children who reside in Germany. The health care system consists of a social health care system that is mandatory for low- and middle-income earners[36] and private, contractual health care that is elected by some nine percent of the population.[37] Both the social and the private health care systems provide family coverage, thus covering children. For the few that would fall through the cracks of this tight social net, health benefits are granted as a welfare service, either by granting benefits in kind or by paying the social health insurance contributions for the needy person.[38]

The social health care system dates back to the 19th century and is based on employment, being financed largely by equal employer and employee contributions. However, to the extent that coverage extends to non-contributing individuals such as university students and interns, it is funded in part by the system and in part by federal subsidies. The benefits are extensive, and they include natal care, pre- and postnatal care, preventive care, ambulatory and stationary care, dental care, nursing care, rehabilitation, and sick pay.

Social Welfare

Currently social services for children and youths are provided on the basis of Title Eight of the Social Code.[39] However, it remains to be seen how long this federal law will remain fully in effect in the various states, since the constitutional reform of 2006 gave the states legislative power over welfare matters that would allow the states to override federal legislation and enact their own laws. Currently, the social services community is concerned about the potential developments.[40] One reason for the constitutional change was that under the heretofore prevailing system the federation could impose burdensome unfunded mandates on the local communities and the states.

Title Eight of the Social Code grants every young person the right to obtain assistance for his or her development and the right to an education that makes the young person a responsible member of the community.[41] To ensure these rights, various forms of assistance are granted to children, juveniles below the age of eighteen, the parents of these beneficiaries, and, to some extent, even to young adults up to the age of twenty-one. Inclusion of the family in the benefit schemes lives up to the German creed that the parents are primarily entitled to and responsible for raising their children. An important aspect of social assistance for young people is to make up for disadvantages that may result from circumstances such as poverty or a lack of integration in society. The protection of young people from dangerous influences also is an important task. A variety of programs and subsidies are provided to deal with problems that young people may face. These include counseling, placement in day care centers, foster parenting, some medical assistance, and support payments. These are applied case-by-case, based on expert evaluations.

Social assistance to young people is provided primarily through the youth offices of the municipalities and states. There is, however, much cooperation between the public and the private sector. Many organizations that assist young people are private volunteer organization or are sponsored by a religious community.

IV. EDUCATION, INCLUDING SPECIAL NEEDS

The legislative and executive power over primary and secondary education always has been vested in the states and most of the states have constitutional provisions on education and extensive legislation on the educational system.[42] Some uniformity among the states is achieved through the efforts of a permanent conference of the education ministers of the states.[43] In 2006, a major reform of the German Constitution[44] has strengthened the role of the states by granting them power over framework legislation on universities, which prior to the reform had been vested in the Federation. However, the same reform gives the Federation the power to institute uniform standards for examinations at universities.

Attendance at school is mandatory for all children in Germany from the age of six until the age of eighteen, and home schooling is not permissible. Children often have a choice between public and private schools. The latter may be religious or secular, and either can obtain governmental subsidies if they are properly accredited.[45] Aside from a few private universities, attendance at colleges and universities is free,[46] and stipends and loans are provided to students who cannot defray their living expenses while studying.[47]

The German education system is structured into preschool (below the age of six), primary school (grade 1-4, ages six to ten), secondary schooling (up to age nineteen), and tertiary schooling at universities and colleges. Secondary schooling branches out into tracks at age eleven, with more opportunities to choose at age fifteen. These tracks differentiate between a general education, a college-preparatory track, and a vocational track. In some states, the college-preparatory track already starts at age eleven, although opportunities for changing the direction of a child's education exist at various levels. This track system that makes children chose their career path at an early age has recently come under criticism. Vernor Muñoz, Special Rapporteur on the Right to Education, reported to the United Nations General Assembly that the German school system disadvantages children of low socio-economic backgrounds, in particular, the children of immigrants.[48]

Germany has a longstanding tradition of providing special schools for children with special needs. Yet until a few years ago, education for the disabled and other special children was provided in segregated schools. Since 1994, however, the awareness has been growing that this form of special schooling discriminates against the disabled, and efforts have since then been underway to integrate special education into the regular school system.[49] The issue has constitutional overtones, since an amendment to the Constitution now prohibits discrimination of the disabled.[50] Decisions of the Federal Constitutional Court have applied this guarantee to the schooling of the disabled, yet change is required only to the extent that is financially feasible.[51]

V. Child Labor and Exploitation

Children below the age of fifteen generally may not be employed in Germany, under legal provisions that are very similar to federal legislation in the United States, [52] yet the German prohibition does not apply to minor jobs such as carrying out newspapers, babysitting, tutoring, taking care of pets, or assisting in agricultural enterprises, provided the work of the child is "light," which is defined as not involving uncomfortable postures or dangers from animals or machinery that a child may not assess accurately or may not have experience in averting. Those below the age of thirteen may not be required to lift objects repeatedly that weigh more than 7.5 kilograms or to lift objects occasionally that weigh more than 10 kilograms. Children may be allowed to participate in artistic performances, for which a permit will be granted if the conditions are suitable. None of these occupations of children may interfere with their attendance at school. For this reasons, daily work is limited to two hours per day during the school year (three hours for farm work), and to four weeks during vacation. [53]

Minors below the age of eighteen may be employed, albeit under numerous prohibitions that apply in principle also to vocational training. Some exceptions are made for properly supervised training. Minors may not be employed in dangerous occupations, which are listed in the Youth Labor Protection Act,[54] such as work that exceeds their physical or mental capacity; work that exposes them to moral dangers; work that involves the risk of accidents; and work that endangers health through excessive heat, cold, wetness, noise, air pollution, radiation, vibration, and chemical or biological agents.

The employment of minors under piece-work pay systems or in units where other workers are paid by the piece is prohibited. Also prohibited is work that is strictly timed, such as assembly line work. In addition, minors may not be employed in underground mines, except for properly authorized and supervised training situations for minors above the age of sixteen. [55]

Various persons with criminal records are prevented from employing minors. Among them are those who have been convicted of a felony and sentenced to imprisonment for two years or more, those who have been convicted of hurting young people in violation of their duties as employers or educators, those who have been convicted of sexual offenses or of violent crimes, and those who have been convicted for violating the laws of protecting minors from presentations of sex or violence in the media.[56]

In addition to these prohibitions, various restrictions apply to the working conditions of minors. Among these are medical requirements, occupational safety requirements, and mandatory working hour rules. Before beginning an employment relationship, a minor must provide the employer with a medical certificate that shows that the minor has been examined and found fit for the particular occupation. The certificate may also make various suggestions relating to the work to be performed. When the minor has been employed for one year, another medical examination is mandatory, and every year thereafter follow-up examinations are recommended.

Employers are also under a special duty of care to instruct minors in the risks and dangers of the work environment that the employer must make as risk-free as possible. Night work is generally not permitted, and after a day's work there must be at least twelve hours of rest. Minors should not be employed for more than forty hours per week, and special rules apply for minors who work as part of a vocational training program. They must be given enough time to attend their classroom instruction. Minors should be employed only for five days a week, and their weekend rest should consist of at least two days. Saturday and Sunday work is only permitted for certain specified workplaces, such as hospitals or agricultural work. Minors below the age of sixteen must get thirty work days of vacation, and a few days less are required for minors who are sixteen or seventeen years old.[57]

Violations of the protective labor provisions for children and minors are punishable primarily by administrative fines, but short prison sentences can be imposed on employers who hurt a youngster by disobeying the rules.[58] In addition, the German Criminal Code makes it a criminal offense to abuse, maltreat, or neglect a minor or helpless person who is in the custody of a teacher, employer, or other person who is in a position of responsibility.[59]

VI. SALE AND TRAFFICKING OF CHILDREN

The German Criminal Code contains stringent provisions against the sexual exploitation of children. Its section 174 penalizes those who have custody or authority over a person below the age of eighteen for the commission of sexual acts upon these minors. The penalty is up to five years of imprisonment. Section 176 makes the commission of sexual acts on persons below the age of fourteen punishable with imprisonment of up to ten years, and the same punishment applies to inducing a child to commit sexual acts with a third person. Punishable with up to five years imprisonment is the commission of sexual acts in front of a child or the inducing of a child to commit sexual act on his or her own body, as well as the showing of material with a pornographic content to a child.

Section 176 a provides a minimum sentence of one year in prison for certain aggravated forms of sexual abuse of children, including acts of penetration, acts committed by more than one person, and acts committed by repeat offenders. Those who engage in sexual abuse of children with the intent of producing pornography are punished with up to two years in prison, while those who seriously harm a child through sexual exploitation are punishable with imprisonment of no less than five years. If death results, the penalty is imprisonment for life or for at least ten years. Section 182 of the Criminal Code penalizes the sexual abuse of minors between the ages of fourteen and sixteen, if sexual conduct is forced upon them through the exploitation of a coercive situation.

Since 1993, Germany prosecutes sex tourism under sections 176 through 176 b and 182. At that time, a change in the rules on criminal jurisdiction was enacted that makes these offenses punishable if a German commits them anywhere in the world.[60] The law is successful; in 1998, a UNICEF report praised Germany for the number of prosecutions.[61]

Provisions against child pornography are contained in section 184 b. It penalizes the production, distribution, marketing, and display of child pornographic material with between three months and five years imprisonment, but twice the punishment is applied to commercial endeavors. In addition, section 232 of the Criminal Code penalizes human trafficking for the purpose of sexual exploitation; if perpetrated on a child, the offense is punishable with imprisonment of one to ten years. Section 180 a, 180 b and 181 contain various prohibitions against forcing others into prostitution.

VII. JUVENILE JUSTICE – AGE REQUIREMENT FOR BEARING CRIMINAL RESPONSIBILITY

Germany has had an enlightened policy on juvenile delinquency since the 19th century. Since then, the goal of the juvenile justice system has been to limit detention time for young offenders and to focus on their rehabilitation through educational measures. Aside from a few years toward the end of the Nazi regime, these principles have been applied consistently in Germany, and today Germany has the lowest juvenile incarceration rate in Europe, despite an increase in juvenile crime in Germany and public outcries against leniency.[62]

When Germany enacted a Youth Court Act in the 1920s, it served as a model for other countries. Since then, this Act has been refined repeatedly, and some of its reforms were inspired by the practice in the United States, in particular, the principle of diversion.[63] In its current version, the Youth Court Act[64] continues to live up to the principles of diversion, "depenalization," and "decarceration."[65]

The Act applies to offenders who were between the ages of fourteen and eighteen at the time of their offense. The Act states that these juveniles should be punished only if they were mature enough to realize the wrongfulness of their conduct and were also capable of acting accordingly.[66] Yet, even though these circumstances are commonly investigated by social and psychological evaluations, the Courts usually find young offenders guilty and punishable, within the more lenient framework of the Youth Court Act.[67] The Act also allows for its application to offenders between the ages of eighteen and twenty, if they lack the maturity to be tried as adults.[68]

Juvenile offenders are tried for the same criminal offenses as adults, albeit with different consequences. Prison time is kept to a minimum by not imposing prison sentences of less than six months and by making ten years in prison the maximum penalty that can be meted out. Juvenile offenders are never imprisoned together with adults, and the youth prisons are staffed with personnel with educational expertise. Recently, a bill has been drafted by the Cabinet that would allow for the detention of very dangerous young criminals after they have served the prison sentence, in order to protect the public from their continued violent predisposition. Such an institution already exists for adult offenders,[69] and a need seems to exist to extend this institution to the few juvenile offenders who continue to be very dangerous.[70]

Prison sentences are imposed on juveniles only as a measure of last resort, and, if at all possible, prison penalties are suspended or educational and disciplinary measures such as fines and community services are imposed instead. This practice lives up to the principle that rehabilitation is the primary purpose of a youth sentence. While the offender is usually deemed legally responsible for the deed, the penalty considers the overall situation of the offender, his background and education, and devises a plan for reforming him. All this has to be accomplished under observation of the principle of proportionality that calls for applying the least intrusive measures possible that still will achieve their purpose.[71]

Usually, a youth crime proceeding begins with a criminal investigation that is referred to the prosecutor for a decision on whether to drop the charges or prosecute. At a very early stage in the investigation, social workers are involved to evaluate the background and psychological development of the young person. If the case comes to trial, the social worker must report his findings to the judge, and the social worker is often influential in shaping the sentence. Youth criminal trials are not open to the public; only the parents of the accused and the victim may attend the trial.

Statistics seem to indicate that the German juvenile justice system is working. There has been an increase in crime, particularly after 1990, that is often ascribed to a rise in unemployment, especially in the eastern part of Germany. However, most of the reported incidents involved petty crimes, and serious offenses have remained rare occurrences, though some of them were much publicized. . Moreover, only thirty percent of the young offenders have committed repeat offenses.[72]

VIII. MISCELLANEOUS ISSUES

Germany protects young people against exposure to alcohol, tobacco, and descriptions of sex and violence in the media. Children below the age of sixteen may not purchase tobacco products or hard spirits; however, other alcoholic beverages may be consumed in public by children between the ages of fourteen and sixteen if they are accompanied by an adult. Children below certain age limits may not visit drinking and dancing places at certain hours of the night. [73]

The protection of young people against sex, violence, and racial hatred extends to virtually all media including books, serial publications, audio and video recordings, television, radio, and the Internet. Restrictions are contained in the federal Youth Protection Act,[74] and these apply primarily to written materials and recordings. Proliferation of sex and violence in the broadcast media and the Internet is governed by an agreement between the German states.[75]

Concluding Remarks

Germany has an effective legal framework for protecting the young and promoting their welfare. However some problems are encountered in integrating the children of immigrants and in providing a quality education for them.

Prepared by Edith Palmer
Senior Foreign Law Specialist
August 2007

End Notes

[1] Convention on the Rights of the Child, Nov. 20, 1989, 1577 U.N.T.S 3, ratified by Germany Feb. 17, 1992, BUNDESGESETZBLATT [BGBl, official law gazette of Germany] II at 121.

[2] Bekanntmachung, Jul. 10, 1992, BGBl II at 990.

[3] Id.

[4] Germany kept this promise in 1997, by introducing joint custody for divorced parents [Kindschaftsrechts-reformgesetz, Dec. 16, 1997, BGBl I at 2942.

[5] Grundgesetz für die Bundesrepublik Deutschland [GG], May 23, 1949, BGBl 1.

[6] For instance, Verwaltungsgericht Berlin, decision of Dec. 11, 1996, docket number 36 X 643.95, available at the subscription database JURIS.

[7] G. RENNER, AUSLÄNDERRECHT 494 (München, 2005).

[8] G. RENNER, AUSLÄNDERRECHT IN DEUTSCHLAND 165 (München, 1998).

[9] National Coalition für die Umsetzung der Kinderrechtskonvention in Deutschland, Themennetzwerk Kinder ohne deutschen Pass, at the non-official website http://www.national-coaltition.de (last visited Aug. 4, 2007).

[10] May 25, 2000, 39 INTERNATIONAL LEGAL MATERIALS [I.L.M.] 1285 (2000), ratified by Germany by Gesetz, Sept. 16, 2004, BGBl II at 1354.

[11] Id.

[12] Optional Protocol on the Sale of Children, Child Prostitution, and Child Pornography, May 25, 2000, 39 I.L.M. 1285 (2000).

[13] See references to EU legislation against trafficking in human beings and the sexual exploitation of children at the official website http://ec.europa.eu/justice_home/doc_centre/crime/trafficking/doccrimehuman trafficking_en.htm (last visited Aug. 4, 2007).

[14] International Covenant on Civil and Political Rights, Dec. 16, 1966, res. 2200A (XXI); UN Doc. A/6316, ratified by Germany Nov. 15, 1973, BGBl II at 1533, effective date for Germany, Mar. 23, 1976, BGBl II at 1218.

[15] Id.

[16] European Convention for the Protection of Human Rights and Fundamental Freedoms, Nov. 4, 1950, 213 U.N.T.S. 221, ratified by Germany Aug. 7, 1952, BGBl II at 685.

[17] Hamburgisches Oberverwaltungsgericht, June 17, 2004, docket no. 1 Bf 198/00, available at the subscription database JURIS.

[18] Dec. 19, 1966, 999 U.N.T.S. 171, ratified by Germany Nov. 23, 1973, BGBl II at 11569.

[19] Dec. 18, 1979, 19 I.L.M. 33 (1980), ratified by Germany Apr. 25, 1985, BGBl II at 647.

[20] C. STARCK, DAS BONNER GRUNDGESETZ, art. 24 1, comment 20 (München, 1999).

[21] Charter of the United Nations, June 26, 1945, 59 Stat 1031; 993; 3 BEVANS 1153. Germany became a member of the United Nations in 1973 [Gesetz, Jun. 6, 1973, BGBl II at 430].

[22] Universal Declaration of Human Rights, G.A. res. 217A (III), U.N. Doc A/810 at 71 (1948).

[23] C. SCHREUER, DECISIONS OF INTERNATIONAL INSTITUTIONS BEFORE DOMESTIC COURTS 144 (Dobbs Ferry, 1981).

[24] Supra note 16.

[25] Verwaltungsgericht Hamburg, decision of Feb. 27, 2006, docket no. 15 E 340/06, available at the subscription database JURIS.

[26] Id.; Renner, supra note 8.

[27] Convention Concerning the Powers of Authorities and the Law Applicable in Respect of the Protection of Minors, Oct. 5, 1961, 658 U.N.T.S 143, ratified by Germany Apr. 30, 1971, BGBl II at 217.

[28] Council Regulation (EC) 2201/2003, Nov. 27, 2003, OFFICIAL JOURNAL OF THE EUROPEAN UNION (L338) 1.

[29] Oct. 19, 1996, 35 I.L.M. 1396.

[30] B. V. HOFFMAN & K. THORN, INTERNATIONALES PRIVATRECHT 374 (München, 2005).

[31] Apr. 24, 1967, 635 U.N.T.S 255, ratified by Germany Aug. 25, 1980, BGBl II at 1093.

[32] May 29, 1993, 32 I.L.M. 1134 (1993), ratified by Germany Oct. 10, 2001, BGBl II at 1034.

[33] Jan. 25, 1996, 35 I.L.M. 651 (1996).

[34] Gesetz, Nov. 5, 2001, BGBl II at 1074.

[35] I. Baer & A. Marx, Das Europäische Übereinkommen über die Ausübung von Kinderrechten, 44 ZEITSCHRIFT FÜR DAS GESAMTE FAMILIENRECHT 1185 (1997).

[36] Sozialgesetzbuch Fünftes Buch Gesetzliche Krankenversicherung [SGB V], Dec. 20, 1988, BGBl I at 2477, as amended.

[37] R. Schlegel, Comment: German Health Care – Towards Universal Access: An Overview of the Principles of Access and Benefits 18 JOURNAL OF CONTEMPORARY HEALTH LAW AND POLICY 673 (2002).

[38] Sozialgesetzbuch XII, Dec. 27, 2003, BGBl I at 3022, §§ 47 – 52.

[39] Sozialgesetzbuch VIII [SGB VIII], Dec. 8, 1998, BGBl I at 3456, as amended.

[40] R. Wabnitz, Neugestaltung des Artikel 84 Grundgesetz und Auswirkungen auf die Kinder- und Jugendhilfe, SOZIALRECHT AKTUEL l 153 (2006).

[41] SGB VIII, § 1.

[42] In Bavaria, for instance, Bayerisches Gesetz über das Erziehungs- und Unterrichtswesen, repromulgated May 31, 2000, BAYERISCHES GESETZ- UND VERORDNUNGSBLATT [BayGVBl] 414, as amended.

[43] Kutusministerkonferenz im Schulwesen, at its official website http://www.kmk.org/ (last visited Aug. 4, 2007).

[44] Grundgesetzänderungsgesetz 2006, Aug. 28, 2006, BGBl I at 2034.

[45] GG, art. 7.

[46] Hochschulrahmengesetz, Jan. 19, 1999, BGBl I at 18, as amended.

[47] Bundesausbildungsförderungsgesetz, June 6, 1983, BGBl I at 645, s amended.

[48] United Nations Human Rights Council, Implementation of General Assembly Resolution 60/ 251, Mission to Germany (Feb. 2006), http://www.netzwerk-bildungsfreiheit.de/html/munoz.html, click "Mission in Germany."

[49] H. AVENARIUS, EINFÜHRUNG IN DAS SCHULRECHT 22 (Darmstadt, 2001).

[50] GG, art. 3 3.

[51] Avenarius, supra note 49.

[52] C. Rasnig, Unintended Sibling Legislation? Statutory Regulations of Child Labor in Germany and the United States, 8 FLORIDA JOURNAL OF INTERNATIONAL LAW 141 (1993).

[53] Jugendarbeitsschutzgesetz, [JarbSchG], Apr. 12, 1976, BGBl I at 965, as amended, § 5; Kinder- arbeitsschutzverordnung, Jun. 23, 1998, BGBl I at 1508.

[54] JArbSchG, § 22.

[55] JArbSchG, §§ 23 – 24.

[56] See infra note 73-75 and accompanying text.

[57] JarbSchG, §§ 8 – 21 b.

[58] JarbSchG, §§ 58 – 60.

[59] Strafgesetzbuch [StGB], repromulgated Nov. 13, 1998, BGBl I at 3322 § 225.

[60] StGB § 5 no. 8. A. Fraley, Note: Child Sex Tourism Legislation under the Protect Act: Does It Really Protect?, 79 ST. JOHN' S LAW REVIEW 445 (2005).

[61] A. Fraley, id, at 445.

[62] H. Albrecht, Youth Justice in Germany, 31 CRIME AND JUSTICE 443 (2004).

[63] G. Blau, Diversion und Strafrecht, JURA 25 (1987).

[64] Jugendgerichtsgesetz [JGG], Dec. 11, 1974, BGBl I at 3427, as last amended by Gesetz, Apr. 13, 2007, BGBl I at 513.

[65] Albrecht, supra note 62.

[66] JGG § 3.

[67] Albrecht, supra note 62.

[68] JGG § 105.

[69] StGB, § 66.

[70] Sicherungsverwahrung für Jugendliche, FRANKFURTER ALLGEMEINE ZEITUNG 1 (July 19, 2007).

[71] Albrecht, supra note 62.

[72] Id.

[73] Jugendschutzgesetz, July 23, 2002, BGBl I at 2730, as amended.

[74] Id.

[75] Jugendmedienschutz-Staatsvertrag der Länder, Sept. 27, 2002, BayGVBl 147 (2003).

In: Children's Rights
Editors: Brooke Dabney and Michael Eldridge

ISBN: 978-1-62948-252-1
© 2013 Nova Science Publishers, Inc.

Chapter 10

GREECE: CHILDREN'S RIGHTS[*]

Theresa Papademetriou

EXECUTIVE SUMMARY

Based on the constitutional mandate to protect and safeguard children and on its international obligations arising from ratifications of agreements on children's rights, which have the status of domestic law upon ratification, Greece has enacted various laws and has adopted a number of measures and services to promote and advance the rights of the children. The topics covered in this report are health and social welfare, education, labor and exploitation, and juvenile justice. In 2002, the Greek Parliament adopted a new law on human trafficking, and the government has allocated a number of resources in an effort to eliminate this scourge. In 2003, the juvenile system was reformed. An additional law was enacted in 2006 to combat intra-family violence, which also encompasses a prohibition of corporal punishment of children.

I. INTRODUCTION

The Greek Constitution contains a number of solemn proclamations affecting the status of children: that childhood shall be under the protection of the State; that families with a large number of children, war orphans, and everyone who suffers from incurable physical or mental illness have the right to special care by the State; and that the latter also have the right to enjoy measures that secure and facilitate their independence, their professional integration, and their participation in the financial, political, and social life of the country. It also states that the State cares for the health of its citizens and takes special measures for the protection of the children. Furthermore, it proclaims that housing for those in need is the responsibility of the State.[1] Another guiding principle enshrined in the Greek Constitution and legislation

---

[*] This document was released by the Law Library of Congress September 2007.

that also has a bearing on children is the prohibition of discrimination based on race, gender, physical or mental disability, language, or social status.[2]

While the Constitution does not further elaborate on the scope and the extent of these general pronouncements, subsequent statutes and secondary legislation that have been enacted are based on the constitutional mandate to secure the rights of children and to prohibit discrimination. Furthermore, the various policies, services, and programs designed for children that are adopted and implemented by the State at a central or regional level and that are discussed below reflect to a large extent the country's efforts to protect its children. Nevertheless, Greece still faces numerous challenges, especially in the areas of violence against women and children, trafficking of persons, and discrimination against Roma children.[3]

In Greece, children under the age of fifteen constitute about 15.5 percent of the overall population (11,000,000), which is below the average percentage in the European Union.[4] Greece, as other European countries, has experienced in the last few years a high rate of influx of immigrants. As a result, a new multi-cultural and multi-ethnic society has emerged. There are approximately 130,000 immigrant students, mostly from Albania and other Balkan countries, that attend local schools and benefit from the services and programs offered by the Greek State.[5]

In Greece, there is no centralized agency designated to provide care and assistance and to supervise the various services provided by the State. Instead, a number of government agencies are responsible for providing social welfare and health services, as well as free education and child care. Generally speaking, the Ministry of Health and Welfare is responsible for health services, and the Ministry of Social Assistance is responsible for assistance to children who are vulnerable, that is orphans, the handicapped, and trafficked children. The Ministry of Health and Welfare and the Ministry of the Interior have joint responsibility at the national level for early childhood care. Local authorities are responsible for preschools and child care services; the Ministry of Education supervises the early childhood programs at the national level. The Ministry of Labor and Social Security handles the social insurance benefits and the family allowances for each child. The Social Insurance Institute (IKA) administers benefits through local offices.[6]

II. IMPLEMENTATION OF INTERNATIONAL RIGHTS OF THE CHILD

The Greek Civil Code defines a child indirectly. Articles 34 through 36 state that a person, from the moment of its birth, is subject to rights and obligations, as long as it is born alive, irrespective of its viability.[7] From the civil law perspective, minors attain the age of majority upon completion of the seventeenth year. Since 2003, for criminal law purposes, the age of majority has been raised from the seventeenth year to the eighteenth.

Greece signed the Convention on the Rights of the Child on January 26, 1990,[8] and ratified it by Law 21101/1992.[9] Pursuant to article 28, paragraph 1 of the Constitution, this Convention has the force of law from the date of ratification and publication in the Official Gazette.[10] It also takes precedence over any conflicting domestic legislation. In addition, on September 11, 1997, Greece ratified the European Convention on the Exercise of Children's Rights. This Convention has as its chief objective to protect the best interests of the child and also provides that children have the right to express their opinions in judicial proceedings concerning custody issues.[11] On September 7, 2000, Greece signed the Optional Protocol to the Convention the Rights of the Child on the Sale of Children, Child Prostitution, and Child Pornography.[12] On October 22, 2003, Greece also ratified the Optional Protocol to the Convention on the Rights of the Child on the Involvement of Children in Armed Conflict.[13]

On June 7, 1983, Greece ratified the Convention on the Elimination of All Forms of Discrimination against Women. In 2001, Greece ratified the Optional Protocol to the Convention on the Elimination of all Forms of Discrimination against Women.[14] In 2002, the General Secretariat for Gender Equality and the Office of the United Nations High Commission in Greece signed a Memorandum of Cooperation in a joint effort to promote the rights of women and minor girls who have been granted asylum status.

Institutions Dealing Specifically with Children's Rights

Greece has established the following institutions designed to tackle issues and questions related to children:

- The National Observatory on the Rights of Children, to ensure effective implementation of the Convention on the Rights of the Children;
- The Department of Children's Rights;
- The Child Health Institute, in the area of child abuse and neglect; and
- The National Human Rights Committee.

While the first three deal exclusively with children's rights, the jurisdiction of the fourth is broader and includes anyone whose human rights are infringed upon.

Department of Children's Rights

The Department of Children's Rights was established within the office of the Greek Ombudsman in 2003, by law 3094/2003.[15] The scope of its mandate is to investigate actions, omissions, or any complaints about individuals and legal entities that violate the rights of children or endanger their wellbeing. The Department is composed of a Deputy Ombudsman and fifteen investigators with expertise in a variety of areas. During the first year following its establishment, the Ombudsman and his team established closer relations with agencies working with children and reviewed a number of complaints issued either by minors themselves or by adults about infringements of children rights. During the period 2004-2005, the Department accomplished the following:

- published a leaflet on "Defending Children's Rights" designed to raise public awareness about the role of the Child Ombudsman and the services provided by his office. It is disseminated to schools and other institutions working with children;
- created a special website for children and those interested in the wellbeing of children and a free telephone line for children in need;

- published and distributed a booklet on "Guidelines for the Treatment of Unaccompanied and Separated Minors," in cooperation with United Nations High Commissioner for Refugees (UNHCR), with the objective of safeguarding the rights of those children who arrive in Greece without any escort or who are separated from relatives;

- assisted the Ministry of Justice in the preparation of a new law on corporal punishment; and

- within the framework of a project undertaken in cooperation with the Council of Europe, the Deputy Ombudsman exchanged visits with institutions working on children rights in neighboring countries in order to promote exchange of information and best practices.[16]

III. CHILD HEALTH AND SOCIAL WELFARE

The general framework law on social care is Law 2646/1998 on Reorganization of the National System of Social Care and Other Provisions.[17] Based on the constitutional mandate that social care is the responsibility of the state, the Law reaffirms the right of access to social care and welfare services provided by the National Health System to everyone who legally resides in Greece. Thus, the main objective is to ensure participation of all people in the services provided, in order to ensure that all people have an acceptable standard of living.

Consequently, as long as foreign nationals and their children have proof of legal residence, they are eligible for the welfare services and programs offered, including daycare centers, infant care centers, state-run holiday camps, and others.

The institution of foster parents was introduced in 1992.[18] Minors under the age of eighteen who have no place to stay or who live in unhealthy family living conditions could in theory be placed with foster families until they attained the age of majority. Children with special needs could stay with foster families beyond that age. However, the Greek Ombudsman reported in 2005 that the foster parent program was not put into operation.[19]

Since 1973, the state-run orphanages have been converted into child care centers. Abandoned children or those with no place to stay, from the age of five to fifteen, are accepted free of charge. The decision to place a child in a child care center is made based on a report prepared by the social worker assigned to the case and upon verification that living with family or relatives is not feasible. Orphans who have lost one or both parents are given preference, followed by children whose single parent is blind, deaf-mute, handicapped from birth, mentally ill, or incarcerated.[20]

Children between the ages of three and six are accepted at state-run kindergartens. There are also state-run nurseries that cover the needs of children from the age of eight months until they are accepted at elementary schools.[21]

Since 1960, Law 4051 on Supporting Unprotected Children has offered financial benefits to children who meet certain qualifications. Eligible children are those below the age of fourteen (and in some instances up to sixteen) who live with their own families and are:

- orphans who have lost both parents;
- orphans without fathers;

- children whose fathers cannot support them for reasons of health; or
- children born outside marriage.

Children who live in state-run institutions do not qualify for these allowances. Other state-run institutions also provide a small allowance to children of single parents, to those close to the poverty line, or to those children whose families experience medical or social hardships.[22]

The government also makes monetary contributions of a lump-sum, at the beginning of each school year, to families with children up to sixteen years old who attend public schools and whose annual income is no more than €3,000 (about US$4,161, at the exchange rate of €1=US$1.39, effective Sept. 17, 2007).[23] Another allowance is €1000 to families with children studying in cities other than the place of residence of their families.

Other laws directly or indirectly assist low-income families with children. An annual allowance of €15 to purchase school items is given to families of the unemployed and to single-parent families. Another example is Law 3227/2004, on Measures against Unemployment, which gives an incentive to employers to hire unemployed mothers of at least two children. The incentive consists of a subsidy of an amount equal to the employer's insurance contribution liability for providing insurance coverage for the employed mothers. The subsidy is equal to a year's contribution for each child of the employed mother.

Moreover, the same law exempts women farmers from contributing to the Farmers' Fund (Agricultural Insurance Organization O.G.A.) for every child born after the first child. The government also provides pensions for low-income families in rural areas and financial incentives for children who attend school. Other government programs also provide a certain amount of money for families with three children.[24]

It should also be noted, that the National Center for Emergency Social Care, which operates as a legal entity, under the authority of the Ministry of Health and Welfare, has extended its services in almost all regions of Greece. Thus, separated children or victims of human trafficking may receive emergency assistance in such centers.

IV. EDUCATION

As article 16 of the Greek Constitution provides, education is provided to all Greek citizens for free at all levels in all public institutions. Parents have no option to offer home schooling to their children. They are legally obliged to send their children to schools for nine years. This is the minimum mandatory duration of education.[25] Schoolbooks in all subjects and at all levels of education are provided for free to all students, as well as transportation if the students live far from the schools. Instruction in the Christian Orthodox religion, which is the predominant religion in Greece, is mandatory. Students of other religions are exempted from this obligation, upon written request.[26]

The State provides financial aid to those students who are eligible based on merit or financial need. During the last fifteen years, Greece has focused its attention on the creation of vocational training. In 1992, it established the Organization of Vocational Education and Training to oversee services related to vocational training. Vocational guidance is given only to those who are able to speak Greek.

Disabled children may be schooled in the traditional mainstream schools, including high school, provided that they are able to do so. There are thirty-five special schools for deaf children and twenty for the physically challenged. Blind children are free to attend regular secondary schools. All handicapped children may attend higher education in universities without undergoing the necessary entrance examinations. Vocational training for the disabled is also offered, but to a limited extent. There are seven special vocational schools under the aegis of the Minister of Education. A number of workshops operated within rehabilitation centers offer opportunities for disabled children to acquire new skills. Such centers operate in big urban centers, so they are not able to meet the needs of children with special needs in remote areas.[27]

The rehabilitation centers offer either in-center job placement or community job placement. In most instances, they also offer follow-up services to ensure that children have adjusted well to the real world environment. By law, employers are required to hire a certain number of disabled workers.

Statistics from the Ministry of Health and Welfare provide a grim picture of children with special education needs. In 2004, there were approximately 180,000 to 200,000 such children, of whom only 18,585 were attending school, either because there were not enough schools in close geographic proximity to their residences or because those schools were not physically accessible for those with special needs.[28]

Minority Children and Children of Immigrants

Greece also has minority schools to meet the needs of children who are Muslims; they are located mainly in Thrace, a province in northern Greece.[29] The curriculum is taught in Turkish and Greek. There are also two Koranic schools for the Muslim minority. In 2001, Thrace had 225 minority primary schools and four such schools for secondary education.[30]

Roma children, as a group and because of their family's lifestyle, have particular needs. Since 1997, under the aegis of the Ministry of National Education and Religious Affairs, a program has been established to ensure school attendance and to offer counseling to Roma families about education, outreach to teachers and other professionals, information on health and hygiene issues, and other programs.[31] The Ministry of Education provides an annual benefit of €300 for every child in primary education to Roma families who have annual incomes of less than €3,000.[32] This benefit was later extended to other migrant parents who meet the low income threshold.[33]

There are also the so-called intercultural schools that provide a school environment suitable to children whose native language is other than Greek in order to meet their special needs, such as social, cultural, or other problems. Such schools have been operating since 1996, with the objective of facilitating the children's integration into mainstream society. A public school is designated by law as intercultural when the number of foreign students "reaches or exceeds forty-five percent of the total number of students."[34] The school curricula are the same as that of regular public schools, with additional Greek language training. During the 2002-2003 school year, twenty-six intercultural schools were operating, located mainly in Athens and Thessaloniki to accommodate children of Greek emigrants, ethnic Greeks from Albania, and children of other nationalities.[35]

Children of immigrants have also the right to attend public schools, including those whose parents live in Greece illegally. In September 2003, the Greek Minister of Internal Affairs issued a circular which banned the children of immigrants without valid residence permits from enrolling in public schools.

The Minister withdrew the circular after a strong protest from the Department of Children's Rights. The latter argued that the Greek authorities, pursuant to legal obligations arising from the Constitution and the ratification of the Convention of the Rights of the Child, must provide every child with access to basic education, regardless of the legal status of the parents.[36]

Public Institutions

In the last ten years, Greece has paid more attention to the issue of balancing family responsibilities and work.[37] Greece has established numerous institutions run by the state to accommodate working mothers and also to provide a safe environment for children. In Greece there are 3,964 primary and 2,169 nursery schools. There are also 1,306 public day care centers, which serve children from two and a half years of age until the age of six, and 132 daycare centers for infants and children that accommodate approximately 10,000 children from eight months old until they reach the age of six. These public day care centers fall under the competence of local administration authorities.[38] Moreover, 164 daycare centers for children and infants have been transferred to the competent authorities of the municipalities and communities where they operate.[39] The European Union, through its Community Support Framework, has provided funds for these institutions and others, such as Creative Occupation Centers for children with disabilities and the Program for Employment and Vocational Training.

Corporal Punishment

Corporal punishment in schools has not been permitted by law since 1998, when Presidential Decree No 201/98 explicitly banned it. However, the Children Rights Department, other notable individuals, and various NGOs expressed concerns over the lack of effective civil and criminal penalties in cases of corporal punishment by teachers and parents.

Even though the principle of the best interests of the child permeates many pieces of legislation and especially the family law provisions on relations between children and parents, it has been argued that corporal punishment has been interpreted as permissible under the Civil Code. Specifically, article 1518 of the Greek Civil Code states that parents have the right to take any disciplinary measures, as long as such measures are necessary and do not violate the children's dignity.[40] However, on October 19, 2006, the Greek Parliament adopted Law 3500/2006 on Combating Intra-Family Violence.[41] This Law explicitly prohibits physical violence against children within the family. Parents who use physical punishment as a disciplinary method will be considered as abusing their parental authority, which may result in removal of parental authority by the courts.

V. Child Labor and Exploitation

Government statistics released in 2001 estimated that there were approximately 80,000 adolescents aged fourteen to nineteen who assist the family through work, mostly in agricultural jobs; in fishing; as car mechanics; or in hotel, restaurant, or construction jobs. This estimate does not include young children who are forced to work without money, the children of economic migrants, or "traffic light kids," the approximately 5,800 street children between the ages of three and fifteen who clean the windshield wipers of cars at traffic lights or sell small items on the streets.[42]

Since 1989, the minimum age for employment has been established at fifteen.[43] A Presidential Decree No 62/1998 prohibits the employment of children below the minimum age of employment in family businesses in the agricultural, forestry, and livestock sectors.

In 2001, Greece enacted another law that extends the ban on night work to young persons employed in family business in the agricultural, forestry, and livestock sectors[44] and in the maritime and fishing industries.[45]

In 2003, Greece outlawed activities such as begging and other forms of labor in the streets, including selling flowers, cleaning shoes, or cleaning car windshields. There is no punishment for the above crimes, except the crime of begging. Article 409 of the Criminal Code punishes anyone who forces persons under his care to beg for financial benefit with imprisonment of up to six months or a fine. It is an aggravating circumstance if it involves children under the age of eighteen, or those who are older who but are mentally or physically challenged.[46]

Greece has also ratified the 1999 ILO Convention No. 182 on the Worst Forms of Child Labor.[47]

VI. Sexual Exploitation of Children

Child Pornography

Greece outlawed child pornography in 2002.[48] Article 348A of the Criminal Code punishes those who, for profit, manufacture, offer, provide, possess, or sell pornographic material in any format of a real or a virtual act involving a minor with imprisonment of at least one year and a fine of €10,000 to €100,000 (about US$13,890 to $138,900). It is an aggravating circumstance if the pornographic materials involve exploitation of the need or mental incapacity, deafness, or inexperience of an under age person or involve the use of violence against him or her. In such cases, perpetrators are punishment by imprisonment for up to ten years and a fine of €50,000 to €100,000. If the victim is injured, then the punishment is at least ten years of imprisonment and the fine is augmented from €100,000 to €500,000.

Pimping

The Criminal Code also punishes those who encourage prostitution of minors with imprisonment for up to ten years and a fine of €10,000 to €50,000. The punishment is more severe if the crime involves a minor under the age of fifteen or is committed by parents or step-parents, relatives, guardians, custodians, or teachers.[49]

Lewd Acts against Minors

Adults who commit lewd acts against minors in exchange of money or other material exchange or adults who cause lewd acts among minors committed before other people are punished as follows:

- If the victim is less than 10 years old, by imprisonment of at least ten years and a fine of €100,000 to 500,000;
- If the victim is between 10-15 years old, by imprisonment of up to ten years and a fine of €50,000 to 100,000; and
- If the victim is more than fifteen years old, by imprisonment of one year at least and a fine of €10,000 to 50,000.
- If the victim dies, by life imprisonment.[50]

Seduction of Minors

Article 339 of the Criminal Code[51] punishes one who commits the offense of seduction of a person younger than fifteen years old. More severe punishment is provided if the victim is younger than ten.

VII. SALE AND TRAFFICKING OF CHILDREN

Trafficking of children, as a serious social phenomenon raising legal and humanitarian concerns, emerged in Greece in the early 2000s, when several major cities witnessed an influx of street children, selling small items or flowers or cleaning the windshields at traffic lights. These children came to be known as "street children" or "traffic light children." According to surveys, the children came mainly from Albania, following relatives and friends or even unknown people, with the promise of a better future.[52] They were required to work hard and pass their earnings to those who facilitated their entry through the Greek borders. This problem grew rapidly, and the situation facilitated the creation of a profitable market for traffickers due to two factors: a) the failure of the Greek government to act promptly and to coordinate its actions efficiently, and b) the generosity of the local people, who were willing to give money to the street children, which enabled their street lives. Finally, the issue caught the attention of the press and various NGO's dealing with human rights.

A number of organizations, including the Greek Helsinki Monitor and others, reported in 2003 that during the period of 1998 and 2002, 502 children disappeared from the state-run institution Aghia Varvara.[53] The center was established to temporarily accommodate street children. The Greek authorities did not investigate the issue until the Albanian Ombudsman sent a formal request to his Greek counterpart to conduct an investigation. The 2004 report of the Greek Ombudsman apparently dealt only with problems that the institution faced, such as absence of guards, insufficient funding etc.

According to more recent estimates, the number of Albanian children being trafficked into Greece in 2005 and 2006 has decreased. However, there are reports that Albanian Roma children are still trafficked for labor exploitation.[54]

Legislative Action

The Ministry of Public Order took a step in the right direction through the establishment of the Group against Human Trafficking (OKEA) to study the phenomenon and to set the legislative process in motion. In 2002, the Greek Parliament unanimously adopted Law No 3064/2002 on Measures to Combat Trafficking in Human Beings, Sexual and Economic Exploitation, and Child Pornography.[55] An implementing Presidential Decree, No. 233, followed in 2003.

Article 323 of the Law punishes trafficking of human being for labor purposes. The Article provides for punishment of up to ten years and a fine of €10,000 to €50,000 for anyone who, by force, threat, or other coercive means, including abuse of power, hires or transports someone within or outside the Greek territory with the purpose of exploiting his or her labor. A punishment of at least six months is provided to someone who knowingly accepts the labor of such a person.[56] If the act involves a minor, then the punishment increases to imprisonment of at least ten years and a fine of €50,000 to €100,000. The same punishment is extended under that article to anyone who recruits a minor in order to use him or her in armed conflict.

Article 351 punishes trafficking of human beings for sexual exploitation. It provides for imprisonment of up to ten years for anyone who by force, threat, or other kinds of coercive means transports, within or outside the country; hands over a person to someone else with or without something in exchange; or receives from somebody a person with the purpose of sexually exploiting that person either personally or by another person. The same punishment is also provided to a person who, sexually exploits another even if he receives the consent of a person in need by making promises, giving presents, or providing payment or other benefits or by the use of fraudulent means. The Criminal Code provides more severe punishment if the act of human trafficking involves a minor. Thus, in such a case, a perpetrator receives a sentence of at least ten years and a fine of fifty to one hundred euros in the following if the crime was: committed against a person younger than eighteen years or was committed by a relative or adopted parent, a guardian, or another person with a close relationship to a minor.

If the human trafficking results in serious physical injury to the victim, an imprisonment of at least ten years is imposed, and in case of the death of the victim, the law provides for the maximum penalty, which is life imprisonment.

Assistance to Victims of Trafficking

The law also provides that victims of trafficking whose life, physical well-being, and personal and sexual freedom are endangered be offered protection. Assistance is also provided in the form of shelter, food, psychological support, and medical care. Legal counsel and translation services are provided. If minors are involved, they are provided all the above services and are placed in educational and vocational programs, as appropriate.[57] If the minors reside in Greece illegally, the law provides for safe repatriation, provided that they wish to be repatriated. In such a case, the minor must express his will in writing before a designated official. The district attorney assigned to juvenile cases must also concur in the minor's repatriation.[58] If the minor does not wish to be repatriated, the law provides that the minor must be allowed to stay temporarily. Presidential Decree 233/2003 requires that Greek authorities not repatriate foreign victims, including minors.

Despite the enactment of the human trafficking law, problems still remain in this area. In a report released on June 13, 2007,[59] Amnesty International criticized the Greek government for failing to guarantee protection and justice to a large number of trafficked women and children forced into prostitution.

Under Greek immigration law, victims of trafficking against whom deportation proceedings are pending are offered a reflection period. The reflection period is given by the Prosecutor and lasts one month for adults and for two months for minors. The purpose is to give the victims time to consider whether they wish to cooperate with the police. At the end of this period, if the victims are willing to cooperate, residence permits are issued.[60]

Since 2004, victims of human trafficking have been entitled to residence and work permit for a period of six months. Their permit is renewable, until a court decides on their fate.

Presidential Decree 233/2003 establishes the various forms of assistance to victims, which include the following: a) medical; b) psychological; c) legal through the assignment of the case involving a minor to a special "legal assistant"; d) educational; e) protection of witnesses in trials involving human trafficking; f) non-repatriation in case of foreign victims; and g) equal protection of all victims, including foreigners.

Agreement between Greece and Albania on Child Victims of Trafficking

Greece has signed several agreements with neighboring countries concerning human trafficking. On February 27, 2006, Greece signed a bilateral agreement with Albania against trafficking in children. This is the first agreement that Greece has entered into with another country that relates specifically to children. Since this agreement is the first of its kind, it is intended to be used as a model for similar agreements with other states. Its objective is to protect and provide assistance to children from Albania who are trafficked to Greece and to reduce the risk of trafficking of children in Albania. The success of this agreement naturally will lie in its full implementation by both governments.[61] The Ministry of Foreign Affairs is in the process of negotiating a child trafficking agreement with Malta.

Financial Assistance

The Greek government has also financed a number of measures to fight trafficking of human beings. There are four shelters, in Athens and in northern Greece, offering protection to victims, including social and psychological support and also assistance in eventual repatriation of the victims. These are funded by the Ministry of Foreign Affairs. There are also two hostels operated by the Ministry of Health and Welfare, in Athens and Thessaloniki, offering assistance for the first hours after a victim is located. Another measure provides funds for a protection center for unaccompanied or neglected children after their return to their homeland. In addition, there are a number of shelters run by NGOs in major cities.

The Ministry of Health and Welfare operates the national center of Emergency Social Care. Victims can call a hotline (#197) and file complaints regarding detention; they also receive psychological support, medical advice, and further referrals to appropriate institutions for legal advice or to health centers for medical and pharmaceutical care.

A Permanent Committee for the Protection and Assistance of Victims of Human Trade was established in 1993.[62] Its mandate and competencies have been strengthened in the last few years. The Ministry of Justice has undertaken the task of providing seminars to train and familiarize active judges, as well as future judges graduating from the National School of Judges. In spite of the statutory framework, a number of problems persist. A 2005 report prepared by the Special Rapporteur on the Sale of Children, Child Prostitution, and Child Pornography identifies the lack of an effective system in place to identify minor victims of trafficking and exploitation. Consequently, children who may be victims are caught, arrested, and deported along with adults on grounds of illegal entry. Even though the law prohibits deportation until a final hearing, apparently children have been deported in great numbers.[63]

VII. JUVENILE JUSTICE

In 2003, the juvenile justice system underwent significant changes.[64] The impetus for these changes was the desire to harmonize the criminal law provisions with those of the Convention of the Rights of the Child and also to bring the juvenile system in line with the constitutional mandate regarding the responsibility of the state to protect children.[65]

Some cosmetic changes are noteworthy, since they reflect a changed attitude of the society at large and of the criminal justice system in particular towards criminal acts committed by minors. First, the word "delinquent" was eliminated from those articles of the Criminal Code dealing with minors. Secondly, rather than confinement in an institution, the term "confinement in a special institution for minors" was used. Another important change concerns the lower and upper limits of the period during which a person is considered a minor for the purposes of criminal responsibility. These were changed from seven to seventeen years of age to eight to eighteen. Since the Convention defines a child as anyone under the age of eighteen, without further differentiation, the Criminal Code has now been brought into line with the Convention.[66]

Criminal Responsibility

The Criminal Code absolves a minor between the ages of eight and thirteen from any criminal responsibility for wrongdoing. Such a person is subject only to reformative or therapeutic measures. If a minor at the time of commission of a criminal offense has completed the thirteenth year of age, the court takes into consideration all the circumstances surrounding the case and may decide that it is optimal to order the confinement of the minor in a special institution for youth for a specific period of time.[67] Confinement may last from five years up to twenty years, if the same act committed by an adult would require confinement from ten years to life imprisonment. In all other cases, confinement lasts from six months to ten years.

The court may impose reduced punishment on anyone who has committed a criminal act when at the time of the commission he had completed the eighteenth year of age but not the twenty-first. [68]

If a minor commits a misdemeanor, then he is only subject to two reformative measures: a) a reprimand; and b) assignment of the minor under the responsible care of his parents or guardians.[69]

If a minor who has completed the thirteenth year of age commits a criminal act and is brought to trial after the completion of the eighteenth year of age, the court may order that the minor be subject to a reduced sentence, rather than be confined in a special institution. In such a case, minors must be kept in separate quarters from adult criminals.

Reformative and Therapeutic Measures

As stated above, minors are subject only to reformative or therapeutic measures. Minors between the ages of thirteen and eighteen who engage in criminal acts are tried by special courts. The Code of Criminal Procedure provides that those are either: a) a single-member Court for Minors; b) a three-member Court; or c) the Court of Appeals. Appeals from the single-member court for minors are heard before the Court of Appeals and not before the three-member court.

The 2003 amendments of the juvenile justice system specify twelve possible reformative measures, listed in order of severity. These include: a) a reprimand; b) placing the child under the responsible care of his parents or to his guardians; c) assignment of the care of the child to foster parents;[70] d) placing the child in the care of "societies for the protection of children" or institutions designated for the care of children; e) communication between victim and underage perpetrator, so that the latter will have the opportunity to express apologies and remorse; f) compensation of the victim; g) community service performed by the minor; h) attending social and psychological programs in special institutions; i) attending vocational schools or enrolling in training; and several other measures. In exceptional cases, the courts may impose two or three measures concurrently.

The therapeutic measures are designed to assist minors who need special treatment, especially due to mental or physical illness or due to addiction to drugs or alcohol, and who are unable to assist themselves. In such cases, the court, based on an expert's diagnosis and opinion, may assign the care of such a minor either to his parents, guardians, or a foster family or may order the care of such a minor in protection agencies.[71] These measures are imposed by a single-member court, based on an opinion issued by a team of doctors, psychologists, and social workers. The reformative measures cease *ipso jure* when the minor attains majority. In exceptional circumstances, the court has the right to extend these measures until the minor reaches the twenty-first year of age.[72] On the other hand, the therapeutic measures do not come to an end automatically. Only the team that ordered them in the first place has the right to order that such measures be terminated.

Greece has established a public prosecutor for minors in the Athens court district.[73] His responsibilities include assignment of custody, provision of cooperation and assistance to offices of public and private agencies designed to prevent and combat juvenile crime, submission of applications for security measures to the courts for minors, and initiation of legal actions to remove parental custody or child supervision.

Prepared by Theresa Papademetriou
Senior Foreign Law Specialist
September 2007

End Notes

[1] Art. 21, 1 of the Constitution. Ephemeris tes Kyverneseos tes Ellenikes Demokratias [EKED], Part A, No. 85, Apr. 18, 2001.

[2] Art. 5, 2 of the Constitution, id.

[3] Roma, also called "gypsies" are members of "a people with dark skin and hair who speak Romany and who traditionally live by seasonal work and fortunetelling; they are believed to have originated in northern India but now are living on all continents (but mostly in Europe, North Africa, and North America)," according to Wordnet, http://wordnet.princeton. edu/perl/webwn (last visited Sept. 14, 2007). For more information see U.S. Department of State, Greece, COUNTRY REPORTS ON HUMAN RIGHTS PRACTICES, Mar. 6, 2007, available at http://www.state.gov/g/drl/rls/hrrpt/2006/78815.htm.

[4] United Nations High Commissioner for Refugees, Country Operations Plan, Overview: Greece, Planning Year: 2006, at 2, Web site of the Clearinghouse on International Developments in Child, Youth, and Family Policies of Columbia University, http://www.childpolicyintl.org/countries/greece.html (last visited Sept. 13, 2007).

[5] See remarks of the Minister of Education Integration Through Education: Migrant Workers in Greece, Woodrow Wilson Center Web site, Mar. 29, 2006, available at http://www.wilsoncenter.org/index.cfm?fuseaction = events.event summary&evnet_id=1775.

[6] Id.

[7] PENELOPE AGALLOPOULOU, BASIC CONCEPTS OF GREEK CIVIL LAW 39 (2004).

[8] For implementation of this Convention in Greece, see P.NASKOU-PERRAKI Et. Al., HE DIETHES SYMBASE GIA TA DIKAIOMATA TOU PAIDIOU KAI HE ESOTERIKE ENNOME TAKSE [The International Convention on the Rights of the Child and the Greek Legal Order] 34 (2002).

[9] Episemos Ephemeris tes Hellenikes Demokratias (EEHD), Part A No. 192 (1992).

[10] Art. 28, 1 provides that the "generally recognized rules of international law, as well as international conventions as of they time the are sanctioned by statute and become operative according to their respective conditions, shall be an integral part of domestic Greek law and shall prevail over any contrary provision of the law. The rules of international law and of international conventions shall be applicable to aliens only under the condition of reciprocity."

[11] European Convention on the Exercise of Children's Rights, Jan. 25, 1996, Web site of the Council of Europe, http://conventions.coe.int/Treaty/en/Treaties/Html/160.htm.

[12] Optional Protocol to the Convention on the Rights of the Child on the Sale of Children, Child Prostitution and Child Pornography New York, 25 May 2000, Web site of the Office of the United Nations High Commissioner for Human Rights, July 13, 2007, http://www.ohchr.org/english/countries/ratification/11_c.htm.

[13] Status of Ratifications of the Optional Protocol to the Convention on the Rights of the Child on the Involvement of Children In Armed Conflict, Web site of the Office of the United Nations High Commissioner for Human Rights, Nov. 14, 2003, http://www.unhchr.ch/html/menu2/6/crc/treaties/status-opac.htm.

[14] Law No. 2952/2001.

[15] Constitution, EKED, Part A. (2003).

[16] GREEK OMBUDSMAN ANNUAL REPORT 2005 (2006), available at, http://www.synigoros.gr/en_ annual_ 2005.htm.

[17] It was amended by law 3106/2003.

[18] Law 2082/1992 on Reorganization of Social Welfare and Introduction of New Methods of Social Welfare.

[19] GREEK OMBUDSMAN ANNUAL REPORT 2005, supra note 16, at 46.

[20] Royal Decree 273/1973 on Reorganization of National Orphanages to Centers of Child Care, as amended.

[21] Law 1431/1984 on Regulation of Issues of Offices of Social Welfare-Child Protection and Other Institutions, as amended.

[22] Information based on a questionnaire on separated Children prepared by Greek authorities in 2003. Greece - Questionnaire for Country Assessment, Website of the Separated Children in Europe Programme (jointly published by the organization Save the Children and the United Nations High Commissioner for Refugees, http://www.separated-children-europeprogramme.org/separated_children/publications/assessments/greece_ engq.htm (last visited Sept. 12, 2007).

[23] See Ministerial Order 2/37645/0020/2002.

[24] See Statement by the Vice-Minister for Health and Social Welfare to the United Nations Special Session on Children, United Nations, May 10, 2002, available at http://www.un.org/ga/children/greeceE.htm.

[25] According to the 2001 census, 99.4% of school-age children attend school. The majority also complete the mandatory education requirement. Within the Roma community, however, there is a persistent problem of non-compliance with this requirement. According to statistics, 63% of Roma children do not attend school. There have also been a number of incidents of parents withdrawing their children from schools because of the presence of Roma children attending the same schools. U.S. Department of State, supra note 3, at 14.

[26] For more information on the educational system in Greece, see National Report of Greece, International Conference on Education, Geneva, Sept.8-11, 2004, available at http://www.ibe.unesco.org/International/ ICE47/english/Natreps/ reports/greece.pdf.

[27] Greece, Overview, Web site of the European Agency for Development in Special Needs Education, http://www. european-agency.org/transit/overview/greece/overview.html (last visited Sept. 5, 2007).

[28] U.S. Department of State, supra note 3, at 16.

[29] The legal status of the Muslim minority is governed by the 1923 Treaty of Lausanne and other subsequent bilateral agreements.

[30] National Report of Greece, supra note 26, at 15. GREEK OMBUDSMAN ANNUAL REPORT 2005, supra note 16

[31] Ministry of the Interior of Greece, Public Administration and Decentralization, General secretariat for Gender Equality, Report on Progress for the Implementation of the Platform for Action of the 4th world Conference on Women of the United Nations (Beijing , 1995) and the Outcome of the 23rd Special Session of the General Assembly of the United Nations (New York, 2000), June 2004, available at http://www.isotita.gr/en/ index.php/docs/c2/ (Web site of the General Secretary for Gender Equality).

[32] See Ministerial Decision 2/37645/0020/08.72002.

[33] European Racism and Xenophobia Information Network, National Focal Point for Greece, RAXEN NATIONAL REPORT 2004 DATA COLLECTION, at 25, http://www.antigone.gr/listpage/reports_on_greece/2004/ NAR_ 2004_GR_01. 12.2005.pdf (last visited Sept. 13, 2007).

[34] Law 2413/1996 , EKED, Part A. No. 124 (June 17, 1996)

[35] National Focal Point for Greece, supra note 33.

[36] GREEK OMBUDSMAN ANNUAL REPORT 2005, supra note 16.

[37] The European Union, through its public awareness campaigns and funds, has greatly assisted Greece in reaching this objective.

[38] See art. 12 of Law 2880/2001.

[39] Art. 8 of Law 3106/2003.

[40] See Greek Civil Code, Family Law.

[41] EKED, Part. A, No.

[42] See Greece, Non-Governmental Organizations' Report in Application of the United Nations Convention on the Rights of the Child 23 (2001).

[43] Law 1837/1989.

[44] Law 29956/2001.

[45] Presidential Decree No. 407/2001.

[46] The aggravating case was added to the Criminal Code provision in 2003, by art. 2, 7 of Law. 3189/2003, EKED, Part. A. 243.

[47] Convention No. C-182, web site of the International Labor Organization http://www.ilo.org/ilolex/cgi-lex/ratifce.pl?C182 (last visited Sept.13, 2007).

[48] Art. 6 of Law 3064/2002, EKED, Part. A 248.

[49] Art. 349 of the Criminal Code.

[50] Art. 351A of the Criminal Code.

[51] It was amended in 2002 and 2003 by Law 3064/2002 and Law 3160/2003.

[52] For more information see Transnational Action against Child Trafficking Transnational Protection of Children, The Case of Albania and Greece 2000-2006, Web site of the European Network of Ombudsmen for Children, Oct. 18, 2006, available at http://www.crin.org/enoc/resources/infoDetail.asp?ID=10732&flag=report.

[53] This was established in 1998 under the aegis of the Deputy Minister of Health and Welfare, in order to promote the protection and social welfare of street children.

[54] U.S. Department of State, supra note 3, at 15.

[55] Law No. 3064/2002/.

[56] PHILIPPOS N. ANDREOU, POINIKOS KODIKAS [Criminal Code] 1274 (2005).

[57] Law 3064/2002, art. 13.

[58] Id., art. 14 .

[59] Greece: Uphold the Rights of Women and Girls Trafficked Sexual Exploitation, Amnesty International Web site, http://web.amnesty.org/actforwomen/gre-120607-action-eng (last visited Sept. 6, 2007).

[60] Law 3386/2005, effective Jan. 1, 2006; it harmonizes the provisions of the Council Directive 2004/81/EC of Apr. 29, 2004.

[61] Albania and Greece Sign First Bilateral Agreement on Trafficking, USAID/ALBANIA, Feb. 27, 2006, available at http://albania.usaid.gov/(bu2s504zz32wb45kpafj45)/en/Story.aspx?id=87.

[62] By virtue of art. 9 of Presidential Decree 233/2003.

[63] Rights of the Child, Addendum to the Report of the Special Rapporteur on the Sale of Children, Child Prostitution and Child Pornography (Nov. 8-15, 2005)

[64] Law 3189/2003, Part. A, No. 243.

[65] For more information see C. D. SPINELLIS AND A. TSITOURA, THE EMERGING JUVENILE SYSTEM IN GREECE (2006).

[66] PHILIPPOS N. ANDREOU, supra note 56.

[67] Criminal Code, art. 127.

[68] Id., art. 133.

[69] Id., art. 128.

[70] The institution of foster parents was established in 1992. Law No. 2082 provides that children under the age of eighteen who have no place to stay or who live under conditions that are unhealthy and dangerous to their physical and mental well-being may be placed under the care of foster families until they reach the age of majority.

[71] The Criminal Code, as amended, art. 123.

[72] Id., art. 125.

[73] Regulation of the Internal Service of the Prosecution of the Athens Court of first Instance, Part. B 1017.

In: Children's Rights
Editors: Brooke Dabney and Michael Eldridge

ISBN: 978-1-62948-252-1
© 2013 Nova Science Publishers, Inc.

Chapter 11

ISLAMIC REPUBLIC OF IRAN: CHILDREN'S RIGHTS[*]

G. H. Vafai

I. INTRODUCTION

The Islamic Revolution of 1979 introduced drastic and fundamental changes in the social, economic and political structure of Iran. It marked the end of a 2,500 year- old monarchical regime and brought to power a religion-oriented government based on the Shiite school tenets of Islam.

The change in the nature of the regime from secular to religious had its impact both on domestic legislation and international conventions, as explained below.

II. INTERNATIONAL CONVENTIONS

The Islamic Republic of Iran (Iran) is a party to Convention on the Rights of the Child. Iran adhered to the Convention in September 1991, and ratified it on July 13, 1994.[1] Iran, however, has made the following reservation "If the text of the Convention is or becomes incompatible with the domestic laws and Islamic standards at any time or in any case, the Government of the Islamic Republic shall not abide by it."[2] Iran has so far (according to the available sources in the Law Library of Congress) not passed legislation calling for the implementation of the Convention.

Iran is also a signatory to the International Covenant on Civil and Political Rights, as of April 4, 1968, adhering to this Covenant on June 24, 1975.[3] Iran, however, has not passed any legislation implementing the Covenant (according to the available sources in the Law Library of Congress).

---

[*] This document was released by the Law Library of Congress August 2007.

III. Domestic Legislation

The Law Aggravating Punishment for Employing Children under 12 Years of Age in the Carpet Industry of February, 1969 provides for a jail term of six months to one year and a fine of five thousand to fifty thousand rials for violators.[4] Other than the carpet industry, the Labor Law sets age fifteen as the minimum age for employment.[5]

In addition, the Regulations regarding the Maximum Weight to Be Lifted Manually by Women and Teenagers of February 1991 provide that the load to be lifted manually by a woman should not exceed ten kilograms. For a male teenager, it should not exceed twenty kilograms.[6]

Prepared by G.H. Vafai
Senior Foreign Law Specialist
August 2007

End Notes

[1] See list of countries ratifying the Convention on the Rights of the Child, Office of the United Nations High Commissioner for Human Rights, http://www.ohchr.org/english/countries/ratification/11.htm (last visited Aug. 9, 2007).

[2] HUQUQI KOODAK, SHIRIN EBADI,183 (1996) (in Farsi).

[3] See list of countries ratifying the International Covenant on Civil and Political Rights, Office of the United Nations High Commissioner for Human Rights, // http://www.ohchr.org/english/countries/ratification/4.htm# reservations (last visited Aug. 9, 2007).

[4] MAJMUAHI QAVANIN SALI 1347, 495 (1968) (in Farsi).

[5] COLLECTION OF LABOR LAWS (Yar Bakhat 1993).

[6] Id.

In: Children's Rights
Editors: Brooke Dabney and Michael Eldridge

ISBN: 978-1-62948-252-1
© 2013 Nova Science Publishers, Inc.

Chapter 12

ISRAEL: CHILDREN'S RIGHTS[*]

Ruth Levush

EXECUTIVE SUMMARY

Israel adheres to international conventions to which it is a signatory and maintains a special set of laws to protect children. In addition to health benefits applicable to all Israeli residents, special benefits apply specifically to pregnant women and children. Special welfare benefits are also directed at assisting families with children and, particularly, the disabled. The law requires at least ten years of compulsory education and protects children from labor and sexual exploitation. The system recognizes different rules in the adjudication of juveniles.

I. INTRODUCTION

Israel maintains an extensive system of laws designed to protect children's rights. It is a signatory to numerous international conventions and provides many health and welfare services to children. Special protections apply in the areas of child labor and sexual exploitation. Children enjoy different treatment in the juvenile justice system than adults do in the regular justice system. The age of majority in Israel is eighteen.[1]

II. IMPLEMENTATION OF INTERNATIONAL RIGHTS OF THE CHILD

Israel has ratified the following treaties:[2]

1. the International Covenant on Economic, Social and Cultural Rights;[3]
2. the International Covenant on Civil and Political Rights;[4]

---

[*] This document was released by the Law Library of Congress August 2007.

3. the International Convention on the Elimination of All Forms of racial Discrimination;[5]
4. the Convention on the Elimination of All Forms of Discrimination Against Women;[6]
5. the Convention Against Torture and Other Cruel, Inhuman or Degrading Treatment or Punishment;[7]
6. the Convention on the Rights of the Child;[8] and
7. the Optional Protocol to the Convention on the Rights of the Child on the Sale of Children, Child Prostitution and Child Pornography.[9]

The United Nations (UN) Convention on the Rights of the Child (hereafter CRC) was signed by the State of Israel on 3 July 1990, ratified by the Knesset (Israel's Parliament) on August 4, 1991, and went into effect on November 2, 1991. Although the Convention does not have the status of law, it is often cited in rulings of both the supreme and the lower courts as a legal source and a basis of interpretation. The fundamental principles declared in the Convention, however, seem identical to the fundamental principles on which laws concerning children are based in Israel, and to principles underlying Israeli law.

Israel's periodic report to the United Nations Committee on the Rights of the Child[10] notes additional international conventions concerning children to which Israel is a signatory.

For example, since 1953, Israel has been a party to conventions of the International Labor Organization (ILO), primarily the Convention Concerning Medical Examination of Children and Young Persons in Non-industrial Occupations (No. 78, 1946); the Convention Concerning Medical Examination for Fitness for Employment in Industry of Children and Young Persons (No. 77, 1946); the Convention Concerning Night Work for Children and Young Persons in Industrial and Non-industrial Occupations (No. 90, 1948 and No. 79, 1949). Since 1980, Israel has been a party to the International Labor Convention Concerning Minimum Age for Admission to Employment (No. 138, 1973). In addition, Israel is a party to the Hague Convention on International Private Law. Since 1991, Israel has been a party to the Hague Convention Concerning Civil Aspects of Child Kidnapping (No. 513 XXVIII, 1980), and since 1995, Israel has been a party to the Hague Convention Concerning the Protection of Children and Cooperation in Respect of Inter-country Adoption (1993).[11]

Principles enumerated in these conventions have been incorporated in Israeli domestic legislation. Some examples are discussed in this report. Additionally, in accordance with the Registration of Information on the Influence of Legislation on the Child's Right Law, 5762-2002, [12] members of Parliament and the government are required to review, in the process of preparing a bill for a first hearing, the bill's potential influence on the rights of children, in the spirit of the CRC.

III. Child Health and Social Welfare

A. Access to Healthcare Services

Health services in Israel are provided under the National Health Insurance Law, 5754-1994,[13] as amended. Although the law was first implemented in 1995, the existing health system can trace its roots to the 1920s, well before the founding of the State in 1948.[14]

The National Health Insurance Law 5754-1994,[15] stipulates that all of Israel's residents are eligible for health services based on principles of justice, equality, and mutual assistance. The law mandated the provision of a basket of health services, which are largely provided by sick funds - non-profit corporations whose income is used to provide these services. The government finances health services, primarily through an earmarked, progressive tax paid by all residents. The law further stipulates that health services must be provided while maintaining human dignity and the patient's right to privacy and medical confidentiality.

The basket of services must cover the following areas of health service:[16]

1. individual preventive care and health education;
2. medical diagnosis;
3. ambulatory medical care, including psychiatric care, whether in a clinic, at home, or in an institution (e.g., old-age home, day care center);
4. acute, psychiatric, psycho-geriatric hospitalization and chronic nursing care;
5. rehabilitation, including medical and psychological rehabilitation, physical, speech, and occupational therapy, and social work in the area of speech;
6. medications;
7. medical instruments and assistive devices;
8. preventive dental care for children up to an age specified by regulations;
9. first aid and transportation to a hospital or clinic;
10. medical services at work; and
11. medical and psychological care for addicts and alcoholics undergoing rehabilitation.

B. Preventive Services

Preventive services for pregnant women and children from birth to age five are provided by family health centers. These centers provide pre-natal examinations, inoculations, early detection of physical and emotional disabilities, health education, and counseling.[17] In addition, they identify families that are unable to provide proper care for their children and refer them to the social welfare system. When developmental problems are suspected or identified by a center's primary care physician or nurse, the children are referred to a center for child development. These centers offer early diagnosis, counseling and care for children up to age five (and, in special cases, older children) who may have a developmental or functional disability. Their multi-professional staffs provide diagnostic and paramedical services, and sometimes support and training for parents. Children over age five who need care are usually referred to a special education or other medical framework. Additional special preventive programs are available for special populations, including new immigrants, HIV positive patients and the *Bedouin*[18] population.[19]

C. Health Education

Health education programs on preventing accidents in the home, at school, and on the roads are conducted at family health centers. In addition, some of the centers offer enrichment programs, programs to improve children's cognitive development, and parenthood preparatory programs, in cooperation with social welfare services.

The State of Israel is a cosignatory of the 1990 WHO- and UNICEF-sponsored "Innocenti Declaration", whose aim is to promote breastfeeding. In compliance with the declaration, Israel has placed limits on advertisements for and efforts to market baby formula in maternity wards, although these are apparently not strictly enforced. In 1998, the National Commission on Child Medicine, which operates within the Ministry of Health and examines policy concerning children's health, established the committee for the promotion of breastfeeding, whose goal is to encourage breastfeeding, in part by creating conditions that will make it easier for mothers to breastfeed their children (e.g., longer maternity leave and private rooms in work places where mothers can pump milk).[20]

D. Preventive Services for School Children

Health services for elementary and secondary school students in Israel are financed by the State. In elementary schools, the nurses conduct routine examinations, such as testing vision and hearing and measuring height; give inoculations; and teach nutrition, personal hygiene, and sex education.

The health services provided in secondary schools are primarily educational and focus on preventing drug and alcohol addiction and communicable diseases such as AIDS, and on safety and accident prevention. In addition to the health services provided at schools, preventive services are offered to adolescents through specialty service centers, which are financed by the Ministry of Health, social welfare agencies, and one of the health funds' Health Services.

These centers specialize in adolescent health and provide sex education, medical testing, and treatment of problems that arise during adolescence, such as acne and weight problems. Countrywide youth counseling centers further provide youth with instruction, counseling, and referral in a variety of areas, including health.[21]

E. Social Welfare Services

Israel maintains an extensive system of social security and income support, as well as a national system of welfare services in the framework of the health and education systems, to meet the needs of vulnerable populations. These services are provided through the National Insurance Institute.

The National Insurance Institute is a statutory corporation charged with implementing the National Insurance Law [Consolidated Version] 1995,[22] and other laws that grant residents of the State social benefits and other transfer payments.

Among child-related benefits is the children's monthly allowance, as well as the disabled child allowance for families that care for a disabled child, to ease the burden of personal and nursing care and maternity insurance. As part of maternity insurance, women who have given birth or adopted children are entitled to a hospitalization grant (for expenses of the birth, and of the hospitalization of the mother and baby (including premature babies)), maternity benefits, and equipment grants. In addition, mothers are entitled to maternity leave allowance to compensate the working mother for the loss of wages during her maternity leave and during the pregnancy if for reasons related to the pregnancy she was forced to cease working for thirty days.

Additional child-related benefits paid by the National Insurance Institute are an education grant paid to single parents for each of their children, benefits paid to parents whose finances are below the poverty line, and custodians of orphans or children immigrating to Israel without their parents.[23]

IV. EDUCATION, INCLUDING SPECIAL NEEDS

A. General Education

The State Education Law 1953[24] stipulates that education will be provided, as a rule, by the State on the basis of an educational program that is supervised and approved by the Ministry of Education. The law recognizes two streams of education: State education, and State religious education. The law also sanctions non-government education institutions, recognized but not official institutions that are supervised by the Ministry of Education, and independent institutions that are not supervised by the Ministry. Although parents have the right to choose the stream of education which their children will attend[25] they are not allowed to choose the specific school their children will attend. The local school board refers children to schools, in accordance with the policy of social integration.[26]

The Compulsory Education Law 1949[27] stipulates that education in Israel is compulsory for children ages three to fifteen inclusive, or until the completion of ten years of schooling, and beginning at age five. The law allows the Minister of Education to grant an exemption from compulsory education in special cases, such as when a child is educated privately, or cannot be integrated into a regular school.[28]

According to the Compulsory Education Law 1949, children and youth ages three to seventeen have the right to free education. Although complete implementation of free education for children ages three to four has been deferred for budgetary reasons; such free education is provided in some towns and neighborhoods.[29] In the remaining towns, free education is provided from age five, although the local authorities in these towns provide pre-compulsory education from age three-four for a fee. This preschool tuition is progressive, and is set according to socio-economic criteria.

Another law designed to increase equal opportunity in education and to enable children to fulfill their potential is the Extended School Day and Enrichment Education Law 1997.[30] The law stipulates that at least four school days a week will be eight-hour school days. It is being implemented gradually, first in neighborhoods and towns whose education systems need reinforcement.[31]

B. Special Education

The Special Education Law 5748-1988,[32] as amended, establishes the right of children with physical, mental, emotional, or behavioral disabilities to an education suited to their needs and development, and ensures that education frameworks are adapted appropriately. The law stipulates how eligibility for special education is to be determined, and that an individual study plan is to be made for each and every child, so as to enable him to fulfill his potential.

The law also expands the type and scope of services provided in the framework of special education. Under the law, special education is provided to children and youth ages three through twenty-one; the law also increased the number of special education hours, lengthened the school day and year (special education schools are open during vacations), and established the right of children to paramedical services (e.g., physical, occupational, and speech therapy), expressive therapies, and assistive devices.

The law expresses a policy of integrating disabled children into regular schools to the extent possible, by requiring that children be given the assistance they need in the "least restrictive environment." Services provided under the law, however, are allocated mostly to children in special education schools and classes, while funds allocated to children who have been mainstreamed are limited and considered insufficient.

The Free Education to Sick Children Law, 5761-2001[33] authorizes the Minister of Education to determine a program for education for children who are hospitalized or are sick and stay at home for a period exceeding twenty-one days. The program will reflect the needs of such children, their medical disabilities, and their education program before they became sick. Education under this program will be provided to the sick child at home or at the hospital.[34] The law provides that the State and the local education authority will finance the education of a sick child.[35]

The Rehabilitative Day-Care Centers Law 5760-2000[36] is meant to ensure toddlers ages one-three, who suffer from a disability, mental retardation, or some other handicap, an appropriate rehabilitative, therapeutic, and educational framework, financed by the State.

C. Humane School Discipline

Students' Rights Law, 5761-2000,[37] as amended, declares its objective:

> To prescribe principles for students rights in the spirit of human dignity and the principles of the United Nations Conventions on the Rights of the Child, while guaranteeing the dignity of the student, the education worker and the education institution team, as well as guarding the specialty of the different education institutions... and in order to encourage the creation of an atmosphere of mutual respect in the educational institution's community.[38]

The law prohibits discrimination against a student based on ethnic, socio-economic, and political grounds in registration, admission, or removal of a student, determining educational programs and class composition, as well as student's rights and obligations, including implementation of disciplinary rules. The law recognized a right of a hearing for a student and his parents prior to a permanent removal from an educational institution.

The law provides that discipline in an educational institute must be implemented in a way that befits human dignity, including the right not to be subjected to physical or degrading disciplinary measures. Additionally, an educational institution must not employ a punitive measure against a student for an act or an omission by his parents.

V. CHILD LABOR AND EXPLOITATION

A. Employment of Minors

The principal law dealing with the employment of minors is the Youth Employment Law 1953- 1953.[39] Another supplementary law is the Apprenticeship Law 5713-1953,[40] which covers minors who acquire a trade through apprenticeship. The Youth Employment Law and the Apprenticeship Law, which were enacted at the same time, were designed to protect working minors and set the frameworks and conditions of their employment. In 1998, the Youth Employment Law was amended in an effort to adapt it to the standards of the CRC.

The Youth Employment Law prohibits the employment of a minor who is under the age of fifteen.[41] The law further prohibits minors from working in certain places,[42] and certain types of work.[43] It is prohibited to employ minors who are obligated to be in school under the Compulsory Education Law 1949, unless the Minister of Education is convinced that the minor is unable to study in an ordinary manner at a recognized educational institution, or the minor is working as an apprentice under the Apprenticeship Law. Because the Compulsory Education Law applies to minors up to age sixteen, in practice minors may only really be employed on a regular basis from the age of sixteen. During official school vacations, however, it is permissible to engage minors over the age of fourteen in light work that is unlikely to harm their health or development.[44]

The law authorizes the Minister of Labor to prohibit certain types of work, if these are liable to adversely affect the minor's physical, mental, or educational development. The Youth Labor (Prohibited and Restricted Work) Regulations 1995,[45] as amended, restrict the employment of minors, and specify the places and types of work in which it is prohibited to employ a minor. These include work involving potentially hazardous mechanical, physical, chemical, and biological elements.

The Youth Employment law and the Youth Employment (Medical Examinations) Regulations, 5760-2000[46] implementing this law require a thorough medical examination prior to employment of a minor to assess whether he is physically fit to do the work. In addition, minors are to be examined periodically, to ensure that the work they are doing is not having an adverse effect on their development and health.

B. Hours of Work and Rest

The law restricts the number of days and hours a minor may work per week. A minor may not be employed for more than eight working hours a day and forty working hours a week.[47] The employer is obligated to allow a minor to take breaks to rest and eat.[48] Minors may not be employed on the weekly rest day of their religion. The Law prohibits a minor from engaging in night work,[49] between 20:00 and 08:00 for minors to whom the Compulsory Education Law applies, and between 22:00 and 06:00 for those to whom it does not. The Minister of Labor and Social Affairs may make exceptions to these restrictions. Even when a permit has been granted a minor must be guaranteed a rest of at least fourteen hours between one working day and the next. Overtime employment of a minor, beyond the hours permitted by law, is a criminal offense, although the minor himself is not regarded by the law as having committed the offense or even as having been an accessory to the offense of his employer.

C. Children in Armed Conflict

Although the age of compulsory military recruitment under the Defense Service Law [Consolidated Version] 5746-1986[50] is generally eighteen years of age, persons over the age of seventeen may make a written request to be inducted into the armed forces with the consent of their parents (or one parent, if there is real difficulty determining the opinion of the other parent) or guardian.[51]

V. Sale and Trafficking of Children

A. Sexual Exploitation and Sexual Abuse

The Penal Law 5737-1977 explicitly prohibits the sexual exploitation of minors.[52] The law imposes particularly harsh penalties on sexual contact with a minor, especially if initiated by force, through exploitation of a relationship based on control or authority, or with a minor under the age of fourteen.[53] The law prescribes a twenty-year imprisonment for rape and forced sodomy of a minor who has not yet reached the age of sixteen.[54] A penalty of five years' imprisonment is imposed for sexual intercourse with a minor between the ages of fourteen and sixteen who is not married to the perpetrator of the act, even if it is committed with her consent.[55] A defendant, however, may claim in his defense that the age difference between him and the girl with whom he engaged in sexual intercourse does not exceed three years, that the girl consented to the act, and that the act was committed in the context of a relationship based on mutuality, and not through the exploitation of the defendant's status.[56] The same criteria also applies to sexual relations between males.[56] A maximum penalty of five years is imposed on a person who has sexual intercourse with a minor over the age of sixteen, even if she consented to the act, if the act involved the exploitation of a relationship based on control, domination, educational authority, or supervision, or a false promise of marriage when the offender is already married. An act of sodomy with a minor over the age of fourteen is punishable by five years' imprisonment, regardless of whether the minor consented to the act or the perpetrator exploited his authority or control over the minor.[57]

The Penal Law 1977 prohibits physical, mental and sexual violation of a minor, and prescribes a maximum sentence of seven years' imprisonment for such offenses, or nine years' imprisonment if the perpetrator is responsible for the child.[58] Harsher penalties are imposed on perpetrators of harm to minors and helpless persons especially when committed by a person who is responsible for a minor, by relatives and care givers. Any person knowing of an offense against a minor committed by a person who is responsible for that minor is obligated to report the offense.[59]

B. Child Prostitution

In Israeli law, prostitution is not an offense, although pimping and soliciting are offenses. A person who solicits another to prostitution is liable to seven years of imprisonment or ten if the person solicited is a minor under the age of fourteen years.[60]

Additional offenses prescribed by the Penal Law include advertisement of prostitution services provided by minors;[61] claiming that a provider of prostitution services is a minor even if this is not true;[62] and publication of pornographic material that involves the body of a minor.[63]

C. Trafficking in Children

The Penal Law 1977 provides that "[A] person who offers or gives compensation for the permission to take custody of a minor who has not yet reached the age of 14, and a person who requests or receives compensation for the right to take custody of a minor is subject to three years' imprisonment."[64] Additionally, "A person who takes or detains a minor who has not yet reached the age of 14, by fraud or force or enticement, or who receives or hides such a minor ... with the intent of depriving his parent, or guardian, or another person legally responsible for him of his custody, is subject to seven years' imprisonment."[65]

D. Child Pornography

The publication of an advertisement that includes an image or an imitation of an image or a drawing of a minor is subject to five years penalty. The use of a minor for the creation of such advertisement is subject to seven years imprisonment. If the perpetration of the above offenses is by a person responsible for the minor, or with the consent of such a person, the responsible person is subject to ten years imprisonment.[66]

VI. JUVENILE JUSTICE

A. Age of Criminal Responsibility

Children under the age of twelve are not criminally liable.[67] A child under age twelve may not be arrested, interrogated as a suspect or brought to trial. Generally, such children are put in the care of the child protection services, and their acts are likely to constitute grounds for determining that the minor needs protection under the Youth (Care and Supervision) Law 5720-1960.[68] Accordingly, "a minor is in need of protection if ... he has performed an act that is a criminal offense, but has not been brought to trial."[69] Criminally liable minors (i.e. youths between the ages of twelve and eighteen) are treated differently than adults.

B. Presumption of Innocence

A defendant in a criminal trial is presumed innocent, unless his guilt is proven beyond a reasonable doubt.[70] The prosecution has the burden of proof.[71]

C. Prompt Indictment and Trial

A suspect must be released if an indictment has not been filed against him within 75 days of his arrest; if a trial has not commenced within 30 days of filing the indictment; and if sentencing has not been passed within nine months.[72] These periods may be extended by the Supreme Court in special circumstances. When an indictment has been filed, the court must set the earliest date possible for commencement of the trial.[73] In the case of a defendant who is a minor, "save with the consent of the attorney general, a minor will not be brought to trial for an offense if a year has passed since its commission" [74]

D. Defense against Self-incrimination

A suspect in a criminal investigation and a defendant on trial have the right to remain silent. The law provides that "a person interrogated [at a police station] ... is required to respond correctly to all questions posed to him during the investigation by the police officer in question, or any other authorized officer, with the exception of questions the answer to which may put him in danger of incriminating himself."[75] During trial, the court is obligated to notify the defendant that he has the right not to testify or to testify, in which case he may be cross-examined.[76] The court is also obligated to explain to the defendant that a decision not to testify is likely to be considered in support of any other incriminating evidence.[77] Failure to explain his rights to a suspect or defendant may, under certain circumstances, constitute cause to disqualify an admission which the suspect made during investigation.[78]

E. Appeal

All court decisions regarding the extension of arrest, bail, or other release conditions may be appealed to a higher court. [79]

F. The Right to an Interpreter

The law provides that if the court finds that a defendant does not understand Hebrew, it is required to appoint an interpreter for him at the expense of the State Treasury, or else the judge must act as an interpreter.[80] In addition, testimony heard in a language other than Hebrew must be translated into and recorded in Hebrew, unless the court instructs otherwise.

CONCLUSION

Israel maintains a comprehensive system of laws protecting children's rights. Health benefits cover pregnancy and childhood and include preventive services as well as health education programs. Primary, secondary, vocational, and higher education, as well as students' rights, are guaranteed by law. The State offers an extensive system of welfare services including a children's monthly allowance and special benefits to disabled children and their families. Compulsory education is applicable to primary, secondary and vocational education. Special arrangements are made for the disabled with the goal of their integration into regular schools to the extent possible.

Special laws regulate youth labor and protect children from exploitation. The juvenile justice system also applies different rules than those normally applicable to adults in the adjudication of children.

Prepared by Ruth Levush
Senior Foreign Law Specialist
August 2007

End Notes

[1] Capacity and Guardianship Law, 5722-1962, 16 Laws of the State of Israel (LSI) 106 (5722-1961/62).
[2] CONVENTION ON THE RIGHTS OF THE CHILD, adopted and opened for signature, ratification and accession by General Assembly resolution 44/25 of 20 November 1989, Status of Ratifications, United Nations Office of the High Commissioner website, available at http://www.unhchr.ch/pdf/report.pdf; see also International Conventions on Human Rights, Israel Ministry of Foreign Affairs Website, http://www.israel-mfa.gov.il/mfa/mfaarchive/1990_1999/1999/1/international% 20conventions% 20on%20human%20rights (last visited July 20, 2007).
[3] Jan. 3, 1992.
[4] Jan. 3 1992.
[5] Feb. 2, 1979.
[6] Nov. 2, 1991.
[7] Nov. 2, 1991.
[8] Nov. 2, 1991.

[9] Nov 14, 2001.

[10] United Nations Committee on the Rights of the Child, Consideration of Reports Submitted by States parties, Under Article 44 of the Convention, Periodic reports of States parties due in 1993, ISRAEL (Feb. 20, 2001) par. 61, available at http://domino.un.org/UNISPAL.NSF/fd807e46661e3689852570d00069e 918/cf2615a 74f16b41d85256c47004a10bc!OpenDocume nt.

[11] Id., para. 62.

[12] Sefer Ha-Hukim (Book of Laws, Official Gazette, hereafter S.H.) No. 1859 p. 486 (5762-2002).

[13] S.H. No. 1469 p. 156 (5754-1994).

[14] UNITED NATIONS COMMITTEE ON THE RIGHTS OF THE CHILD, Periodic reports of ISRAEL, supra note 9, para. 800.

[15] S.H. No. 1469 p. 156 (5754-1994).

[16] Id. § 6a.

[17] For information on pre-natal health services, see the Ministry of Health website, http://www.health.gov.il/pages/ default.asp?pageid=860&parentid=854&catid=116&maincat=35 (last visited July 23, 2007).

[18] Bedouins are desert dwelling nomads who reside in the Negev and Sinai desert.

[19] UNITED NATIONS COMMITTEE ON THE RIGHTS OF THE CHILD, Periodic reports of ISRAEL, supra note 9, para. 808-818.

[20] Id. para. 817.

[21] Id. para. 819.

[22] S.H. No. 1522 p. 210 (5755-1995).

[23] National Insurance Law [Consolidated Version] 1995, id.

[24] 7 Laws of the State of Israel (hereafter LSI) 113 (5713-1952/53).

[25] Id. § 10.

[26] UNITED NATIONS COMMITTEE ON THE RIGHTS OF THE CHILD, Periodic reports of ISRAEL, supra note 9, para. 905.

[27] 3 LSI 125 (5709-1948/49).

[28] Id. § 5.

[29] The Compulsory Education (Implementation in Nursery Schools) Ordinance 1999 and 2001, KOVETZ HATAKANOT (Subsidiary Legislation, hereafter KT) no. 5990 and 6104, of 5759-1999 and 5761-2001, respectively.

[30] S.H. No. 1997 p. 421 (5757-1997).

[31] Id. § 4.

[32] S.H. no. 1256 p. 114 (5748-1988).

[33] S.H. No. 1773 p. 12 (5761-2001).

[34] Id. § 2.

[35] Id. § 4.

[36] S.H. No. 1735 p. 169 (5760-2000).

[37] S.H. No. 1761 p. 42 (5761-2000).

[38] Id. § 1.

[39] 7 LSI 94 (1953-1953).

[40] 7 LSI 86 (1953-1953).

[41] Id. § 2.

[42] Id. § 5.

[43] Id. §6.

[44] Id. § 2A.

[45] KT No. 5722 p. 243 (5756-1995).

[46] KT No. 6044 p. 714 (5760-2000).

[47] Youth Employment Law 1953-1953, § 20.

[48] Id. § 22.

[49] Id. § 25.

[50] S.H. No. 1170 p. 107 (5746-1986).

[51] Id. § 14.

[52] Penal Law, 5737-1977, §§ 345-354, LSI Special Volume (5737-1977).

[53] Id. § 345.

[54] Id. § 347.

[55] Id. § 346.

[56] Id. § 353. 56 Id.

[57] Id. § 347.

[58] Id. § 368B & C.

[59] Id. §3 68D.

[60] Id. § 203.

[61] Id. § 205a.

[62] Id. § 205b.

[63] Id. §§ 214(b) to 214(b3).

[64] Id. § 364.

[65] Id. § 367.

[66] Id. § 214.

[67] Id. § 34f.

[68] 14 LSI 44 (5720-1960).

[69] Id. § 2(3).

[70] Penal Law, 5737-1977, §341, LSI Special Volume (5737-1977).

[71] Criminal Procedure Law (Consolidated Version) 5742-1982, S.H. No. 1043 p. 43 §152a.

[72] Criminal Procedure (Enforcement Powers - Arrests) Law 1996 § 59-61.

[73] Criminal Procedure Regulations 5734-1974. Reg. 19, KOVETZ HATAKANOT (Subsidiary Legislation) No. 3172 p. 1200.

[74] Youth (Trial, Punishment and Modes of Treatment) Law § 14.

[75] The Criminal Procedure (Witnesses) Law, 5718-1957 § 2c.

[76] Criminal Procedure Law (Consolidated Version) 5742-1982 § 161.

[77] Id. § 162.

[78] UNITED NATIONS COMMITTEE ON THE RIGHTS OF THE CHILD, Periodic reports of ISRAEL, supra note 9, http://domino.un.org/UNISPAL.NSF/fd807e46661e3689852570 d00069e918/cf2615a74f16b 41d 85256c47004a10bc!OpenDocume nt, para. 1274.

[79] Criminal Procedure (Enforcement Powers - Arrests) Law 1996 § 53.

[80] Procedure Law (Consolidated Version) 5742-1982, S.H. No. 1043 p. 43 §§ 140-142.

In: Children's Rights
Editors: Brooke Dabney and Michael Eldridge

ISBN: 978-1-62948-252-1
© 2013 Nova Science Publishers, Inc.

Chapter 13

JAPAN: CHILDREN'S RIGHTS[*]

Sayuri Umeda

EXECUTIVE SUMMARY

Japan is a signatory of many international conventions which aim to protect the rights of children. There are various domestic laws to promote children's well-being. Almost all children in Japan are covered by health care insurance. Families with small children which do not have a high income level can receive an allowance from the government. Local governments support pregnant women's and infants' health and give advice to them. Schools also provide health examinations. Parents are obliged to have their children attend primary and secondary schools for nine years. The government provides this mandatory education free of charge. There are provisions which punish acts that harm children, both in special laws and in the Criminal Code. There is a juvenile justice system which is separated from the normal criminal justice system.

I. INTRODUCTION

This report lists the international treaties to which Japan is a signatory in the field of children's rights. It presents a summary of the relevant legislation concerning children's rights, including child health and social welfare, child education, child labor and exploitation, the sale and trafficking of children, and juvenile justice.

II. IMPLEMENTATION OF INTERNATIONAL RIGHTS OF THE CHILD

Japan has ratified the following conventions:

---

[*] This document was released by the Law Library of Congress August 2007.

- the U.N. Convention on the Rights of the Child 1989 (CRC);[1]
- the Optional Protocol to the CRC on the Sale of Children, Child Prostitution and Child Pornography;[2]
- the Optional Protocol to the CRC on Involvement of Children in Armed Conflict;[3]
- the International Covenant on Civil and Political Rights;[4]
- the International Covenant on Economic, Social and Cultural Rights;[5]
- the Convention on the Elimination of all Forms of Discrimination against Women;[6]
- the Convention concerning the Prohibition and Immediate Action for the Elimination of the Worst Forms of Child Labour;[7] and
- the Convention concerning Minimum Age for Admission to Employment.[8] Japan has not signed the following conventions:
- the Hague Convention on the Civil Aspects of International Child Abduction;[9]
- the Hague Convention on the Protection of Children in Intercountry Adoption;[10]
- the Hague Convention on Jurisdiction, Applicable Law and Recognition of Decrees Relating to Adoptions;[11] or
- the Hague Convention on Jurisdiction, Applicable Law, Recognition, Enforcement and Co-operation in Respect of Parental Responsibility and Measures for the Protection of Children.[12]

III. CHILD HEALTH AND SOCIAL WELFARE

Japan has a system of universal health coverage. Almost all residents in Japan are covered by health insurance.[13] Patients can choose to visit any licensed health care providers. Working-age adults and children over three years old pay, in general, thirty percent of the cost of treatment. Infants under three years old may pay twenty percent of it. Seniors who are seventy years old or older pay ten or twenty percent of it, depending on their income.[14] Japan has a system to support pregnant women and infants. The Mother and Child Health Law obliges municipal governments to provide counseling service for pregnant women, their spouses, and parents or custodians of infants. [15] When the municipal government deems it necessary, it may dispatch a medical doctor, health care officer, or midwife to a family with a newborn.[16] The municipal government must arrange health examinations for children whose ages are between one and one-half and two years old and between three and four years old.[17]

Local governments also give advice to parents with premature babies.[18] If a family with a premature baby has financial difficulties, the local government may lend the family money for the infant.[19] The mortality rates in Japan for infants and children under five years of age are one of the world's lowest.[20] Schools also take care of children's health. Schools must implement measures to maintain and enhance school children's health and conduct health check-ups. [21] The education committee of the local government must arrange health checks for children before they enter elementary school at the age of six.[22] Schools subsequently conduct annual health check-ups for their students.[23]

Based on the Child Welfare Law, anyone who finds a child who needs protection must report it to the local government's welfare office or child guidance center.[24] Concerning child abuse, the Child Abuse Prevention Law obliges teachers, medical practitioners, and child welfare officers to make an effort to detect child abuse cases early.[25] These offices will investigate the situation of the child. If necessary, the local government sends the child to a child guidance center for medical, psychological, or other examinations.[26] The local government may give a warning to the child or its parents or guardian, place the child or its parents or guardian under the guidance of a welfare worker, or place the child under foster care, or in one of various child welfare facilities.[27]

The government provides financial support for low to moderate income families with infants. When a parent has a child who is younger than three years old, the parent can receive a child allowance from the government unless the parent's income is more than the amount specified by the Child Allowance Law.[28] The amount is 5,000 yen [US$43] to 10,000 yen [US$87] per child per month.[29] The government supports mothers who do not have spouses and their children. The government lends money to a woman who does not have a spouse and lives with a minor child or children when the mother starts up a business or keeps a business, or when the children needs money to attend schools.[30] A mother without a spouse also receives a priority when she opens a beauty shop or a kiosk in public facilities, or applies for a license to sell tobacco in public housing and admission into child care facilities.[31] When a mother or a father without a spouse has a hardship in taking care of daily life due to his or her illness, the local government may dispatch a helper to his or her house.[32]

IV. EDUCATION

The Japanese Constitution guarantees children's rights to an education. The Constitution provides "All people shall have the right to receive an equal education correspondent to their ability, as provided by law. All people shall be obligated to have all boys and girls under their protection receive ordinary education as provided for by law. Such compulsory education shall be free."[33] Parents are obliged to have their children whose ages are between six and fifteen receive six years of primary education and three years of secondary education at schools which are authorized by the government.[34] School textbooks are distributed to students for free. The primary and secondary school enrollment ratio in Japan is almost 100 percent.[35] School teachers are prohibited from inflicting corporal punishment.[36]

The right to an education is also guaranteed for children with disabilities. The Education Basic Law obliges the government to take measures in order to make sure that children with a disability can receive sufficient education, depending on their disability level.[37] The local government is obliged to establish special schools for disabled children, including special schools for the blind, the deaf, the physically disabled, the mentally retarded, and sickly children.[38] Schools can establish special classes, such as a special class for the physically disabled, the mentally retarded, children with weak eyesight or weak hearing.[39] The local government provides financial support to parents if it is difficult for them to have their children attend schools due to financial hardship.[40]

V. CHILD LABOR AND EXPLOITATION

The Constitution provides that children shall not be exploited.[41] The Labor Standards Law has provisions to protect child workers. The Labor Standards Law prohibits employers from employing children until the March 31 immediately following the child becoming fifteen years old.[42] March 31 is the end of a school year. Children are obliged to go to school usually until that time. Children thirteen years old or older, however, may be employed if the labor is light and not injurious to their health and welfare, and if the employer obtains permission from the local Labor Standards Administration office.[43] Children under thirteen years old can be employed only in motion picture production and theatrical performance enterprises, upon permission of the Labor Standards Administration office.[44] An employer cannot employ a person under eighteen years old for extended-hour or night-time work.[45] An employer also cannot assign a person under eighteen years old to dangerous work, *e.g.*, maintenance or repair of machinery during its operation and mining.[46]

A parent or a guardian cannot make a labor contract for a minor, in this case a person under twenty years old.[47] This provision aims to prohibit a parent or guardian from forcing a minor to work for a parent or guardian's economic benefit. The parent or guardian cannot receive the wages earned by the minor in place of the minor.[48]

VI. SALE AND TRAFFICKING OF CHILDREN

There are several laws which punish or provide measures to prevent the sexual exploitation of children and trafficking of children, and which support those victims. Japan is among "tier 2" countries in the United States State Department assessment, whose governments do not fully comply with the United States Trafficking Victims Protection Act's minimum standards, but are making significant efforts to bring themselves into compliance with those standards.[49]

A. The Law for Punishing Acts Related to Child Prostitution and Child Pornography, and for Protecting Children

The Law for Punishing Acts Related to Child Prostitution and Child Pornography, and for Protecting Children prohibits child prostitution, providing child pornography for others and preparation of it, and child trafficking for child prostitution purposes.[50] Child prostitution means the act of performing sexual intercourse or other sexual acts (*i.e.*, an act similar to sexual intercourse, or an act for the purpose of satisfying one's sexual curiosity, including touching genital organs or other body parts on a child or of making a child touch one's genital organs or other body parts) in return for giving or promising to give remuneration to the child, by the person who acts as an intermediary in sexual acts with the child, the protector of the child (parents, a guardian, or anyone is taking actual care of the child), or a person who has placed the child under his control.[51] A person who commits child prostitution is punished with imprisonment for up to five years or a fine not in excess of one million yen [US$8,700].[52] The same punishment is applied for a person who acts as an intermediary in child prostitution or who solicits another person to commit child prostitution for the purpose of intermediating in child prostitution.[53] A person who acts as an intermediary in child prostitution or a person who solicits another person to commit child prostitution for the purpose of intermediating as his business is punished with imprisonment for up to seven years and a fine not exceeding five million yen [US$43,500].[54]

A person who distributes, sells, or lends, as a business, child pornography is punished with imprisonment for up to three years or a fine not exceeding three million yen [US$26.000].[55] A person who produces, possesses, transports, imports to or exports from Japan child pornography for the purpose of conducting any of the acts mentioned in the preceding sentence shall be punished with the same penalty.[56] A person who distributes child pornography for an unlimited audience or many people, or displays it in public, including the Internet, is punished with imprisonment for up to five years and/or a fine not exceeding five million yen [US$43,500].[57]

A person who buys or sells a child for the purpose of making the child be a party to sexual intercourse or other sexual acts, or for the purpose of producing child pornography by depicting a child in certain poses is punished with imprisonment for between one and ten years.[58] A Japanese national who, for any of such purposes, transports a child, who has been abducted, kidnapped, sold, or bought in a foreign country, out of that country is punished with imprisonment for two years or more.[59]

B. Law to Regulate Solicitation of Children through Matching Business via the Internet

Recently in Japan, some teenage girls voluntarily have been involved in meeting/dating strangers for expensive presents, nice meals, or money. In some cases, the girls know sex would be required and still pursue the date, and, in some cases, girls are raped.[60] The government recognizes the situation and has taken countermeasures. One of them was the passage of the Law to Regulate Solicitation of Children through Matching Business via Internet. Matching business sites in the Internet contributed to child prostitution and the rape of children.[61] Matching business sites targeted in the law provide websites where users can post advertisements and make their email addresses available for other users. Such matching business operators are obliged by the law to verify that the user is eighteen years old or older and to specify in the site that a person under eighteen years old cannot use the site.[62] If the matching business operator fails to do so, the Public Safety Committee of the prefecture orders them to follow the law.[63] If the operator does not follow the order, he or she will be punished with imprisonment for up to six months or a fine not exceeding one million yen (US$8,700).[64] The Law also punishes the following acts with a fine not exceeding one million yen (US$8,700): (1) soliciting a child for sexual intercourse or other sexual acts; (2) soliciting a person who is eighteen years old or older to have sexual intercourse or other sexual acts with a child; (3) soliciting a child for dating by offering compensation; and (4) soliciting a person who is eighteen years old or older to have a date with a child if the person pays a fee.[65]

C. Penal Code

A person who, through violence or intimidation, has sexual intercourse with a female person of thirteen years of age or older is punished with imprisonment for between two and twenty years. The same punishment applies to a person who has sexual intercourse with a female person less than thirteen years of age, with or without violence or intimidation.[66] A person who commits rape and thereby kills or injures the victim is punished with imprisonment for five years or more.[67] A person who, through violence or intimidation, forces a person of thirteen years of age or older to do any act of a sexual nature is punished with imprisonment for between six months and seven years. The same applies to a person who forces a person under thirteen years of age to do any act of a sexual nature, with or without violence or intimidation.[68] When such a criminal act has resulted in the victim's death or injury, the person is punished with imprisonment for three years or more.[69]

A person who buys a minor is punished with imprisonment for between three months and seven years. [70] If such sale is made for a commercial sexual exploitation purpose, harming the body of the victim, or killing the victim, the person is punished with imprisonment for between one and ten years.[71] The person who sells another person is punished in the same manner.[72] A person who transports to another country a person who has been kidnapped or sold is punished with imprisonment for between two and twenty years.[73]

D. Child Welfare Law

The Child Welfare Law punishes acts of having a child have sex with others or doing other acts of sexual nature with imprisonment for ten years or less and/or fine not exceeding three million yen (US$26,000).[74] The Child Welfare Law also punishes acts of having a child under fifteen years old go into a bar, a dance hall, a night club, or a restaurant in connection with the child's duty to sell or distribute goods, collecting goods or providing service, or using a child as an attendant at a table where alcohol is served, with imprisonment for three years or less and/or a fine not exceeding one million yen (US$8,700).[75] A person who hands over a child acknowledging the circumstances that the child will be under the control of a person who will commit one of the crimes listed in this paragraph will be also punished.[76]

E. Child Abuse Prevention Law

The Child Abuse Prevention Law prohibits anyone from committing sexual acts on a child or having a child do an act of sexual nature.[77] The Law obliges the national and local governments to support children who have been abused or are under risk of abuse, and to educate their parents and custodians. Based on the law, the head of an institution which takes care of an abused child, upon the local government's direction, can prohibit parents and custodians from meeting or contacting the child.[78]

VII. JUVENILE JUSTICE

The Juvenile Law adopts special measures with respect to the criminal cases of juveniles. For the criminal cases of juveniles who are under twenty years old, the Juvenile Law is applied, instead of the Criminal Procedure Law. The Family Court has primary jurisdiction over such cases.[79] Children under fourteen years old, however, are handled primarily by the child guidance center, as provided by the Child Welfare Law, when they have committed acts, which, if committed by a person aged fourteen or over, would constitute a crime. These children under fourteen years old come under the jurisdiction of the family court only when the governor of the prefecture or the chief of the child guidance center refers them to the family court.[80]

When a case is filed in a family court, a judge assigns the case to a family court probation officer for the investigation.[81] The officer undertakes a social inquiry into the personality, personal history, family background, and environment of the juvenile. When the judge decides that the juvenile needs to be taken into a juvenile classification home for investigation, the judge may detain the juvenile for up to two weeks. The detention period may be extended once. If the case concerns a grave crime, for which the maximum punishment includes capitol punishment or imprisonment, the detention period can be extended up to eight weeks.[82] If the juvenile is dissatisfied with the decision about detention measures, the juvenile and his or her legal representative or attendant may lodge an objection with the family court.[83]

Instead of defense counsel, "attendants" of the juvenile are involved in the family court procedure. A juvenile and his or her parents or guardians may appoint up to three attendants with the permission of the family court. If an attorney is to be appointed as the attendant, no permission by the court is required.[84] In a case where the family court decides the public prosecutor should be involved in the proceedings, an attorney is required as an attendant on the juvenile side. If an attorney is not retained by the juvenile, the court must appoint an attorney as the attendant.[85]

Upon completion of the social inquiry, the family court probation officer submits a report to the judge. If the judge thinks that further investigation is necessary before a determination can be made, the juvenile may be placed under the supervision of a family court probation officer. During this period of supervision, juveniles may continue to live with their parents or guardians under conditions imposed by the family court or they may be placed under a suitable institution, agency, or individual.[86] A public prosecutor may be involved in the proceedings if the family court decides that it is necessary to prove the facts, that the juvenile is over fourteen years old, and when he or she has committed crimes resulting in death with criminal intent or crimes whose statutory penalties include capital punishment or imprisonment for two years or more.[87] Provisions of the Code of Criminal Procedure are applied for the investigation proceedings so far as the provisions of the Code are not at variance with the nature of juvenile proceedings.[88] The judge may set a non-public hearing.[89]

The judge may make one of the following decisions: (1) to dismiss the case; (2) to refer the case to the governor of the prefecture or the chief of the child guidance center; (3) to place the juvenile under probation, a support facility, or a juvenile training school; and (4) to refer the case to the public prosecutor.[90] The last decision can be made when the juvenile is fourteen years old or over at the time of the criminal acts and when the judge finds it is appropriate for the juvenile to be treated under the regular criminal procedure. As a general rule, when the juvenile is sixteen years old or over and has caused death by an act done with criminal intent, the court refers him or her to the public prosecutor.[91] When the court chooses decision (3), the juvenile may file an appeal of the case to the higher court.[92]

CONCLUSION

It appears that Japan maintains a comprehensive system to protect children's rights.

Prepared by Sayuri Umeda
Foreign Law Specialist
August 2007

End Notes

[1] Convention on the Rights of the Child, Treaty No. 2 of 1994 .

[2] Optional Protocol to the CRC on the Sale of Children, Child Prostitution and Child Pornography, Treaty No. 2 of 2005.

[3] Optional Protocol to the Convention on the Rights of the Child on Involvement of Children in Armed Conflict, Treaty No. 10 of 2004.

[4] International Covenant on Civil and Political Rights, Treaty No. 7 of 1979.

[5] International Covenant on Economic, Social and Cultural Rights, Treaty No. 6 of 1979.

[6] Convention on the Elimination of all Forms of Discrimination against Women, Treaty No. 26 of 1985.

[7] Convention concerning the Prohibition and Immediate Action for the Elimination of the Worst Forms of Child Labour, Treaty No 182 of 2001.

[8] Convention concerning Minimum Age for Admission to Employment, Treaty No. 5 of 2000.

[9] Hague Convention on the Civil Aspects of International Child Abduction, Oct. 25, 1980, T.I.A.S. No. 11,670, 1343 U.N.T.S. 89 (1980).

[10] Hague Convention on the Protection of Children and Cooperation in Respect of Intercountry Adoption, May 29, 1993, 32 I.L.M. 1134 (1993).

[11] Hague Convention on Jurisdiction, Applicable Law and Recognition of Decrees Relating to Adoptions, Nov. 15, 1965.

[12] Hague Convention on Jurisdiction, Applicable Law, Recognition, Enforcement and Co-operation in Respect of Parental Responsibility and Measures for the Protection of Children, Oct. 19, 1996, 35 I.L.M. 1391 (1996).

[13] Kokumin kenkō hoken hō [National Health Insurance Law], Law No. 192 of 1958, as amended, arts. 5 and 6.

[14] Id. art. 42; and Kenkō hoken hō [Employee Health Insurance Law], Law No. 70 of 1922, as amended, art. 74.

[15] Boshi hoken hō [Mother and Child Law], Law No. 141 of 1965, as amended, arts. 9 and 10.

[16] Id. art. 11.

[17] Id. art. 12.

[18] Id. art. 19.

[19] Id. art. 20.

[20] UNICEF, The State of the World's Children 2007, Table 1. Basic Indicators.

[21] Gakkō kyōiku hō [School Education Law], Law No. 26 of 1947, as amended, art. 12.

[22] Gakkō hoken hō [School Health Law], Law No. 56 of 1958, as amended, art. 4.

[23] Id. art.6.

[24] Jidō fukushi hō [Child Welfare Law], Law No. 164 of 1947, as amended, art. 25.

[25] Jidō gyakutai no bōshi tō ni kansuru hōtitsu [Child Abuse Prevention Law], Law No. 82 of 2000, as amended, art. 5.

[26] Child Welfare Law, Law No. 164 of 1947, as amended, art. 25-7.

[27] Id. art. 27.

[28] Jidō teate hō [Child Allowance Law], Law No. 73 of 1971, as amended, arts. 4 and 5.

[29] Id. art. 6.

[30] Boshi oyobi kafu fukushi hō [Mother and Child and Women without Spouses Welfare Law], Law No. 129 of 1964, as amended, art. 13.

[31] Id. art.

[32] Id. art. 17.

[33] Nihon koku kenpō [Constitution of Japan] (1946), art. 26.

[34] Kyōiku kihon hō [Education Basic Law], Law No. Law 120 of 2006, art. 5. School Education Law, Law No. 26 of 1947, as amended, arts. 17, 19, 22, 35, 37, and 39.

[35] UNICEF, supra note 20, Table 5.

[36] School Education Law, Law No. 26 of 1947, as amended, art. 11.

[37] Education Basic Law, id. art. 4, para. 2.

[38] School Education Law, Law No. 26 of 1947, as amended, art. 74.

[39] Id. art. 75.

[40] Id. arts. 25 and 40.

[41] Constitution (1946), art. 27, para. 3.

[42] Rōdō kijun hō [Labor Standards Law], Law No. 49 of 1947, as amended, art.56, para. 1.

[43] Id. art. 56, para. 2.

[44] Id.

[45] Id. arts. 60 and 61.

[46] Id. arts. 62 and 63.

[47] Id. art. 58, para. 1.

[48] Id. art. 59.

[49] UNITED STATES DEPARTMENT OF STATE, TRAFFICKING IN PERSONS REPORT 2007, 27 (2007).

[50] JidO baishun, jidO poruno ni kakaru kOi tO no shobatsu oyobi jidO no hogo ni kansuru hOritsu [Law for Punishing Acts Related to Child Prostitution and Child Pornography, and for Protecting Children], Law No. 52 of 1999, as amended. An unofficial English translation of the law as of 1999 is available at Interpol's website, http://www.interpol.int/Public/Children/SexualAbuse/NationalLaws/csaJapan.asp (last visited July 30, 2007). The 2004 amendment of the law is not reflected in the translation.

[51] Id. art. 2, para. 2.

[52] Id. art. 4.

[53] Id. art. 5, para. 1 and art. 6, para. 1.

[54] Id. art. 5, para. 2 and art. 6, para. 2.

[55] Id. art. 7, para. 1.

[56] Id. art. 7, para. 2.

[57] Id. art. 7, para. 4.

[58] Id. art. 8, para. 1.

[59] Id. art. 8, para. 2.

[60] SeishOnen ikusei suishin kaigi [Youth's Well Growth Promotion Conference], "Deai kei saito" ni kakaru jidO kaishun tO no higai kara nenshOsha o mamoru tameni tOmen kOzu beki sochi [Measures to be taken in order to protect youth from child prostitution in relation to "Matching business site" at this time] (Oct. 21, 2002), available at http://www8.cao.go.jp/youth/suisin/deaikei.html.

[61] Explanation attached to the bill of the Law to Regulate Solicitation of Children for Matching Business via Internet.

[62] Inänetto isei shOkai jigyO o riyO shite jidO o yuin suru kOi no kisei tO ni kansuru hOritsu [Law Concerning Regulations of Acts of Soliciting Children through Matching Business via Internet], Law No. 83 of 2003, arts. 7 and 8.

[63] Id. art. 10.

[64] Id. art. 15.

[65] Id. art. 16.

[66] Penal Code, Law No. 45 of 1907, as amended, art. 177.

[67] Id. art. 181, para. 2.

[68] Id. art. 176.

[69] Id. art. 181, para. 1.

[70] Id. art 226-2, para. 2.

[71] Id. art 226-2, para. 3.

[72] Id. art 226-2, para. 4.

[73] Id. art. 226-3.

[74] Child Welfare Law, Law No. 164 of 1947, as amended, art. 60, para. 1 and art. 34, para. 1. item 6.

[75] Id. art. 60, para. 2 and art. 34, para. 1, items 4-3 and 5.

[76] Id. art. 60, para. 2 and art. 34, para. 1, items 7.

[77] Child Abuse Prevention Law, Law No. 82 of 2000, as amended, arts. 2 and 3.

[78] Id. art. 12.

[79] Shōnen hō [Juvenile Law], Law No. 168 of 1948, as amended, arts. 2 and 3.

[80] Id. art. 3.
[81] Id. art. 8.
[82] Id. art. 17.
[83] Id. art. 17-2.
[84] Id. art. 10.
[85] Id. art. 22-3.
[86] Id. art. 17.
[87] Id. art. 22-2.
[88] Id. arts. 14 and 15.
[89] Id. art. 22.
[90] Id. arts. 23 and 24.
[91] Id. art. 20.
[92] Id. Chap. 2, Sec. 3.

In: Children's Rights
Editors: Brooke Dabney and Michael Eldridge

ISBN: 978-1-62948-252-1
© 2013 Nova Science Publishers, Inc.

Chapter 14

LEBANON: CHILDREN'S RIGHTS[*]

Issam Saliba

EXECUTIVE SUMMARY

Despite the armed conflict that consumed the country and its institutions for a long period until 1989, Lebanon ratified the Convention on the Rights of the Child relatively quickly. The existing Lebanese laws comply with most of what is required under the Convention, and the Lebanese government adopted a number of amendments in its attempt to comply fully with the balance of such requirements.

I. INTRODUCTION

Lebanon endured about fifteen years of civil strife, coming close to a full-blown state of chaos and civil war before a political agreement was reached among the warring factions in October 1989 in the city of Taef in Saudi Arabia. The recovery from the devastating damage to the infrastructure of that period is still proceeding as of this date. On the social level, and especially with respect to children the harm was more complex to assess and more difficult to repair.

Lebanon became a party to the 1989 Convention on the Rights of the Child in 1991,[1] and to the Optional Protocol on the sale of children, child prostitution and child pornography, in 2004.

On February 11 2002, Lebanon signed (but has not yet ratified) the Optional Protocol on the involvement of children in armed conflict.[2]

---

[*] This document was released by the Law Library of Congress August 2007.

II. IMPLEMENTATION OF INTERNATIONAL RIGHTS OF THE CHILD

It is not clear to what extent the Lebanese government has been able so far to produce tangible results in protecting the rights of children, but the legal framework is in place to provide such protection.

A. Definition of Child

The Lebanese law adopts the same definition of child adopted by the Convention on the Rights of the Child (CRC). For the purpose of civil obligations and contracts, a child is any person who has not yet reached the age of eighteen.[3] The same definition applies in matters of criminal responsibility,[4] with further distinction as to punishments among:

children under seven years old;
children between seven and twelve years old;
children between twelve and fifteen years old; and children between fifteen and eighteen years old.[5]

B. Rights of Children to Registration, Nationality, and Protection of Identity

Lebanese law requires that a birth certificate be prepared and filed for registration within thirty days from the date of birth.[6] As to nationality, the child acquires Lebanese citizenship by being either:

born to a Lebanese father,
born in Lebanon and not acquiring by birth a foreign nationality, or born in Lebanon to unknown parents or to parents without a nationality.[7]

There are a number of provisions in the Penal Code aiming at protecting the sanctity of the identity of children. The following acts are criminal offenses:

- the abduction or hiding of a child under seven years old, any substitution of one child for another, or any attribution of a child to a woman not its natural mother are felonies punished by three to fifteen years hard labor;[8]
- the placement of a child in a foundling shelter and the concealment of its identity as reflected in the personal status records, whether the child is legitimate or illegitimate but recognized, is also a felony punished by three to fifteen years hard labor;[9]
- any other acts not mentioned above aiming at eliminating or altering the personal status records of a person are felonies punished by three to fifteen years hard labor;[10] or
- the abduction or taking of a child, even with his consent, away from the authority of his legal guardian is a misdemeanor punished by six months to three years imprisonment and by a fine of 50,000 to 200,000 Lebanese pounds (US$33 to 133).[11]

C. Protection against Neglect, Abuse, and Delinquency

Lebanese law gives the judicial authority the power to interfere *sua sponte* whenever a child's interest is at risk.[12] The following situations may trigger a judicial action for imposing protective or corrective measures whenever:

- A child is in an environment exposing him to exploitation, or adversely affecting the child's health, safety, morality, or upbringing;
- Was exposed to sexual or violent corporal attack beyond the customary non-harmful disciplinary measures; or
- Was found in a state of mendacity or vagrancy.[13]

In any of these situations the judge has the discretion of taking whatever measures deemed necessary for the protection of the child, including rehabilitative measures when appropriate.[14]

III. CHILD HEALTH AND SOCIAL WELFARE

The Lebanese Law gives the government the right to enter into contracts with medical doctors and nurses for supervising the medical environment in the public schools and of attending to the health of their students.[15]

In a report prepared in 1994 the Lebanese Government informed the Committee on the Rights of the Child that the Lebanese Ministry of Public Health had set several objectives to be achieved in 1995 regarding the health and welfare of children through various programs in cooperation with the Ministry of Social Affairs, UNICEF, and non-governmental organizations. Among these objectives were:

- the reduction of the infant mortality rate;
- the reduction of severe malnutrition; and
- the reduction of the incidences of intestinal diseases, measles cases, and deaths.[16]

In its report prepared in 1989 the Lebanese Government reported that the health status of the Lebanese population had improved and that this was evident in "the increase in life expectancy at birth, in the reduction of child mortality, and in other positive indicators."[17] The report also concluded that "the health sector in Lebanon ... suffers from a number of structural and functional deficiencies which have an adverse effect on its performance and also have particular implications for the health status of children."[18]

In 2000, a new law gave disabled persons, including children, specific rights; among them is the right to free health services paid by the Government.[19]

IV. EDUCATION AND SPECIAL NEEDS

Since at least 1955, the Lebanese Government has adopted a policy of providing free education at the primary level to all Lebanese children.[20] In addition, in 1998primary education up to age twelve became mandatory.[21] Children with disability have the same right to an education[22] and the Government covers all expenses in this regard.[23]

The educational system prior to entering college is divided into four phases, kindergarten to be completed in two years, elementary school to be completed in five years, secondary school to be completed in four years, and high school to be completed in three years.[24].

The primary purpose of education during the kindergarten years is to nurture the development of children's motor functions and senses in general, accustom them to spontaneous reactive impulses through imitation, games, drawing, and free manual work, train them for the correct use and pronunciation of words and expressions relevant to their daily life, and strengthen in them the spirit of taking initiatives, assuming responsibilities, respecting cooperation, and adopting good traditions and moral behavior.[25] The main purpose during the elementary years is to nurture the physical, mental, and cultural capabilities of children through reading, writing, conversations, mathematics, and the study of the natural and human environments.[26] The secondary years are intended to help the student discover his or her personal capabilities and interests and to direct him or her to take the courses compatible with these capabilities and interests.[27] The high school years are intended to help the student attain intellectual maturity and obtain the essential knowledge necessary to choose the appropriate field of higher education compatible with his or her capabilities, preparing him or her to pursue such a field of study.[28]

V. CHILD LABOR AND EXPLOITATION

The employment law in Lebanon basically divides children into two categories, those aged between fourteen and eighteen and those under fourteen. The law categorically prohibits the employment of children who have not completed thirteen years and requires a medical certificate proving that a child above thirteen is fit for the job he is hired to perform.[29] In certain types of work deemed harmful or detrimental the law prohibits employing any child under the age of sixteen years. Furthermore, in addition to other restrictions no child shall be employed for more than six hours per day and be given at least one hour rest whenever the total working hours exceed four per day.[30]

Lebanon has joined and ratified the following International Labor Conventions:

- C 136 Benzene Convention of 1971 relating to prevention of hazardous poisoning resulting from benzene ratified on February 23, 1999;[31]
- ILO Convention 182 related to the prohibition and immediate action for the elimination of the worst forms of child labor, ratified on Sept. 11, 2001;[32]and
- C 138 Convention of of 1973 concerning Minimum Age for Admission to Employment, ratified on June 10, 2003.[33]

VI. SALE AND TRAFFICKING OF CHILDREN

There is no specific law prohibiting the sale and trafficking of children. The Lebanese Penal Code, however, specifically make the abduction or taking of a child a criminal offense punished by three months to three years imprisonment or by temporary hard labor if the child is under thirteen years of age, or was taken or abducted by force or by ploy.[34]

Furthermore, anyone who repeatedly entices children or other persons under the age of twenty into prostitution or immoral acts, or helps and facilitates the commission of such acts shall be punished by one month to one year imprisonment and a 50,000.00 to 500,000.00 Lebanese pounds fine (US$33 to 330).[35]

VII. JUVENILE JUSTICE

In 2002, the Lebanese Parliament overhauled the juvenile justice system by enacting a self-contained law titled "Protection of Children in Violation of the Law or Exposed to Danger" to deal with juvenile courts emphasizing educational and rehabilitative measures rather than punishment.[36] The law requires compliance with the following principles in its implementation:

1. the juvenile is in need of special help that enables him or her to play a role in society;
2. under all circumstances, the interest of the child shall be taken into consideration to protect it against delinquency;
3. a juvenile who violates the law should benefit from humane and fair treatment; the manner by which he or she is prosecuted, investigated, and tried shall be subject to special procedures that save him or her, to the extent possible, from normal criminal procedures through adopting amicable settlements and solutions, away from liberty depriving measures. The juvenile judge shall have the most discretion in this regard with the authority to amend or rescind whatever measures ordered, based on the results of its implementation on the child.
4. The juvenile court is the authority in charge of juveniles and the application of the law and the competent ministries provide all necessary means needed to this implementation.[37]

Measures and punishment that may be imposed upon juveniles are:

1. public blame;
2. placement under probation;
3. protection;
4. supervised freedom; and
5. to provide labor to the benefit of the public or to compensate the victim.[38]

Prepared by Issam Saliba
Senior Foreign Law Specialist
August 2007

End Notes

1 The Convention on the Rights of the Child, with a Preamble and fifty-four articles, was adopted by the U.N. General Assembly Nov. 20, 1989, and entered into force Sept. 2, 1990. G.A. Res. 44/25, annex, 44 U.N. GAOR Supp. (No. 49) at 167, U.N. Doc. A/44/49 (1989); 28 I.L.M. 1448 (1989). For an online text, see the OHCHR Web site, http://www.ohchr.org/english/law/crc.htm (last visited July 23, 2007).

2 The Child Soldiers Protocol entered into force Feb. 12, 2002. G.A. Res. A/RES/54/263 of May25, 2000. For an online text, see the OHCHR site, http://www.ohchr.org/english/law/crc-conflict.htm (last visited July 23, 2007).

3 Civil Code, issued Mar. 9, 1932, art. 4.

4 Law Number 422 of 2002 (Protection of at-Risk Children or Children Violating the Law), art. 1

5 Id., art. 6.

6 Personal Status Records Registration Law of 1951, art. 11.

7 Lebanese Nationality law issued by Decree Number 15 of 1925, art. 1.

8 Lebanese Penal Code, art. 492.

9 Id. art. 493.

10 Id. art 494.

11 Id. art 495.

12 Law Number 422 of 2002, art. 26.

13 Id., art. 25.

14 Id.. art. 26.

15 Legislative Decree Number 26 of 1955, art. 19.

16 See CRC/C/8/Add.23, 3 February 1995, para. 63.

17 See CRC/c70/Add.8, 26 September 2000, para. 286.

18 Id., para. 288.

19 Law Number 220 of 2000, art.27.

20 Legislative Decree Number 26 of 1955, art. 17.

21 Law Number 686 of 1998.

22 Law Number 220 of 2000, art. 59.

23 Id., art 61.

24 Presidential Decree Number 9099 of 1968, art. 1.

25 Id., art. 2.

26 Id., art. 3.

27 Id., art. 4.

28 Id., art. 5.

29 Labor Code of 1946, as amended, art. 22.

30 Id., art 23.

31 Ratification date as reflected at: http://www.ilo.org/ilolex/cgi-lex/ratifce.pl?C136.

32 Ratification date as reflected at: http://www.ilo.org/ilolex/cgi-lex/ratifce.pl?C182.

33 Ratification date as reflected at: http://www.ilo.org/ilolex/cgi-lex/ratifce.pl?C138.

34 Lebanese Penal Code, issued by Legislative Decree No. 340 of Mar. 1, 1943, art.495.

35 Id., art. 523.

36 Law Number 422 of 2002.

37 Id., art 2.

38 Id., art. 5.

In: Children's Rights
Editors: Brooke Dabney and Michael Eldridge

ISBN: 978-1-62948-252-1
© 2013 Nova Science Publishers, Inc.

Chapter 15

MEXICO: CHILDREN'S RIGHTS[*]

Gustavo Guerra

EXECUTIVE SUMMARY

The Mexican Constitution provides that the State has the duty to promote respect for the dignity of all children and the full exercise of their rights. It also provides that children have the right to satisfy their nutritional, health, educational, and recreational needs. Several laws have been enacted in order to implement this mandate, most importantly the federal Law on the Protection of the Rights of Children and Adolescents. In addition, Mexico is a signatory to several treaties that impact children's rights.

I. INTRODUCTION

Mexico is a federal republic formed by thirty-one states and a federal district, best known as Mexico City. The rights of the child are protected by legislation enacted at the federal and the state level. However, federal legislation on this topic tends to be more relevant, because the most significant and extensive initiatives on the rights of the child in Mexico are regulated by federal law. This report provides a summary of relevant federal laws concerning children's rights, including health, welfare, education, child labor and exploitation, trafficking of children, and juvenile justice. The report also provides a list of international treaties ratified by Mexico in the field of children's rights.

Definition of a Child

The Federal Civil Code provides that the age of majority is eighteen.[1] However, there are some instances in which individuals under the age of eighteen may be allowed to assume

---

[*] This document was released by the Law Library of Congress August 2007.

control over their actions and decisions. For example, the Federal Civil Code provides that, under certain circumstances, persons under eighteen may be allowed to marry.[2]

II. IMPLEMENTATION OF INTERNATIONAL RIGHTS OF THE CHILD

Among other relevant treaties and agreements, the following treaties with provisions that affect children, have entered into force in Mexico:

- International Covenant on Civil and Political Rights;[3]
- Convention on the Elimination of All Forms of Discrimination against Women;[4]
- Convention on the Rights of the Child;[5]
- Hague Convention on the Civil Aspects of International Child Abduction;[6]
- Hague Convention on the Protection of Children and Cooperation in Respect of Intercountry Adoption;[7]
- Optional Protocol to the Convention on the Elimination of All Forms of Discrimination against Women;[8]
- Worst Forms of Child Labor Convention;[9]
- Optional Protocol to the Convention on the Rights of the Child on the Sale of Children, Child Prostitution and Child Pornography;[10]
- Optional Protocol to the Convention on the Rights of the Child on the Involvement of Children in Armed Conflict;[11]
- Protocol To Prevent, Suppress And Punish Trafficking In Persons, Especially Women And Children, Supplementing The United Nations Convention Against Transnational Organized Crime.[12]

III. CHILD HEALTH AND SOCIAL WELFARE

Health Care

The Mexican Constitution provides that every person has the right to health protection.[13] Furthermore, the Constitution provides that children have the right to satisfy their nutritional, health, educational, and recreational needs.[14]

The General Law on Health (GLH) sets forth the objectives of the right to health protection as well as the objectives of the National Health System.[15] The GLH provides that basic health services are classified under the following categories: 1) health education and the promotion of sanitation; 2) prevention and control of priority communicable diseases, the most frequent non-communicable diseases, and accidents; 3) medical care, including preventive measures, rehabilitation, and emergency treatment; 4) maternal and child care; 5) family planning; 6) mental health care; 7) the prevention and control of oral diseases; 8) the availability of medicaments and other essential supplies; 9) promotion of improved nutrition; and 10) social welfare for at-risk groups.[16]

The provisions in chapter 5 of the GLH prioritize and define maternal and child care and call for the protection of minors, activities to support families and contribute to maternal and child health, appropriate standards of school hygiene, and health services for schoolchildren. Health care for children includes pre- and post-natal care, nutrition advice, immunization, and eye and ear care.[17] Public health care services are provided by the federal Department of Health, with support from social security institutions and state and local authorities.[18]

Welfare

The Law on Social Welfare (LSW) regulates social services in Mexico.[19] The LSW states that social welfare services are provided by the federal Department of Health, with support from social security institutions, such as the National System for Integral Family Development (DIF), state and local authorities, and private institutions.[20]

IV. EDUCATION

Article 3 of the Mexican Constitution provides that every individual has the right to education.[21] The State – federation, states, Federal District, and municipalities – shall provide preschool, primary, and secondary education.[22] Preschool, primary, and secondary education through grade 9, constitute the basic compulsory education.[23] The General Law on Education regulates education in Mexico.[24]

The Mexican education system is organized into four levels: Preschool (K1-K3), basic education (grades 1-9), upper secondary education (grades 10-12), and higher education.[25] Although the government is only officially responsible for providing compulsory basic education, it is also involved at the other levels through public funding of upper secondary and higher education.[26]

Humane School Discipline

The Law on the Protection of the Rights of Children and Adolescents provides that teachers must avoid any form of harm, injury, aggression, abuse, or exploitation of children or adolescents.[27]

V. CHILD LABOR AND EXPLOITATION

The Mexican Constitution provides that the State has the duty to promote respect for the dignity of all children and the full exercise of their rights.[28] It also provides that the use of labor of minors under fourteen years of age is prohibited.[29] Persons above that age and less than sixteen shall have a maximum work day of six hours.[30]

The Federal Labor Law provides that children under sixteen may not engage in unhealthy or hazardous work or in industrial night work.[31] Unhealthy or hazardous occupations are those which, by the nature of the work; by the physical, chemical, or biological conditions of the environment in which it is conducted; or by the composition of the raw material used, may be detrimental to the life, development and physical and mental health of children.[32]

Children between the ages of fourteen and sixteen must obtain a medical certificate indicating their fitness to work.[33] Without the certificate, no employer may lawfully employ them.[34] Working children will be subject to periodical medical examinations conducted by labor authorities.[35] Children under the age of eighteen cannot be hired for purposes of working outside of Mexico, except in the case of children with technical or professional training, artists, athletes, and specialized workers.[36]

The Department of Labor is charged with protecting workers' rights.[37] It has been reported that government enforcement is more effective at large and medium-sized companies, especially in industries under federal jurisdiction, than it is at the smaller companies and in the agriculture, construction, and informal sectors. It is in the informal, unregulated sector, however, that most children work.[38]

VI. SALE AND TRAFFICKING OF CHILDREN

The Law on the Protection of the Rights of Children and Adolescents recognizes the right of children and young persons to be protected against any acts or omissions affecting their physical or mental health, their normal development, or their right to education, including neglect; negligent treatment; abandonment; emotional, physical, or sexual abuse; exploitation; the use of drugs and narcotics; abduction; and trafficking.[39] This law also provides that mothers, fathers, and anyone having custody of children must protect them against any form of ill treatment, prejudice, harm, aggression, abuse, trafficking, and exploitation.[40] In addition, the Federal Criminal Code and the Federal Law on Organized Crime provide that corruption of minors, child prostitution, and child pornography are felonies.[41]

These legal provisions notwithstanding, it has been reported that Mexico is a point of origin, transit, and destination for persons trafficked for sexual exploitation.[42] While a majority of non-Mexican trafficking victims are from Central America, others have been brought to Mexico from Brazil, Cuba, Ecuador, China, Taiwan, India, and Eastern European countries.[43] The government estimates that approximately 20,000 children are sexually exploited each year.[44]

Sexual tourism and sexual exploitation of minors take place frequently in the northern border area and in resort areas.[45] Undocumented migrants from Central America and the poor are particularly vulnerable to trafficking. Many illegal immigrants become victims of traffickers along the Guatemalan border, where the growing presence of gangs made the area especially dangerous for unaccompanied women and children migrating north. Young female migrants recounted being robbed, beaten, and raped by members of criminal gangs and then forced to work as prostitutes under threat of further harm to them or their families.[46]

Individual police, immigration, and customs officials reportedly participated in, facilitated, or condoned trafficking, primarily for money. Poorly paid officials often extort money from victims and traffickers. In September 2005 a judge issued arrest warrants for seven immigration agents in connection with their participation in a human smuggling ring; however, none were charged.[47]

VII. JUVENILE JUSTICE

The Federal Law for the Treatment of Juvenile Offenders provides that children between eleven and eighteen years of age are subject to special courts for juvenile offenders.[48] Juveniles are assisted by Guardianship Councils, which are responsible for the care and protection of juvenile defendants.[49] Children that are accused of committing an infraction must be treated fairly and humanely.[50] Ill treatment, *incommunicado* detention, psychological coercion or any other action impairing the child's dignity or physical or mental integrity during legal proceedings are prohibited.[51]

The Law on the Protection of the Rights of Children and Adolescents provides that children shall be protected against any act that violates their constitutional guarantees or the rights recognized by law or by international treaties subscribed to by Mexico.[52] This law also provides guarantees for children accused of having infringed criminal laws, including a presumption of innocence, prompt notification of any charges, prohibition of self incrimination, and prompt trial.[53]

Minors who are found responsible of committing an infraction may be subject to a wide variety of measures, including:

- Counseling
- Educational and vocational training programs, and other rehabilitating measures.[54]
- Warning
- Admonition
- Prohibition to go to certain places
- Prohibition to drive motor vehicles
- Placement in custodial homes
- Confinement in educational institutions[55]

CONCLUSION

Mexico has a vast legal framework designed to protect children's rights. This legislation notwithstanding, the rights of children are not always fully protected.

Prepared by Gustavo Guerra
Senior Foreign Law Specialist
August 2007

End Notes

[1] Código Civil Federal (Federal Civil Code, as amended), art. 646, Diario Oficial de la Federación (D.O.), May 26, 1928, http://www.diputados.gob.mx/Leyes Biblio/pdf/ 2.pdf. This hyperlink connects to the official Web site of the Mexican House of Representatives.

[2] Id., art. 148 & 149.

[3] The International Covenant on Civil and Political Rights, with a Preamble and 53 articles, was adopted by the U.N. General Assembly Dec. 16, 1966, and entered into force Mar. 23, 1976. G.A. Res. 2200A (XXI), 21 U.N.

GAOR, 21st Sess. Supp. (No. 16) at 52, U.N. Doc. A/6316 (Dec. 16, 1966), 999 U.N.T.S. 171. See also the Promulgation of the International Covenant on Civil and Political Rights, DIARIO OFICIAL DE LA FEDERACIÓN (D.O.), May 20, 1981.

[4] CEDAW, comprising a Preamble and 30 articles, was adopted by the U.N. General Assembly Dec. 18, 1979, and entered into force Sept. 3, 1981. G.A. Res. 34/180, 34 U.N. GAOR Supp. (No. 46) at 193, U.N. Doc. A/34/46. For an online text, see the U.N. Division of the Advancement of Women Web site, http://www.un.org/womenwatch/daw/cedaw/text/ econvention.htm#article1 (last visited August 8, 2007). See also the Promulgation of the Convention on the Elimination of All Forms of Discrimination against Women, D.O., May 12, 1981.

[5] G.A. Res. 44/25, annex, 44 U.N. GAOR Supp. (No. 49), at 167, U.N. Doc A/44/49 (1989). 28 Int'l Legal Materials 1456 (1989) (an unofficial source). See also the Promulgation of the Convention on the Rights of the Child, D.O., Jan. 25, 1991.

[6] The Hague Convention on the Civil Aspects of International Child Abduction, Hague No. 28, was adopted by the Hague Conference on Private International Law Oct. 25, 1980, and entered into force Dec. 1, 1983. T.I.A.S. No. 11,670, 1343 U.N.T.S. 89; 19 I.L.M. 1501 (1980). For an online text, see the HCCH Web site, http://hcch.e-vision.nl/index_en.php?act= conventions.text&cid=24 (last visited Aug. 8, 2007). See also the Promulgation of the Hague Convention on the Civil Aspects of International Child Abduction, D.O., Mar. 6, 1992.

[7] The Hague Convention on the Protection of Children and Cooperation in Respect of Intercountry Adoption, comprising a Preamble and 48 articles, was concluded on May 29, 1993, and entered into force on May 1, 1995. 32 Int'l Legal Materials 1134 (1993). For an online text, see the HCCH Web site, http://www.hcch.net/index_en.php?act=conventions. text&cid=69 (last visited Aug. 8, 2007). See also the Promulgation of the Hague Convention on the Protection of Children and Cooperation in Respect of Intercountry Adoption, D.O., Oct. 24, 1994.

[8] G.A. Res. 54/4 (A/RES/54/4), Oct. 6, 1999. Available from the United Nations Division for the Advancement of Women Web site, http://www.un.org/womenwatch/daw/cedaw/protocol/text.htm (last visited Aug. 8, 2007). Ratified by Mexico on Mar. 15, 2002.

[9] The Worst Forms of Child Labour Convention, with a Preamble and 16 articles, was adopted by the General Conference of the International Labour Organisation June 17, 1999, and entered into force Nov. 19, 2000. See also the Promulgation of the the Worst Forms of Child Labour Convention, D.O., Mar. 7, 2001.

[10] G.A. Res. 54/263, U.N. GAOR, 54th Sess., Annex II, U.N. Doc. A/RES/54/263 (May 25, 2000). Available from the OHCHR Web site, http://www.ohchr.org/english/law/crc-sale.htm (last visited Aug. 8, 2007). Ratified by Mexico on Mar. 15, 2002.

[11] G.A. Res. A/RES/54/263, May 25, 2000, available from the OHCHR Web site, http://www.unhchr.ch/html/menu2/6/protocolchild.htm (last visited Aug. 8, 2007). Ratified by Mexico on Mar. 15, 2002.

[12] G.A. Res. 55/25 (Nov. 15, 2000). See also the Promulgation of the Protocol To Prevent, Suppress And Punish Trafficking In Persons, Especially Women And Children, Supplementing The United Nations Convention Against Transnational Organized Crime, D.O., Apr. 10, 2003, available at http://www.ordenjuridico.gob.mx/TratInt/Penal/OE4QUATER.pdf .

[13] Constitución Política de los Estados Unidos Mexicanos (Mexico Constitution, as amended), art. 4, D.O., Feb. 5, 1917, http://www.diputados.gob.mx/LeyesBiblio/pdf/1.pdf. This hyperlink connects to the official Web site of the Mexican House of Representatives.

[14] Id.

[15] Ley General de Salud, (General Law on Health, as amended), D.O., Feb. 7, 1984, http://www.diputados.gob.mx/LeyesBiblio/pdf/142.pdf. This hyperlink connects to the official Web site of the Mexican House of Representatives.

[16] Id., art. 27.

[17] Id., art. 61.

[18] Id., arts. 7 & 9.

[19] Ley de Asistencia Social (Law on Social Welfare), D.O., Sept. 2, 2004, http://www.diputados.gob.mx/LeyesBiblio/pdf/270.pdf. This hyperlink connects to the official Web site of the Mexican House of Representatives.

[20] Id., arts. 7 & 9.

[21] Constitución Política de los Estados Unidos Mexicanos (Mexico Constitution, as amended), art. 3, D.O., Feb. 5, 1917, http://www.diputados.gob.mx/LeyesBiblio/pdf/1.pdf. This hyperlink connects to the official Web site of the Mexican House of Representatives.

[22] Id.

[23] Id.

[24] Ley General de Educación (General Law on Education, as amended), D.O., Jul. 13, 1993, http://www.diputados. gob.mx/LeyesBiblio/pdf/137.pdf. This hyperlink connects to the official Web site of the Mexican House of Representatives.

[25] RAND Education, Education in Mexico, Challenges and Opportunities, http://www.worldfund.org/assets/files/ RAND_Education%20in%20Mexico.pdf (last visited Aug. 9, 2007).

[26] Id.

[27] Ley para la Proteccion de los Derechos de Ninas, Ninos y Adolescentes (Law on the Protection of the Rights of Children and Adolescents), D.O., May 29, 2000, http://www.diputados.gob.mx/LeyesBiblio/pdf/185.pdf. This hyperlink connects to the official Web site of the Mexican House of Representatives.

[28] Constitución Política de los Estados Unidos Mexicanos (Mexico Constitution, as amended), art. 4, D.O., Feb. 5, 1917, http://www.diputados.gob.mx/LeyesBiblio/pdf/1.pdf. This hyperlink connects to the official Web site of the Mexican House of Representatives.

[29] Id., art. 123 A (III).

[30] Id.

[31] Ley Federal del Trabajo (Federal Labor Law, as amended), art. 175, D.O., Apr. 1, 1970, http://www.diputados. gob.mx/LeyesBiblio/pdf/125.pdf. This hyperlink connects to the official Web site of the Mexican House of Representatives.

[32] Id., art. 176.

[33] Id., art. 174.

[34] Id.

[35] Id.

[36] Id, art. 29.

[37] Ley Orgánica de la Administración Pública Federal (Law on the Federal Executive Branch, as amended), art. 40, D.O., Dec. 29, 1976, http://www.diputados.gob.mx/LeyesBiblio/pdf/153.pdf. This hyperlink connects to the official Web site of the Mexican House of Representatives.

[38] U.S. Department of State, Mexico, COUNTRY REPORTS ON HUMAN RIGHTS PRACTICES - 2006, Mar, 6, 2007, http://www.state.gov/g/drl/rls/hrrpt/2006/78898.htm.

[39] Ley para la Proteccion de los Derechos de Ninas, Ninos y Adolescentes (Law on the Protection of the Rights of Children and Adolescents), art. 21, D.O., May 29, 2000, http://www.diputados.gob.mx/LeyesBiblio/ pdf/185.pdf. This hyperlink connects to the official Web site of the Mexican House of Representatives.

[40] Id., art. 11.

[41] Código Penal Federal (Federal Criminal Code, as amended), D.O., Aug. 14, 1931, http://www.diputados.gob. mx/LeyesBiblio/pdf/9.pdf. See also Ley Federal contra la Delincuencia Organizada (Federal Law on Organized Crime, as amended), D.O., Nov. 7, 1996, http://www.diputados.gob.mx/LeyesBiblio/pdf/101.pdf. These hyperlinks connect to the official Web site of the Mexican House of Representatives.

[42] U.S. Department of State, supra note 38.

[43] Id.

[44] Id.

[45] Id.

[46] Id.

[47] Id.

[48] Ley para el Tratamiento de Menores Infractores para el Distrito Federal en Materia Común y para toda la República en Material Federal (Federal Law for the Treatment of Juvenile Offenders, as amended), art. 6, D.O., Dec. 24, 1991, http://www.diputados.gob.mx/LeyesBiblio/pdf/179.pdf. This hyperlink connects to the official Web site of the Mexican House of Representatives.

[49] Id., art. 4.

[50] Id., art. 3.

[51] Id.

[52] Ley para la Proteccion de los Derechos de Ninas, Ninos y Adolescentes (Law on the Protection of the Rights of Children and Adolescents), art. 44, D.O., May 29, 2000, http://www.diputados.gob.mx/Leyes Biblio/pdf/ 185.pdf. This hyperlink connects to the official Web site of the Mexican House of Representatives.

[53] Id., art. 46.

[54] Id., art. 45 (g).

[55] Ley para el Tratamiento de Menores Infractores para el Distrito Federal en Materia Común y para toda la República en Material Federal (Federal Law for the Treatment of Juvenile Offenders, as amended), arts. 97,

103 & 112, D.O., Dec. 24, 1991, available at http://www.diputados.gob.mx/LeyesBiblio/pdf/179.pdf. This hyperlink connects to the official Web site of the Mexican House of Representatives.

In: Children's Rights
Editors: Brooke Dabney and Michael Eldridge

ISBN: 978-1-62948-252-1
© 2013 Nova Science Publishers, Inc.

Chapter 16

NICARAGUA: CHILDREN'S RIGHTS[*]

Norma C. Gutiérrez

EXECUTIVE SUMMARY

Nicaragua has issued many legislative enactments to comply with the international legal instruments to which it has subscribed. Chief among them are: the inclusion of the Convention on the Right of the Child as an express constitutional mandate; the promulgation of the Code of Childhood and Adolescence and the General Law on Education; extensive amendments to the Penal Code protecting minors; adoption of a new General Law on Health with its Program of Comprehensive Care for Women, Children, and Adolescents; and creation of a new Labor Code, raising the minimum working age and protecting young workers from being exploited.

I. INTRODUCTION

This report covers international treaties on children's issues to which Nicaragua has become a party, Constitutional provisions, and some of the most relevant statutes and national policies issued for the protection of children and adolescents.

II. IMPLEMENTATION OF INTERNATIONAL RIGHTS OF THE CHILD TREATY RATIFICATIONS

Nicaragua is a party to the following international treaties related to the right of the child:

---

[*] This document was released by the Law Library of Congress August 2007.

- Convention on the Rights of the Child, adopted by U.N. General Assembly resolution 44/25 of November 20, 1989.[1] Nicaragua signed the Convention on February 6, 1990, and ratified it on October 5 1990.[2]
- Universal Declaration of Human Rights.[3] Nicaragua voted in favor of it at the time it was adopted by the U.N. Plenary Meeting of the General Assembly, on December 10, 1948.[4]
- International Covenant on Civil and Political Rights, adopted by the U.N. General Assembly, on December 16, 1966.[5] Nicaragua ratified it on March 12, 1980.[6]
- Convention on the Elimination of All Forms of Discrimination Against Women, adopted by the U.N. General Assembly, on December 18, 1979.[7] Nicaragua signed it on July 17, 1980, and ratified it on October 27, 1981.[8]

Other conventions and protocols to which Nicaragua is a party are cited below, on pages 4, 5, and 7. Available sources do not indicate that Nicaragua is a party to the following:

- Hague Convention on Jurisdiction, Applicable Law, Recognition, Enforcement and Co-Operation in Respect of Parental Responsibility and Measures for the Protection of Children;[9]
- Hague Convention on Jurisdiction, Applicable Law and Recognition of Decrees Relating to Adoptions;[10]
- Inter-American Convention on Conflict of Laws Concerning the Adoption of Minors;[11]
- Convention on Protection of Children and Co-Operation in Respect of Intercountry Adoption.[12]

A number of legislative enactments have been issued by Nicaragua to protect children and adolescents and to comply with its international legal obligations. Five years after Nicaragua ratified the Convention on the Rights of the Child, in 1995, that Convention was given constitutional status through an amendment to Article 71 of the Constitution. The amended provision states that "[c]hildhood enjoys special protection and all the rights that its status may require [and] for that reason, the International Convention on Rights of Children *[el Niño y la Niña]* is fully applicable in Nicaragua."[13] The same constitutional reform established the concept of family property to be free of taxes and from seizure.[14] The Constitution prohibits child labor in tasks that can affect normal development or the compulsory education calendar. The Constitution also prohibits any form of economic and social exploitation of children and adolescents.[15]

Other constitutional provisions state that minors cannot be subject to or be the object of judgment, nor can they be submitted to any legal proceeding. Transgressor minors cannot be taken to penal rehabilitation centers, and they must be attended to in centers under the responsibility of a specialized institution. A law must regulate this matter.[16]

The Code of Childhood and Adolescence was promulgated in 1998. The Code defines "children" as those who have not reached thirteen years of age and "adolescents" as those who are between thirteen and eighteen years of age. It deals with family life; civil and political rights of children and adolescents; their rights to health, education, social security, culture, and recreation; duties and responsibilities of girls, boys, and adolescents; the creation of the National Council for Comprehensive Care and Protection of Children and Adolescents, which is attached to the Office of the President; the establishment of the Council's national policy; special protection for children and adolescents and preventive measures; duties of organizations and centers that work in the fields of childhood and adolescence; and a specialized criminal justice system for youth.[17]

In compliance with the mandate of Code of Childhood and Adolescence, Law No. 351 on the Organization of the National Council for Comprehensive Care and Protection of Childhood and Adolescence and the Office of the Children and Adolescents' Ombudsman was promulgated. The Council is a made up of a broad group of government ministries and agencies and representatives of civil society; it is responsible for the government's comprehensive policy on youth. The Youth Ombudsman's Office is responsible for the defense and protection of the rights of children and adolescents as provided in the Code. [18]

Extensive amendments to the Penal Code were promulgated in 1992, strengthening the provisions dealing with rape and statutory rape; procuring, aiding, or encouraging the sexual corruption of a minor; various kinds of sexual abuses and assaults; aiding, assisting, protecting, or procuring the prostitution of another; and other crimes that infringe the physical and moral integrity of persons.[19]

Under the amendments, these criminal offenses are prosecuted *sua sponte* by the public prosecutor if the victim is less than sixteen years old.[20]

The Penal Code was further amended and provisions were added to strengthen the provisions concerning protection against domestic violence and child abuse.[21]

The Law creating the Office of the Government Attorney for the Defense of Human Rights was promulgated in 1996; within this Office, the Office of the Government Attorney for the Defense of Children's Human Rights was created.[22]

The National Commission on Violence against Women, Children, and Adolescents was created by Executive Decree No. 116-2000. The Decree mandates the Commission to develop the National Action Plan for the Prevention of Violence against Women, Children, and Adolescents.[23]

An Executive Decree of 2006 creating the National Program of Gender Equality was promulgated in 2006. Its objective is to encourage gender equality between Nicaraguan women and men during the five year period 2006-2010. This will contribute to and create positive conditions in such areas as the eradication of violence, education, health, employment, and access to and control of productive economic resources.[24]

An Executive Decree No. 20-2006, on the Special Policy of Special Protection of Boys, Girls and Adolescents was promulgated in 2006. Its goal is to contribute to the highest level of well-being and development of children and adolescents that are in situations that require special protection, guaranteeing the restitution of the exercise of their rights in conditions of dignity and equality of opportunity. The Decree endorses the special policy approved by the National Council for Comprehensive Care and Protection of Childhood and Adolescence to comply with Nicaragua's obligations under the UN Convention on the Rights of the Child.[25] The same Decree No. 20-2006 makes reference to the fact that in compliance with the Convention on the Right of the Child, Nicaragua became a party to and ratified the following:[26]: the Optional Protocol to the Convention on the Rights of the Child on the Sale of Children, Child Prostitution, and Child Pornography;[27] and the Optional Protocol to the Convention on the Rights of the Child on the Involvement of Children in Armed Conflicts.[28]

Nicaragua acceded to the Hague Convention on the Civil Aspects of International Child Abduction of October 25, 1980, on December 14, 2000.[29] Nicaragua is also a party to the Inter-American Convention on the International Return of Children, adopted in Uruguay on July 15, 1989.[30]

The Law on the Organization, Jurisdiction, and Procedures of the Executive Branch, which was enacted in 1998 and later amended, includes among the agencies that make up the Presidential Cabinet the Ministry of the Family, the Nicaraguan Institute on Women, and the National Council for Comprehensive Care and Protection of Childhood and Adolescence.[31]

III. Child Health and Social Welfare

The General Law on Health was promulgated in 2002. Nicaragua, in its third period report to the UN Committee on the Rights of the Child, stated that the principles protected by the Convention are reflected in the Law's basic principles; the importance given to the Program of Comprehensive Care for Women, Children, and Adolescents; and the definition of a basic package of health services for the care of children and adolescents.[32]

The Law on Prevention, Rehabilitation and Equal Opportunities for Persons with Disabilities was promulgated in 1995,[33] together with its Regulation.[34] In the same year, the National Council for Comprehensive Care of Children with Disabilities was created.[35]

In addition to statutes and regulations, Nicaragua has created several national policies and plans to reaffirm children's rights and to protect them, such as the National Policy for the Comprehensive Care of Children and Adolescents; the National Plan for the Reduction of Maternal, Perinatal, and Infant Mortality; and the ambitious National Action Plan for Children and Young Persons, 2002-2011.[36] Moreover, in 2001, the Government initiated its Enhanced Economic Growth and Poverty Reduction Strategy, which contains a framework of policies and programs to increase the welfare of people through higher employment, greater investment in human capital, better protection of the most vulnerable, and improved governance.[37]

IV. Education, Including Special Needs

The Constitution states that the State must create programs and develop special centers for the care of minors; minors have the right to measures of prevention, protection, and education from their family, society, and the State, as required by their condition.[38]

After 105 years following the adoption of the previous statute on education, Nicaragua promulgated a new statute regulating the national educational system in 2006.[39] The objective of this statute, known as General Law on Education, is to establish the general guidelines for education and the national educational system, the powers and obligations of the State, and the rights and responsibilities of persons and of society.[40] The Statute establishes that the educational system is made up of the subsystems of formal education, technical and professional education, higher education, non-formal education, and the autonomous educational subsystem of the Atlantic Coast of Nicaragua.[41] The Statute provides for special basic education for the handicapped and other social groups that are vulnerable or socially excluded.[42] Elementary school is compulsory, and government schools provide free education at the elementary and high school levels.[43]

The Law on the Comprehensive Promotion and Development of Youth was promulgated in 2001. Its objective is to promote the human development of young men and women, guarantee the exercise of their rights and obligations, establish institutional policies, and invest resources of the state and the civil society for young people.[44]

V. CHILD LABOR AND EXPLOITATION

The Constitution states that no one must be subjected to servitude. Slavery and trafficking [of persons] of any nature are prohibited.[45] Furthermore, it states that child labor in tasks that can affect normal development or the compulsory education calendar is prohibited. Children and adolescents shall be protected against any form of economic and social exploitation.[46]

A new Labor Code was promulgated in 1996. Under the Code and its amendment of 2003, children are not allowed to work, but adolescents may do so. The amendments raised the minimum age at which a person may begin working from twelve (under the previous Code) to fourteen years.[47] The amendments consider persons between fourteen and eighteen years of age to be adolescents.[48] An adolescent between fourteen and sixteen years old requires parental authorization or the authorization of a legal representative to enter into an employment contract, which must also be supervised by the Ministry of Labor.[49] Adolescents who are between sixteen and eighteen years of age have the legal capacity to enter into an employment contract without parental consent.[50]

The Code prohibits adolescent labor in unhealthy areas, mines, underground workplaces, and dumping areas. It also prohibits work performed with dangerous machines and equipments; work in nighttime entertainment centers, which because of their nature are undignified and contrary to human rights; night work in general; work that requires manipulation of psychotropic or toxic substances; and other risky and dangerous kinds of works, in addition to work in circumstances in which adolescents are exposed to physical or psychological abuse and or commercial sexual exploitation.[51] The Code limits the workday for adolescent to six hours and the work week to thirty hours. Moreover, it provides a list of labor rights of working adolescents.[52] The fines for violations of these provisions have been raised, and inspectors of the Labor Secretariat may close those facilities that breach the law.[53]

Decree 22-97 of April 10, 1997, created within the jurisdiction of the Ministry of Labor the National Commission for the Progressive Eradication of Child Labor and the Protection of Working Minors.[54]

To comply with its international obligations, Nicaragua became a party to and ratified[55] the ILO Convention No. 138, Concerning the Minimum Age for Admission to Employment;[56] and the ILO Convention No. 182, Concerning the Prohibition and Immediate Action for the Elimination of the Worst Forms of Child Labor.[57]

Enforcement

The U.S. Department of State, in its 2006 COUNTRY REPORTS ON HUMAN RIGHTS,[58] in the section on Nicaragua, provides abundant, detailed information on many violations to children's rights and the lack of enforcement of the laws protecting them, despite the fact that the Government has publicly expressed its commitment to children's human rights and welfare.[59] The report also explains how sometimes the government's decisions are not in harmony with its expressed commitment to children's rights and welfare. For instance, the Government did not adequately fund children's programs and primary education.[60] The Government designated an emergency 24-hour hot line for reporting of trafficking in persons incidents and provided a vehicle to bring the victims to safety. However, there were reports that that by year's end, the hot line service was not fully operational and the vehicle was often not available.[61] Despite the law's prohibition, violence against children remains a significant problem.[62] The same can be said with respect to trafficking of women and children.[63] The report also stated, "Rules controlling child labor rarely were enforced except in the small formal sector."[64] Although the law provides free and compulsory education through the sixth grade, according to the Pan American Health Organization, approximately 800,000 school-age children did not attend school.[65] Many other incidents of breach of legal standards and lack of enforcement of the laws protecting youth were cited by the U.S. report. [66]

VI. SALE AND TRAFFICKING OF CHILDREN

The Amendment to the Penal Code of 1992, cited above, dealt also with the trafficking of persons. Consistent with the Constitution,[67] the amendment prohibits the trafficking of persons. The maximum penalty is applied when the victim is less than fourteen years of age or is married to or united by a *de facto union* to the wrong-doer.[68]

VII. JUVENILE JUSTICE

As stated above, the Code of Childhood and Adolescence was promulgated in 1998. It includes a specialized criminal justice system for youth, which provides for rights and guarantees the creation of special courts to hear juvenile cases, proceedings, conciliation, appeals, statute of limitations, measures, definition of measures, and execution of measures. [69]

CONCLUSION

Nicaragua has promulgated a number of laws to protect children and adolescents in compliance with the international conventions to which it has adhered. It has also created several national policies and plans to reaffirm children's rights and protect them. Moreover, the government of Nicaragua has publicly expressed its commitment to children's human rights and welfare. An illustration of this intended commitment is the fact that the government has elevated to the rank of Presidential Cabinet agencies the Ministry of the Family, the

Nicaraguan Institute on Women, and the National Council for Comprehensive Care and Protection for Childhood and Adolescence. However, very often the laws protecting children have not been enforced, as illustrated by the U.S. Department of State 2006 COUNTRY REPORTS ON HUMAN RIGHTS. In addition, it appears that Nicaragua has not become a party to four major conventions on children's issues, cited above.

Prepared by Norma C. Gutiérrez
Senior Foreign Law Specialist
August 2007

End Notes

[1] The Convention on the Rights of the Child, with a Preamble and 54 articles, was adopted by the U.N. General Assembly Nov. 20, 1989, and entered into force Sept. 2, 1990. G.A. Res. 44/25, annex, 44 U.N. GAOR Supp. (No. 49) at 167, U.N. Doc. A/44/49 (1989); 28 Int'l Legal Materials 1448 (1989) (an unofficial source). For an online text, see the Office of the UN High Commissioner for Human Rights [OHCHR] Web site, http://www.ohchr.org/english/law/crc.htm (last visited Aug. 8, 2007).

[2] Id. Ratifications and reservations are available on the OHCHR web site, at http://www.ohchr.org/english/ countries/ ratification/11.htm (last visited Aug. 8, 2007).

[3] The Universal Declaration of Human Rights, with a Preamble and 30 articles, was adopted by the U.N. General Assembly Dec. 10, 1948. G.A. Res. 217 A (III), U.N. Doc. A/810 at 71 (Dec. 10, 1948). For an online text, see the United Nations Web site, http://www.un.org/Overview/rights.html (unofficial source) (last visited Aug. 8, 2007).

[4] The Universal Declaration of Human Rights, Legislative History, Yearbook of the United Nations, 1948-49. It is available on the online web site of the OHCHR, at http://www.ohchr.org/english/issues/ education/ training/udhr.htm (last visited Aug, 9, 2007).

[5] The International Covenant on Civil and Political Rights, with a Preamble and 53 articles, was adopted by the U.N. General Assembly on December 16, 1966, and entered into force on March 23, 1976. G.A. Res. 2200A (XXI), 21 U.N. GAOR, 21st Sess. Supp. (No. 16) at 52, U.N. Doc. A/6316 (Dec. 16, 1966), 999 U.N.T.S. 171. For an online text, see the OHCHR Web site, http://www.ohchr.org/english/law/ccpr.htm (last visited Aug. 8, 2007).

[6] Id., Ratifications and Reservations, available on the same web site, at http://www.ohchr.org/english/ countries/ratification/4.htm (last visited Aug. 8, 2007).

[7] CEDAW, comprising a Preamble and 30 articles, was adopted by the U.N. General Assembly Dec. 18, 1979, and entered into force Sept. 3, 1981. G.A. Res. 34/180, 34 U.N. GAOR Supp. (No. 46) at 193, U.N. Doc. A/34/46. For an online text, see the U.N. Division of the Advancement of Women Web site, http://www.un.org/womenwatch/daw/cedaw/ text/econvention.htm#article1 (last visited Aug. 8, 2007).

[8] CEDAW. The list of the status of signatures, ratifications, and accessions is available on the same Web site, athttp://www.un.org/womenwatch/daw/cedaw/states.htm (last visited July 27, 2007).

[9] The 1996 Convention was adopted Oct. 19, 1996, and entered into force Jan. 1, 2002. 35 INT'L .LEGAL MATERIALS 1391, 1396 (1996). For an online text, see the Hague Conference on Private International Law (HCCH) Web site, http://hcch.evision.nl/index en.php?act=conventions.text&cid=70 (last visited July 27, 2007).

[10] The Hague Convention on Jurisdiction, Applicable Law and Recognition of Decrees Relating to Adoptions, Hague No. 13, was concluded Nov. 15, 1965, and entered into force Oct. 23, 1978. In accordance with its article 23, it will cease to have effect Oct. 23, 2008. For an online text, see the HCCH Web site, http://hcch.e-vision.nl/index_en.php?act= conventions.text&cid=75 (last visited July 27, 2007).

[11] The Inter-American Convention, May 24, 1984, in force May 26, 1988. O.A.S.T.S. No. 62. For an online text of the Inter-American Convention, see the OAS Web site, http://www.oas.org/juridico/english/sigs/b-48.html (last visited July 30, 2007) (scroll to the end of the page for the hyperlink to the treaty text). The URL also lists the status of signatures and ratifications to the Convention.

[12] The Hague Convention on the Protection of Children and Cooperation in Respect of Intercountry Adoption was concluded May 29, 1993, and entered into force May 1, 1995. 32 INT'L LEGAL MATERIALS 1134 (1993). For an online text, see the HCCH Web site, http://www.hcch.net/index_en.php?act=conventions.text&cid=69 (last visited July 27, 2007).

[13] Ley N. 192, Ley de Reforma Parcial a la Constitución Política de Nicaragua, Art. 71 (L.G. July 4, 1995).

[14] Id.

[15] Constitución Política de la República de Nicaragua, art. 84 (L.G. Apr. 30, 1987), as amended many times, available at http://www.asamblea.gob.ni/opciones/constituciones/constitucion.pdf.

[16] Id., art. 35.

[17] Código de la Niñez y la Adolescencia (L.G., May 27, 1998).

[18] Ley de Organización del Consejo Nacional de Atención y Protección Integral a la Niñez y la Adolescencia y la Defensoría de las Niñas, Niños y Adolescentes (L.G., May 31, 2000).

[19] Ley No. 150, Reformas al Código Penal, amending arts. 195-205 (L.G., Sept. 9, 1992).

[20] Id., art. 205.

[21] Ley No. 230, Ley de Reformas y Adiciones al Código Penal (L. G., Oct. 9, 1996).

[22] Ley No. 212, Ley de la Procuraduría para la Defensa de los Derechos Humanos, art. 18 (17) (L.G., Jan. 10, 1996). This statute was amended by Ley No. 471, de Reforma a la Ley No. 212, Ley de la Procuraduría para la Desensa de los Derechos Humanos (L.G., Oct. 9, 2003).

[23] Decreto No. 116-2000, de Creación de la Comisión Nacional Contra la Violencia Hacia la Mujer, Niñez y Adolescencia (L.G., Dec. 13, 2000).

[24] Decreto No. 36-2006, Del Programa Nacional de Equidad de Género (L.G., July 18, 2006).

[25] Decreto Ejecutivo 20-2006, de la Política de Protección Especial a los Niños, Niñas y Adolescentes, art. 1 (L.G., Apr. 4, 2006).

[26] Id. at 2718-2719.

[27] The Sex Trafficking Protocol comprises a preamble and 17 articles. G.A. Res. A/RES/54/263, May 25, 2000. It entered into force Jan. 18, 2002. For an online text, see the UNHCHR Web site, http://www.unhchr.ch/html/menu2/dopchild.htm (last visited Aug. 8, 2007).

[28] The Child Soldiers Protocol, comprising a Preamble and 13 articles, entered into force Feb. 12, 2002. G.A. Res. A/RES/54/263, May 25, 2000. For an online text, see the UNHCHR Web site, http://www. unhchr.ch/html/menu2 6/protocolchild.htm (last visited Aug. 8, 2007).

[29] Convention on the Civil Aspects of International Child Abduction, adopted by the Hague Conference on Private International Law, at its fourteenth session, held at the Hague, Oct. 6-25, 1980. 1343 UNTS 89, 90 (f), 98 (E). For an online text, see the Hague Conference on Private International Law, The Child Abduction Section Web site http://www.hcch.net/ index_en.php?act=text.display&tid=21 (last visited Aug. 8, 2007). The status table of contracting states to this Convention is available on the same web site, at http://www.hcch.net/ index_en.php?act=conventions. status&cid=24 (last visited Aug. 8, 2007).

[30] The Inter-American Convention on the International Return of Children, was adopted at the 4th Inter-American Specailized Conference on Private International Law, held at Montevideo, July 9-15, 1989. OASTS 70; 29 INT'L LEGAL MATERIALS 63, 66 (text); RDU 1989(I):368. For an only text see the OAS, Office of International Law web site, at http://www.oas.org/juridico/ english/treaties/b-53.html (last visited Aug. 9, 2007). Signatures and Ratifications are available on the same web site, at http://www.oas.org/juridico/ english/sigs/b-53.html (last visited Aug. 9, 2007).

[31] Ley No. 290, Ley de Organización, Competencia y Procedimientos del Poder Ejecutivo, arts. 12 & 14 (D.O., June 3, 1998). See also Executive Decree 25-2006, Apr. 20, 2006, art. 18 (2) (L.G., May 11, 2006).

[32] Nicaragua - Third Periodic Reports of States Parties due in 2002, at 14; Committee on the Right of the Child, UN Convention on the Right of the Child, CRC/C/125/Add.3, Oct. 15, 2004, available at http://daccessdds.un. org/doc/UNDOC/GEN/G04/440/12/PDF/G0444012.pdf?OpenElement.

[33] Ley No. 202, de Prevención, Rehabilitación y Equiparación de Oportunidades para las Personas con Discapacidad (L.G., Sept. 27, 1995).

[34] Decreto No. 50-97, Reglamento a la Ley No. 202 de Prevención, Rehabilitación y Equiparación de Oportunidades para las Personas con Discapacidad (L.G., Aug. 25, 1997).

[35] Decreto No. 45-95, Creación del Consejo Nacional de Atención Integral a la Niñez con Discapacidad (CONAINID) (L.G., June 29, 1995).

[36] Ley No. 230, Ley de Reformas y Adiciones al Código Penal (L. G., Oct. 9, 1996); Reports, supra note 34, at 16-17.

[37] Reports, id. at 16.

[38] Constitución Política de la República de Nicaragua, art. 76 (L.G. Apr. 30, 1987), as amended many times, available at http://www.asamblea.gob.ni/opciones/constituciones/constitucion.pdf.

[39] Miguel De Castilla Urbina, Anden y la Ley General de Educación: Los Antecedentes Cercanos, EL NUEVO DIARIO, Sept. 10, 2006, available at http://www.elnuevodiario.com.ni/2006/09/10/opinion/28562.

[40] Ley No. 582, Ley General de Educación (L.G., Aug. 3, 2006).

[41] Id., art. 12.

[42] Id., arts. 6 (i) & 23 (b.5).

[43] Id., arts. 19 & 23 c.

[44] Ley de Promoción del Desarrollo Integral de la Juventud, art. 1 (L.G., July 4, 2001).

[45] Constitución Política de la República de Nicaragua, art. 4 (L.G., Apr. 30, 1987), as amended many times, available at http://www.asamblea.gob.ni/opciones/constituciones/constitucion.pdf.

[46] Id., art. 84.

[47] Ley No. 185, Código del Trabajo, art. 131 (L.G., Oct. 30, 1996), as amended by Ley No. 474, Ley de Reforma al Título VI, Libro Primero del Código del Trabajo (L.G., Oct. 21, 2003).

[48] Id., art 130.

[49] Id., art. 131.

[50] Id.

[51] Id., art. 133.

[52] Id., art. 134.

[53] Id., art. 135

[54] Decreto No. 22-97, Creación de la Comisión para la Erradicación Progresiva del Trabajo Infantil y la Protección del Menor Trabajador (L.G., Apr. 10, 1997).

[55] Decreto Ejecutivo 20-2006, de la Política de Protección Especial a los Niños, Niñas y Adolescentes, art. 1 (L.G., Apr. 4, 2006), at 2718-2719.

[56] Convention (ILO NO. 138) Concerning Minimum Age for Admission to Employment, 1015 UNT 297. For an online text see the International Labor Office web site, at http://www.ilo.org/dyn/declaris/ DECLARATIONWEB. DOWNLOAD_BLOB?Var_DocumentID=6219 (last visited Aug. 9, 2007).

[57] Convention (ILO No. 182) Concerning the Prohibition and Immediate Action for the Elimination of the Worst Forms of Child Labor, 38 Int'l Legal Materials 1207 (1999) (unofficial source). For an online text see the Office of the Special Representative of the Secretary-General for Children and Armed Conflict http://www.un.org/children/conflict/ keydocuments/english/iloconvention1828.html (last visited Aug. 9, 2007).

[58] U.S. Department of State, Nicaragua, COUNTRY REPORTS ON HUMAN RIGHTS PRACTICE – 2006, Mar. 6, 2007. available at http://www.state.gov/g/drl/rls/hrrpt/2006/78899.htm.

[59] Id. at 8.

[60] Id.

[61] Id. at 9.

[62] Id.

[63] Id.

[64] Id. at 11-12.

[65] Id. at 8.

[66] Although the Department of State report on human rights practices in Nicaragua for the most part is accurate, it does contain two errors in its explanation of the law. For instance, contrary to its assertion, the laws against commercial sexual exploitation of minors protect adolescents under 18 year old. In this regard, see Ley No. 185, Código del Trabajo, (L.G., Oct. 30, 1996), as amended by Ley No. 474, Ley de Reforma al Título VI, Libro Primero del Código del Trabajo (L.G., Oct. 21, 2003), arts. 130 and 133. See also Constitución Política de la República de Nicaragua, art. 84 (L.G. Apr. 30, 1987), as amended many times, available at http://www.asamblea.gob.ni/opciones/constituciones/constitucion.pdf, prohibiting children and adolescents from being subject to any form of economic and social exploitation. Similarly, labor trafficking is criminalized. See also Ley No. 150, Reformas al Código Penal, amending art. 203 (L.G., Sept. 9, 1992).

[67] Constitución Política de la República de Nicaragua, art. 40 (L.G., Apr. 30, 1987), as amended many times, available at http://www.asamblea.gob.ni/opciones/constituciones/constitucion.pdf.

[68] Ley No. 150, Reformas al Código Penal, amending art. 203 (L.G., Sept. 9, 1992).

[69] Código de la Niñez y la Adolescencia (L.G., May 27, 1998).

In: Children's Rights
Editors: Brooke Dabney and Michael Eldridge

ISBN: 978-1-62948-252-1
© 2013 Nova Science Publishers, Inc.

Chapter 17

RUSSIAN FEDERATION: CHILDREN'S RIGHTS[*]

Peter Roudik

EXECUTIVE SUMMARY

Protection of children's rights is a serious problem for Russia, particularly because of the worsening demographic situation and progressive involvement of youngsters in criminal and other underground activities. Several presidential programs, together with major pieces of legislation, address this issue, which is at the center of domestic public discussions; because of insufficient budget financing and restrictions on work of nongovernmental organizations, however, legislative declarations remain largely unimplemented. It is expected that the newly created institution of a Children's Rights Ombudsman and introduction of the long delayed juvenile justice system will improve the situation. This paper analyzes legislation that regulates the protection of children's rights and evaluates government attempts to enforce relevant laws.

I. INTRODUCTION

The Russian Constitution, which was adopted in 1993, provides for the state protection of childhood, motherhood, and the family.[1] According to the Constitution, hundreds of laws, presidential decrees, government resolutions, executive regulations of specific agencies, and legal acts of the constituent components of the Russian Federation are supposed to secure rights of children. The primary documents in this field are the Family Code of the Russian Federation[2] and the Federal Law on Basic Guarantees of the Rights of the Child in the Russian Federation of July 21, 1998.[3] Child protection policy is also affected by the implementation of relevant provisions of such legislative acts, as the Civil Code, Labor Code, Housing Code, Criminal Code, Criminal Correctional Code, Fundamentals of Health Care Legislation, Federal Law on State Assistance to Individuals having Minor Children, Federal

---

[*] This document was released by the Law Library of Congress August 2007.

Law on State Support of Youth and Children's Organizations, Federal Law on Social Assistance, and many others.

It appears that from the legal point of view, such basic rights as the right to life, dignity, personal inviolability, housing, education, freedom of movement, social security, protection of health and health assistance, access to cultural values, and others are protected. All the typical problems, however, of the implementation of Russian legislation and the functioning of government institutions are inherent in the area of children's rights protection. Among these problems are that there is no separation of powers between the federal and regional levels of authorities; contradictions within the legislation; no defined division between federal and state budgets in regard to the payment of state subsidies to children; maintenance of social support institutions; and absence of working mechanisms that would provide for rehabilitation and integration of children with disabilities.

The economic and social crisis of the 1990s affected the area of children's rights substantially. Until 2003, payment of social assistance subsidies was constantly delayed, and even if money was received by children and parents having minor children, it did not have a positive impact on the economic situation in the family because of its insignificant amount and inflation. The situation was complicated by the dismantling of the previously existing traditional structures of social protection. Difficulties in family relations impacted the health and welfare of children most. For example, between 1994 and 2003, the population of children in Russia decreased by 4.4 million; approximately eighty percent of all high school graduates have significant health problems.[4]

Several targeted programs aimed at creating opportunities for children's development and protection of their rights were developed by the federal government and the President of Russia. These programs are dedicated to such aspects as the development of gifted children, the organization of summer vacation for children, protection of children whose parents are refugees or forced migrants, treatment of Chernobyl catastrophe victims, family planning, counteraction to drug abuse, and some others. According to Russian tradition, issues included in government or presidential programs receive better financing; their implementation is better controlled by the responsible government agencies; and legislative support is provided.

The system of government authorities is responsible for assisting children in defending their rights and monitoring their implementation. It includes education, health, and youth affairs authorities, as well as interagency bodies, such as guardianship committees and commissions on affairs of minors. This system, however, is not able to respond to children's complaints effectively. Because all these institutions belong to the executive branch of power, the scope of their activities cannot be extended beyond the authority of the agency of which they are a part. Twenty-three out of eighty-seven constituent components of the Russian Federation have established the regional office of a Children's Rights Ombudsman, an office which advocates children's rights, addresses government authorities and courts on behalf of those children who have no other representation or are mistreated, and coordinates the activities of other government and public services involved in the protection of children. In most of the cases, such Ombudsmen are appointed by the Governor and are included in the executive system; during the last two years, however, the appointment, as a rule, is made by the regional legislature or requires its approval. That new procedure gives parliamentary status to the Ombudsman, increases his independence, and expands his authority. The UN Committee on Children's Rights recommended the expansion of this institution in all Russian provinces and the establishment of the federal Children's Ombudsman office.

Among other problems that await a legal solution are the adoption of laws on a specialized juvenile justice system; development of different forms of raising children without parental care; protection of children from mistreatment, commercial, and sexual exploitation; adoption of legal measures aimed at preventing parental kidnapping and illegal transfer of children throughout the sate borders of Russia; the legal education of children, their parents, and officials working with the children; and further involvement of nongovernmental organization in work on the protection of children.

II. IMPLEMENTATION OF INTERNATIONAL RIGHTS OF THE CHILD

As a legal successor to the former Soviet Union, Russia became a party to the International Convention of the Rights of the Child (CRC), which was ratified on August 16, 1990.[5] On February 15, 2001, Russia signed the Optional Protocol to the International Convention of the Rights of the Child on the Involvement of Children in Armed Conflict. After the Convention was ratified, Russia attempted to bring its domestic legislation in accordance with international obligations in the field of children's rights protection. The Federal Law on Basic Guarantees of the Rights of the Child in the Russian Federation of July 21, 1998 repeats all the provisions of the CRC.

It appears that family law was among the most revised areas of legislation in regard to the care of children. In order to secure children's rights, the Family Code of the Russian Federation dedicates a special section to the rights of minors.[6] Almost all provisions of the Code reflect the requirements of the CRC, except the right of the child to be reunited with his or her family. Despite the fact that the Federal Law on Exit from and Entry into the Russian Federation[7] was amended numerously, no provision regarding the protection of migrant children was included in this Law. Different pieces of Russian legislation do not follow the definition of children provided by the CRC uniformly. Despite the fact that article 1 of the CRC states that everyone under eighteen years of age is recognized as a child, most specialized health care programs in Russia do not include children older than fourteen, or older than sixteen, if a child is disabled. Parental consent for medical procedures is required for children under sixteen, and tax legislation treats minors under sixteen, and between sixteen and eighteen years of age differently.

Regardless of the declaration of children's rights in Russian legislation, provisions of Russian laws are not implemented and there is no mechanism that would make the existing legal provisions work. The growing number of orphaned children[8] and the absence of an effective legal defense of children from domestic violence exemplify the non-implementation of declared rights. The Federal Law on Prevention of Orphancy and Crimes Committed by Minors,[9] which established local and regional government commissions on the affairs of minors to coordinate child protection activities, did not meet the expectations. The Law defines the rights of orphaned children who are the subject of police and other government authorities' activities, and protects the rights of children who have committed violations of law. The Law provides for different conditions in correctional institutions, depending on the severity of the violation, age and health of the child. The key problem is the absence of preventive care and work aimed at avoiding the violations. The existing system is aimed at punishment rather than improvement. For example, the termination of parental rights is the most often used form of punishment; it, however, can be applied in very serious situations. Similarly, the authorities usually address the violent behavior of personnel in child care establishments when it becomes aggravated and then is prosecuted as a crime.

Implementation of international legal norms in Russia is complicated by the fact that these norms are rarely publicized and popularized in the country. Educators and social workers involved in child affairs are often ignorant of basic human rights principles and international requirements in regard to the children's rights, and such issues are not taught in Russian universities.

III. CHILD HEALTH AND SOCIAL WELFARE

The right to health care is one of the most important social and economic children's rights. Worsening conditions of children's health in Russia can be explained by social factors, environmental problems, and the increased role of behavioral risks, such as drug and substance abuse. The consequences of the Chernobyl catastrophe continue to influence the state of children's health. Since 2001, the sickness rate of children on the territories affected by radioactive pollution increases by about thirty percent annually.[10] The spreading of AIDS and HIV among youth and young adults is also an alarming factor. It appears that the provisions of the Federal Law on Prevention of Spreading of Diseases Caused by HIV[11] are not implemented. No measures of financial and humanitarian assistance were implemented, and no educational work has been conducted with the youth.

The basic legal principles of health care for minors were defined by the Fundamentals of Russian Federation Legislation on Health Care.[12] This legal act established federal guarantees of receiving free medical assistance by children in all state and municipal health care establishments. Free immunization of children is prescribed by law, and more than ninety percent of Russian children are immunized. Many regions legislated to create state legal norms that provide for additional protection of children's health. They extend the number of medical procedures and treatments provided without charge, in addition to those covered by mandatory medical insurance under federal legislation, allow for free distribution of medicines to children under three years of age, and require qualified medical assistance in all nursing and child care facilities. However, inclusion of these provisions in legislative acts does not secure their implementation because the responsible authorities do not fulfill their duties and obligations. In 2005, inspections conducted by the office of the Russian Prosecutor General found serious violations of a child's right to health care in more than twenty constituent components of Russia. Local and state authorities illegally decreased the amount and forms of health services which should be provided to children for free, approved the performance of paid medical services in state and municipal hospitals, and no region in Russia completely implemented the Government Regulation of June 21, 2003, under which all children under three years of age, and those who have more than three siblings under six years of age were to receive free medicines.[13] Most of the problems exist because of insufficient budget financing, which demonstrates that the government cannot guarantee the implementation of rights which it has declared.

Substantial changes in the area of pediatric health care are expected with the implementation of recently proposed amendments to legislation on organs and tissue transplantation. In July 2007, the Ministry of Health Care and Social Protection of the Russian Federation submitted to the Council of Ministers the draft of a Regulation that permits, upon parental consent, the collection of organs from minors, whose brain death was confirmed by two independent medical panels. Additional safeguards and checks are provided by the Regulation in order to secure minors from medical errors and abuse. Presently, organs can be donated only by or collected from individuals older than eighteen years of age.[14]

An especially difficult situation exists with the implementation of the health care rights of disabled children and children with special needs. Until 1979, disabled children were not legally recognized in the Soviet Union because disability was defined as an inability to perform professional functions due to a sickness or trauma. People who had no labor experience could not qualify for disability benefits. Following the UN requirements, children under age sixteen could be recognized as disabled, according to the Ministry of Health Care Regulation No. 1265 of December 14, 1979. The regulation contained a very limited list of diseases, mostly genetic and incurable, for which children were allowed to receive social security benefits. In 1991, this list was expanded according to the World Health Organization recommendations, and, consequently, the number of those who were recognized as disabled children increased. Since 2000, this category includes minors under eighteen years of age. The number of such children is about 205 per 10,000 children. The primary legal act that provides for the definition of disability, establishes the duties of federal and regional authorities, and determines the economic, legal, and social measures aimed at supporting, compensating, and integrating people with disabilities is the Federal Law on Social Protection of People With Disabilities.[15] The law is based on the concept of equal civil, social, and cultural rights of the disabled individuals, and provides for medical as well as social rehabilitation, including professional education and employment assistance. The rights of disabled children are specified in the Family Code of the Russian Federation, Fundamentals of Health Legislation, and about twenty federal and 800 state legislative acts; most of them, however, lack the norms which would secure the implementation of the adopted legislative decisions.[16]

One of the mistakes in application of the legislation was corrected by the Constitutional Court of Russia by its Ruling No. 231 of June 27, 2005.[17] This ruling extended the right of mothers of disabled children to receive earlier retirement benefits than the fathers of such children, and made one of the parents eligible to receive the federal retirement benefit at fifty years of age, if they have paid social security tax for at least fifteen years and were involved in the upbringing of a child to eight years of age who had been disabled since birth.

According to the Constitution, social welfare is guaranteed to everyone because of age, for the upbringing of children, and in other cases established by law.[18] Under the Federal Law on State Subsidies to Individuals with Children,[19] monetary assistance is provided in the following forms:

- assistance during pregnancy and for childbirth;
- one-time assistance to the women who registered with medical institutions during the early terms of pregnancy;
- monthly assistance during the eighteen-month maternity leave period after the child birth; and

- monthly assistance for each child until the child reaches the age sixteen or graduates from an educational institution, but no later than eighteen years.

All these subsidies do not guarantee constitutional social welfare rights because they are minimal amounts, depend on the woman's family income, are paid irregularly, and do not meet the cost of living requirements. In violation of other legal norms, Russian legislation allows social payments to children until sixteen years of age, and only in exceptional circumstances until eighteen, despite the fact that all individuals under eighteen are minors. Following the 2006 amendments to the Federal Law on Social Protection of Population,[20] aimed at improving the demographic situation in the country, beginning in September 2007, women will receive a one-time payment in the amount of US$10,000 after their second and each following child reaches the age of three years. This money cannot be cashed but can be contributed toward purchase of a home, or invested for education or retirement.

Social welfare policy is not limited to the distribution of monetary subsidies to particular groups in the population. It includes the system of social and psychological support to minors who find themselves in difficult circumstances. These include orphans; homeless children; children with disabilities; victims of armed conflicts, natural calamities, catastrophes, and domestic violence; children forced into prostitution; juvenile criminals; and children involved in drug use. Medical, social, and psychological support services have been established under each regional department of education. According to the Federal Statute on Educational Establishment for Children without Parental Care,[21] such children are entitled to free living and studying at an institution of general and professional education. Special attention is paid to the creation of family style orphanages for five to fifteen children. A number of Government Regulations were issued to secure the legal status, financing, and rights of the people who run such institutions.

Beside the Ministry of Education, which runs educational establishments for children with special needs, the social security system contains forty-five (thirty-four primary and eleven secondary) schools of professional education aimed at the rehabilitation of the disabled youth and providing these people with working skills. The integration of the disabled in the society is complicated by the lack of handicapped access in the majority of Russian buildings.

IV. EDUCATION, INCLUDING SPECIAL NEEDS

The right to education is secured by article 43 of the Constitution and is guaranteed by Federal Laws on Education,[22] on Higher and Continuing Professional Education,[23] on Reimbursement of Food expenditures for Students of State and Municipal Institutions of Professional Education,[24] the Labor Code, and statutes of educational institutions. The Government Regulation of April 28, 1994,[25] on Urgent Measures to Support Education in Russia provided for a program of educational development and contained necessary mechanisms to guarantee social support for students. Administratively, the federal Ministry of Science and Education and its territorial branches is responsible for conducting state policy in the field of education. The first level of organized education consists of preschool institutions, called kindergartens, which cater for children from two months up to six years. Although they are heavily subsidized by the state, parents of children attending kindergartens have to pay a fee depending on family income and the length of daily stay of a child in the kindergarten. Although attendance in kindergartens is not obligatory, many regions legislate that attendance of the last year of kindergarten shall be obligatory in order to prepare the child for attending school. Primary and secondary education in Russian schools is combined, and children between six and eighteen years of age attend the twelve-year school. A ten-year school education is mandatory, according to the Federal Law on Education. Obtaining mandatory secondary education is a constitutional responsibility of each citizen. The obligation to attend school is to be enforced in regard to each individual under fifteen years of age.[26] Schools are designated to cover a certain district, and all children within the district must attend the district school if they are not attending a private or public magnet school. It is illegal to deny acceptance to a child into a public district school, although schools often circumvent this requirement by introducing entry tests and creating special classes with extended study of particular disciplines. Subsidized meals are provided by local authorities. The curriculum and program of schools are developed by the federal Ministry of Science and Education, but some regional variations, depending on local initiatives and/or specifics, are allowed. All students are subject to standardized testing. During the course of market reform, education in Russia became partially fee-based. Pre-school and mandatory secondary education, including professional, at public educational institutions remained free; the growing financial inequality of population, however, substantially limits equal opportunities declared by law. Legislation provides for the following basic principles of the Russian educational system: humanity, respect for universal human values, exclusion of religious influence, unity of the federal educational standards, consideration of ethnic and regional cultural specifics, and adaptation to the abilities of the students. Completion of a secondary school course gives the right to seek admission to institutions of higher education, where about one-fifth of the seats is reserved, according to the federal government plan, for tuition-free education of students with the best grades; the rest are fee based.

Professional schools, which admit students who have completed a nine-year school course, are formally a part of the secondary education system. They offer a course of one to three years leading to a general secondary school diploma and necessary qualifications in industry or agriculture.

Mostly because of insufficient financing and weak law enforcement, the implementation of legal acts regarding education is not satisfactory. The ongoing concentration of educational institutions in towns and district centers leads to the elimination of elementary schools in villages and small settlements, complicating access to education for local children. Development of market relations transforms all education other than the standard basic education into paid services, making it out of reach for an impoverished population. According to news reports, on September 1, 2004 (the official day when school classes begin), 26,220 Russian children did not come into class, and 1,500 were never enrolled in a school. About 100,000 children being rehabilitated in special institutions do not have an education appropriate for their age.[27]

Another great problem is providing education to children who happened to stay outside the established education system. These are children of refugees and migrants, children with deviant behavior, children with insufficient knowledge of the Russian language, and children with behavioral and/or mental problems. The schools try to eliminate such students, who after being excluded from schools remain without supervision. Legislation provides for placing such children into boarding schools.

According to expert evaluations, about 4.5 percent of Russian children (about 1.6 million) have different forms of disability and need special education.[28] Despite the fact that the principle of integrating children with special needs into the society was declared by relevant legal acts, as a rule, children with disabilities do not attend regular educational institutions. This occurs mostly because of a strong bias among the parents of healthy children that presence of children with special needs in a class will disturb teachers and other students. As an experiment, in 2006, several kindergartens in Moscow permitted admittance of a handful of disabled children. In the meantime, 450 thousand children with special needs under six years old attended the so called "compensatory kindergartens." In 2006, Russia had 1,373 boarding schools for 170,000 children with speech, hearing, and language pathology, vision impairment, mental retardation, skeletal diseases, and tuberculosis; and 1,946 day schools for 236,000 disabled students. Most of the children with disabilities are not able to attend schools, which are, as a rule, not accessible,[29] and are subject to home schooling performed by teachers of regular neighboring district public schools. The dropout rate among the disabled is much higher than among students of regular schools and only one percent of people with disabilities continue to study at institutions of higher education.

V. CHILD LABOR AND EXPLOITATION

Under the Labor Code,[30] individuals under eighteen years of age are subject to certain limitations on legal capacity, special limitations, and certain protection in the field of labor relations. The usual age of employment is sixteen, although in special cases, a minor may start work at fifteen, and even at fourteen if additional requirements have been met. The procedure of receiving approvals and permits for hiring a minor under sixteen is cumbersome, and employers usually do not hire minors under sixteen in order to avoid bureaucratic problems. All minors can be hired only after a medical examination. An annual medical examination of all employees under eighteen also is required. Labor law provides special protection to minors in its regulation of working hours and conditions; for instance, a minor's vacation cannot be less than thirty-one calendar days; it cannot be postponed to the next working year or commuted for cash. Article 265 of the Labor Code contains the list of work prohibited for minors because of negative impact on the health and moral development of a minor. This list includes work with hazardous materials, underground work, and work which requires moving heavy weights over the limits established by sanitary norms. This prohibition is mandatory and applies to all enterprises regardless of their legal status and possession. Minors cannot be sent on business travel, they cannot work overtime, at night, or during weekends and holidays.

Article 270 of the Labor Code contains two rules regarding the lessening productivity norms for minors. Because minors are working shorter business hours and have less professional skills, their productivity norms shall be established proportionally to their working time. The second rule affects minors who were hired after they graduated from vocational schools. Lower productivity rates can be established for them as well. Unlike old Soviet legislation, which provided for the same tariff rates for paying the wages of minor workers as for those who were older than eighteen, Russia's Labor Code specifies that the salary of a minor shall reflect his shorter length of work day.

Among other security measures, the legislation states that a minor may not be dismissed, except for cases when the company is liquidated, without the extra approval proceeding by the State Labor Inspection and local Commission on Juvenile Affairs, a state board made up of officials and specialists in juvenile health and upbringing. In all cases when a minor submits his request for employment termination, the employer is obligated to inform the Commission on Juvenile Affairs. The Law charges the Commission with the duty to find out real reasons for this move and assist the minor in staying at his previous place of work or in finding new employment.

Presently, because of numerous bureaucratic formalities and excessive obligations, employers prefer not to hire minors, especially those who are under sixteen, even for short term work during school vacation, or they do not formalize the actual hiring of a minor employee. Presently, the State Duma (legislature) of the Russian Federation is considering amendments to the Labor Code, which would introduce mandatory quotas on a number of positions reserved for minors. There are some problems with the implementation of other Labor Code provisions. In 2004, about 30,000 juveniles were employed in the field of construction, transportation, and communications; 2.8 percent of them worked under conditions which did not meet sanitary and hygienic norms. Because of violation of labor protection rules, twenty-nine individuals under eighteen years of age died.[31] Exploitation of child labor often occurs in agriculture. As a rule, guest workers who are hired for agricultural work arrive with families, including minor children and all children are used as a labor force. Guest workers, especially illegal migrants, are usually not controlled by the authorities, and their children do not attend schools. It is also a widespread practice in rural areas that school students are summoned for agricultural works for several months, especially in autumn during harvesting; students, however, are not paid for this work, and they are not registered as employees of agricultural cooperatives during these periods.

In February 2003, Russia ratified the Convention Concerning the Prohibition and Immediate Action for the Elimination of the Worst Forms of Child Labor.[32] Following the obligations imposed by this Convention, amendments were made to Russian domestic laws. Provisions prohibiting forced labor were added to the Labor Code,[33] and the Criminal Code was amended with provisions prohibiting trade in minors, mercenary activities, recruitment of children to participate in the military, involvement of minors in antisocial behavior, and criminal activities. These crimes are punishable by imprisonment for an average term of six years; the enforcement of these provisions, however, remains inadequate, and orphans, children of migrants, and those from impoverished families are often objects of such crimes. A survey conducted by the International Labor Organization in St. Petersburg revealed that often, children start to work when they are ten to twelve years old, and girls are involved in prostitution at age fourteen. Three-fifths of the working street children are boys; they are usually involved in assistance in trade (cleaning, loading, guarding goods), construction, collecting things for recycling, and agricultural works. Only two-third of such children attend school periodically.[34]

VI. SALE AND TRAFFICKING OF CHILDREN

Russia has a unique role in the international sale and trafficking of children because it is simultaneously a resource for future victims and a recipient of trafficked persons from the former Soviet states. Despite attempts over the years to address the problem of sale and trafficking of children in the Russian Federation, this issue has developed into a cause for serious concern. According to police statistics between thirty and sixty thousand women, most of whom are minors, are transported out of Russia for purposes of sexual exploitation annually. In most cases, minors are taken in and out of Russia under the pretext of employment abroad.[35] In addition, approximately seventy thousand individuals, most of whom are young women, are recognized absent for unknown reasons annually.[36] There is a large chance that these women were abducted in order to use them for slave labor or prostitution in Russia or abroad. According to police information, criminal groups conduct abductions of young and minor women regularly, especially in economically depressed areas. Abducted women are usually brought to criminal bases where they are prepared for transportation to other cities or abroad.[37]

There are no reliable statistics on crimes committed in this sphere due to the latent type of this phenomenon. According to the Ministry of Internal Affairs (police), since 2004, when human trafficking was criminalized in Russia, sixty-six crimes involving trade in humans were registered in Russia; however, only twenty-six criminal investigations were initiated, and twelve people were sentenced by the courts.[38] Russian officials attribute their inability to curb trafficking to the lack of legislation, complaining that prostitution and prostitution-related activities are not subject to prosecution. Also, Russian police cite problems with investigating such violations, because these crimes that begin in Russia are usually completed abroad. The Russian police propose to establish an exact definition of the term "slave trade" in domestic legislation. Presently, Russian authorities are focusing on strengthening control over commercial agencies that could be used as a cover for slave trade.

In 2002, Russia recognized the existence of trade in people in various regions and began to work on adoption of the extremely necessary law in this sphere. In April 2002, the investigation of trafficking-related crimes was transferred to the jurisdiction of police departments charged with combating organized crime,[39] and on October 30, 2002, a working group was created to draft the Law on the Fight Against Trafficking in Humans. The group included representatives from the Administration of the Russian Federation President, the Parliamentary Committee on Legislation, and from interested non-government organizations. The U.S. Department of Justice was to provide operational, technical, and financial support to the working group;[40] all these activities, however, resulted only in amending provisions of the Criminal Code.

Before 2004, all Russian anti-trafficking legislation was confined to the presently void article 152 of the Russian Criminal Code, which dealt with trafficking in minors and article 240, which prosecuted the engagement in prostitution. By referring to trafficking in minors and going after the pimps rather than addressing the issue as trafficking in people in general, the focus of Russian police authorities seemed to be on age and gender issues rather than on the resolution of the problem in general.[41]

At least seven articles of the Criminal Code had some relation to this type of crime, envisaging criminal punishment for forcing one to perform sexual acts (art. 133), trade in minors (art. 152), swapping babies (art. 153), illegal adoption (art. 154), illegal deprivation of freedom not connected with abduction (art. 155), and drawing into the business of prostitution (art. 240). No single article, however, was dedicated to the trade in humans. Because these crimes are not usually committed by single individuals, they were primarily covered by article 210 of the Criminal Code, Organizing a Criminal Community or a Criminal Organization. This relatively large number of provisions did not adequately reflect the current situation and practice to combat these crimes. For instance, article 126, Abduction of People, required proof of the fact of violent detention in order to convict a person under this article. But trafficked people typically are not held forcibly. Understanding that they violate domestic laws of the country where they are present, they prefer not to go to the law enforcement agencies.

Amendments to the Criminal Code, adopted in December 2003, did not establish a comprehensive definition of human trafficking. The Code was supplemented with two new sections criminalizing trade in humans and usage of slave labor. The present version of Russian law follows the UN definition, which from a legal point of view, is extremely complicated. As stated in the Protocol on Trade in Humans, the trade in people is hiring, transporting, transferring, concealing, or receiving people either by threat or fraud, deception, or coercion, or by making or receiving illegal payments or benefits, for the consent of the person who controls another person for the purpose of sexual exploitation or forced labor.[42] Despite the fact that most of these qualifying features were included in Russia's legislation, Russian laws do not distinguish between who is an offender and who is a victim, do not create a mechanism to prosecute recruitment, and do not defend specifically people in a dependent position. Proposals pushed by interested Russian non-government organizations to accept the definition adopted by the U.S. Victims of Trafficking and Violence Protection Act of 2000, which goes beyond the policy definitions used in the UN documents, were not accepted.[43]

Because of gaps in Russian legislation, recruitment into prostitution and fraudulent employment in prostitution-related spheres of business are not covered by Russian law. Article 127-1 of the Criminal Code recognizes recruitment of a person as a preparatory step to commit a sale or purchase of a human individual. Recruitment is not considered an independent crime even if an agreement between a mercenary and an individual has been concluded, and because the Code prosecutes recruitment of each person individually, punishing group recruitment remains problematic. Russian law does not provide punishment for the seizure of minor's identification documents, an activity done in order to isolate minors and prevent them contacting police authorities. Seizure of the victim's document is just a qualifying factor, which makes the punishment of another crime (e.g., exploitation of slave labor) more severe if such a seizure occurred while another crime has been committed. Among the imperfect features of Russian criminal legislation is that the use of threat of force can be prosecuted only if the victim was the subject of trafficking personally.[44] If violence was used in regard to the relatives of the trafficked person, this action is considered as a regular crime unrelated to trafficking. Relatives still cannot bring charges against the traffickers on behalf of the victim, and have almost no rights, except for some coverage under the witness protection program.

VII. Juvenile Justice

In Russia, the system of juvenile courts was established in 1910, and proved to be very successful in correcting underage offenders. Up to seventy percent of young criminals were sentenced to supervision of foster parents instead of imprisonment. Juvenile courts were considered as a system of state oversight rather than the instrument of prosecution. In 1918, the newly established Soviet Government cancelled this practice, subordinating the courts to the politically appointed Commissions on the Affairs of Minors, and minimized the participation of lawyers in such cases.[45] In 1935, the age of full criminal liability was lowered to twelve years for all types of offenses, including minor and unintentional, and permitting courts to sentence to death twelve-year-old children.[46] This approach still affects the state and public attitude toward juvenile justice. In 1964, the USSR Supreme Court recommended the specialization of judges and ordered that cases with minors would be tried by designated judges only; however, the juvenile courts were not established.[47]

Presently, juvenile justice does not exist as an independent branch of the judiciary. The existing Russian court system does not guarantee that all matters would be considered in the best interests of a child without delay by a competent, independent, and impartial authority, as required by Article 40 of the CRC. Because of the general workload increase and low number of judges, criminal cases in regard to minors, which make up approximately twelve percent of all criminal cases tried by the Russian courts, are usually resolved within several years, while the minors await their trials in detention centers. Proposals to establish family and juvenile courts are regularly introduced in the legislature but are not supported by the executive branch. As an experiment, since 1999, the St. Petersburg City Court has included social workers in its staff and involves them in the ongoing trials. The rate of repeated crimes among the youths tried under the new system became significantly lower. Since 2001, this experiment has been extended to two other regions. There was no further development, however, because of budget constraints.

Conclusion

The adoption of legislation that declares children's rights, as well as joining international legal instruments, did not improve the implementation of those rights automatically. It is unlikely that adoption of a few additional pieces of legislation will stop a wide-spread and long-term practice of child abuse and mistreatment. Together with many other related measures, however, such as developing policies to ensure the enforcement of existing laws, extending federal assistance to those who raise children, introducing new forms of care over children without parental oversight, adapting criminal procedures to the needs of minors, protecting victims during the criminal prosecution of traffickers, passing social legislation, and better funding for social, juvenile, and educational services, may change the situation and indicate that Russia has moved to a higher level of legal and political thinking.

In spite of the efforts of the international community and Russia's non-governmental organizations, there is no machinery yet for making Russia a country with a developed legal system and enforceable legislation aimed at the protection of children. It all depends on the degree of realization by Russia's leadership of the gravity of this problem and on its civilized standards for solving it effectively and protecting its underage population.

Prepared by Peter Roudik
Senior Foreign Law Specialist
August 2007

End Notes

[1] Constitution of the Russian Federation, Article 38.

[2] Family Code of the Russian Federation, SZ RF 1996, No. 11, Item 939.

[3] SOBRANIE ZAKONODATELSTVA ROSSIISKOI FEDERATSII (official gazette, SZ RF) 1998, No. 31, Item 3802.

[4] Federation Council of the Russian Federation Federal Assembly. Analytical materials for parliamentary hearings on Protection of Children's Health in the Russian Federation, published in ANALITICHESKII VESTNIK [Analytical Bulletin], No. 7(324), Moscow, 2007, p. 35.

[5] VEDOMOSTI VERKHOVNOGO SOVETA SSSR (then the official gazette) 1990, No. 26b, Item 497.

[6] Family Code of the Russian Federation, SZ RF 1996, No. 11, Sec. 11.

[7] Last amended on Jan.10, 2003, SZ RF 2003, No. 2, Item 159.

[8] According to various estimates, between 700,000 and three million children are orphans; however, only five percent of them have no parents. The rest of the children have parents whose parental rights were terminated because of their antisocial behavior. See note 4, p. 42.

[9] SZ RF 2003, No. 28, Item 2880.

[10] O POLOZHENII DETEI V ROSSIISKOI FEDERATSII [On State of the Children in the Russian Federation, National report], Moscow: Yurizdat, 2005, p. 13.

[11] SZ RF 1995, No.14, Item 1212.

[12] Vedomosti S'ezda Narodnykh Deputatov RF I Verkhovnogo Soveta (then the official gazette), 1993, No. 33, Item 1318.

[13] N.E. Borisova, PRAVOVOE POLOZHENIE NESOVERSHENNOLETNIH V ROSSIISKOI FEDERATSII [Legal Status of Minors in the Russian Federation, in Russian], Moscow: Izdatelstvo MGSU, 2006, p. 164.

[14] Svetlana Sukhaia, Ochered za Zhiznyu [Line for Life, in Russian], TRUD (daily newspaper), Jul. 24, 2007, No.129, p. 4.

[15] SZ RF 1995, No. 32, Item 3198.

[16] Federation Council of the Russian Federation Federal Assembly, supra note 4, p. 42.

[17] SZ RF 2005, No. 29, Item 3097.

[18] Constitution of the Russian Federation, Article 39.

[19] SZ RF 1995, No. 21, Item 1929.

[20] SZ RF 2006, No. 49, Item 4822.

[21] SZ RF 1995, No. 28, Item 2693.

[22] SZ RF 1996, No. 3, Item 150.

[23] SZ RF 1996, No. 35, Item 4135.

[24] SZ RF 1996, No. 32, Item 3847.

[25] SZ RF 1994, No. 2, Item 104.

[26] Federal Law on Education, art. 19.

[27] G. Kaelova, V Rossii 473 Tysiachi Bednyh Semei [There are 473,000 poor families in Russia], INTERFAX News Agency, Moscow, June 23, 2005.

[28] Federation Council of the Russian Federation Federal Assembly. Analytical materials for parliamentary hearings on Protection of Children's Health in the Russian Federation, published in ANALITICHESKII VESTNIK [Analytical Bulletin], No. 7(324), Moscow, 2007, p. 39.

[29] In Moscow, which has much better financial resources than the rest of the country, only about one-fourth of almost 2,000 public schools are accessible.

[30] SZ RF 2002, No. 1, Item 3.

[31] O POLOZHENII DETEI V ROSSIISKOI FEDERATSII [On State of the Children in the Russian Federation, National report], Moscow: Yurizdat, 2005, p. 35.

[32] SZ RF 2003, No. 6, Item 506.

[33] Labor Code of the Russian Federation, Article 4.

[34] ANALITICHESKII VESTNIK, supra note 28, p. 37.

[35] Nabi Abdulaev, Lack of Laws Helping Sex Trade to Flourish, THE ST. PETERSBURG TIMES, Aug. 30, 2002.

[36] Alexasnder Kolesnichenko, Exportnyi Potok [Export Stream], NOVYE IZVESTIIA (daily newspaper), No. 74, Apr. 27, 2006, p. 2.

[37] State Duma of the Russian Federation. REPORT ON FIGHT AGAINST HUMAN TRAFFICKING, Moscow, 2006, p. 74.

[38] Report of the Russian Ministry of Internal Affairs, published on May 16, 2006, available at www.mvd.ru/press/release/4165.

[39] ROSSIISKAIA GAZETA [Government owned daily newspaper], Apr. 29, 2002, at 2.

[40] G. Ilyichev, Bortsy s Aisbergom [Fighters against the iceberg], IZVESTIIA, Oct. 30, 2002.

[41] O. Yablokova, Slavery in Russia, MOSCOW TIMES, July 2, 2005.

[42] UN Protocol to Prevent, Suppress, and Punish Traficking in Perosns, art. 3(a), G.A. Res. A/55/25, Annex III, 55th Sess., U.N. GAOR 56089, Jan. 8, 2001.

[43] P.L. 106-386, Oct. 28, 2000.

[44] Code of Criminal Procedure of the Russian Federation, Sec. 7.

[45] Sobranie Uzakonenii RSFSR (then the official gazette), Part 1, No. 62, Jan. 17, 1918.

[46] Svod Zakonov SSSR [USSR Collection of Laws, official gazette], Part 1, 1935, No. 19.

[47] Biuleten Verkhovnogo Suda SSSR [USSR Supreme Court Bulletin], 1964, No 9, p. 4-5.

In: Children's Rights
Editors: Brooke Dabney and Michael Eldridge

ISBN: 978-1-62948-252-1
© 2013 Nova Science Publishers, Inc.

Chapter 18

UNITED KINGDOM (ENGLAND AND WALES): CHILDREN'S RIGHTS[*]

Clare Feikert

EXECUTIVE SUMMARY

This report provides a basic overview of the laws regarding children's rights in a number of fields. England and Wales has a large number of laws protecting children and guaranteeing them basic rights – both for areas in which there is now an 'entitlement' such as education, as well as in areas in which they need rights to ensure protection, such as in the criminal justice system. Given the large number and complexity of these laws this report provides a broad overview of legislation and common law as it applies to children's rights in England and Wales.

I. INTRODUCTION

Within the United Kingdom of Great Britain and Northern Ireland, England and Wales is the component nation in which largely English law prevails. This report does not address children's rights in Scotland or Northern Ireland, although a number of the provisions discussed in the paper may also apply to them. The common law in England and Wales provides that the responsibility for the care and protection of children is with their parents "as guardians by the law of nature, and on the Crown as *parens patriae,*"[1] with the powers of a child's parents somewhat limited in certain areas by law. There are a number of substantive pieces of legislation affecting children and their rights in a number of different areas. The most substantive piece affecting children and their basic rights to a secure and safe environment is the Children Act 1989. This Act introduces the term 'parental responsibility' rather than the common law concept of custody. Parental responsibility is defined as "all the

---

[*] This document was released by the Law Library of Congress August 2007.

rights, duties, powers, responsibilities and authority which by law a parent has in relation to the child and his property."[2]

The age of majority for children in England and Wales varies; there are many age related rules that distinguish between children of different ages for different purposes. The age of majority typically ranges from between sixteen years of age (in which school no longer becomes mandatory) to eighteen years of age (for voting rights and the consumption of alcohol).

Children's rights are provided by a large number of laws – some that specifically were enacted to protect children, and others that contain just a few sections that pertain to children but provide them with essential rights. There are numerous pieces of legislation that provide children with rights in the areas of education, medicine, employment and the justice system. Given the volume and complexity of these laws, this report provides a necessarily broad overview of the substantive pieces of legislation as they affect children's rights in these areas.

II. IMPLEMENTATION OF INTERNATIONAL RIGHTS OF THE CHILD

The United Kingdom is party to numerous treaties regarding the rights of children, notably the

- United Nations Convention on the Rights of the Child, ratified 12/16/1991;[3]
  - o Optional protocol to the Convention on the Rights of the Child on the sale of children, child prostitution and child pornography, signed 9/7/2000;[4]
  - o Optional protocol to the Convention on the Rights of the Child on the involvement of children in armed conflict, ratified 6/24/2003;[5]
- United Nations Declaration of the Rights of the Child, ratified 1/15/1992;6
- European Convention on the Adoption of Children, ratified 12/21/1967, entered into force 4/26/1968;[7]
- European Convention on the Legal Status of Children born out of Wedlock, ratified 2/24/1981, entered into force 5/25/1981;[8]
- Convention Against Discrimination in Education, accepted by the UK 3/14/1962;[9]
- Convention for the Protection of Human Rights and Fundamental Freedoms, acceded to 2/24/1967;[10]
- Hague Convention on the Civil Aspects of International Child Abduction, ratified 10/20/1986;[11]
- Hague Convention on Jurisdiction, Applicable Law, Recognition, Enforcement and Cooperation in Respect of Parental Responsibility and Measures for the Protection of Children, signed 1/4/2003;[12]
- Hague Convention on the Protection of Children in Intercountry Adoption, ratified 2/27/2003;[13]
- European Convention on the Adoption of Children, ratified 12/21/1967;[14]
- Convention on Consent to Marriage, Minimum Age for Marriage and Registration of Marriages, acceded to 7/9/1970;[15]
- International Covenant on Civil and Political Rights, ratified 5/20/1976;[16]

- Convention on the Elimination of All Forms of Discrimination Against Women, ratified 4/8/1976;[17]
- The European Convention on the Recognition and Enforcement of Decisions Concerning the Custody of Children, ratified 4/21/1986;[18]
- Minimum Age Convention, ratified 7/6/2000;[19]
- Convention concerning the Prohibition and Immediate Action for the Elimination of the Worst Forms of Child Labour, ratified 3/22/2000;[20]
- Universal Declaration of Human Rights;[21] and the International Covenant on Economic, Social and Cultural Rights, ratified 5/20/1976.[22]

III. Child Health and Social Welfare General Access to Healthcare

The United Kingdom does not have a written constitution that provides any guarantees regarding access to healthcare. It does, however, have a comprehensive national health service founded on the principle of providing treatment according to clinical need rather than the ability to pay. The Secretary of State has a number of statutory responsibilities under the National Health Service Act 1977 to ensure that, where possible, a free and comprehensive health service is provided in England and Wales to improve both the physical and mental health of the people of the country and to prevent, diagnose and treat illnesses.[23]

The government has recently introduced a National Service Framework, which provides that healthcare services for children should be designed and delivered around the particular needs of children.[24] The framework intends "to lead to a cultural shift, resulting in services being designed and delivered around the needs of children and families."[25]

Prenatal and Postnatal Care

Healthcare facilities are free and available for British children and infants, and the rate of infant mortality is relatively low, with 3,368 infant deaths (under one year of age) registered in England and Wales in 2006, at a rate of five per 1,000 live births.[26] The new National Service Framework regarding pre- and postnatal care of infants that has been welcomed by the Royal College of Obstetricians and Gynaecologists. The policy aims to provide mothers with a choice of either a midwife or a doctor for prenatal care; a choice of place of birth between a home birth, midwife centre birth, or a hospital birth with a doctor or a midwife. These services are provided at no additional charge through the National Health Service.

Healthcare: Children and Consent

Under the Children Act 1989, the term parental responsibility is defined to include the parents' right to consent to medical treatment.[27] An individual that does not have parental responsibility for the child, but has them in his or her care, for example a doctor or a teacher, "may do what is reasonable in all the circumstances of the case for the purpose of safeguarding or promoting the child's welfare ... though it will presumably only be reasonable to act without first obtaining the consent of the child's parents ... in an emergency or if the treatment is trivial."[28] When children reach the age of sixteen, provided they are mentally competent, they are considered to be *sui juris* and capable of consenting to treatment themselves.[29] Prior to this age, however, a child that has achieved a sufficient degree of understanding and intelligence regarding any treatment that he or she is about to undergo may be considered competent and capable of providing valid consent to this treatment. This level of competence varies according to the seriousness of treatment and "reflects the staged development of a normal child and the progressive transition of the adolescent from childhood to adulthood."[30] This concept is known as Gillick competence,[31] and may be overruled by a parent if the child is refusing to consent to treatment; a parent, however, cannot overrule a Gilleck competent child's consent to treatment.[32]

IV. EDUCATION

Education is funded by the government and the way in which it is provided is governed primarily by statute and a voluminous amount of secondary legislation, although some aspects of the common law continue to exist in the educational setting, such as the duty of care owed by education authorities and their employees regarding the care and supervision of students.[33] The primary legislation in this area is the Education Act 1996;[34] the Education Act 1997;[35] the Education (Schools) Act 1997;[36] the Special Educational Needs and Disability Rights Act 2001;[37] the Further and Higher Education Act 1992;[38] the Learning and Skills Act 2000; the Teaching and Higher Education Act 1998;[39] and the School Standards and Framework Act 1998[40] as amended and supplemented by the Education Acts of 2002[41] and 2005.[42] These Acts together provide the framework for the provision of nursery education for children that are not yet old enough for compulsory education and primary and secondary education for children and teenagers and cover issues such as funding; governance; staffing; admissions and attendance.

It is the duty of the Secretary of State to provide children with education in England and Wales, and this duty is typically performed by Local Education Authorities (LEA) for each county in England.[43] Education in Wales is a devolved area, meaning that it can pass regulations to address educational issues separately from England. Regulations specifically addressing Wales are not addressed in this report.

Compulsory Education

There are three stages of public education in England, comprised of the primary education stage; secondary education stage and further education.[44] Nursery education is also provided for children who are over two years of age but have not yet reached the compulsory school age.[45] Compulsory education in England begins at the age of five years old and continues until the end of the "school leaving year" in which the child is sixteen years old.[46] When a child turns five years old the parents must ensure that their child receives "efficient full-time education suitable to his age, ability and aptitude, and to any special educational needs he may have, either by regular attendance at school or otherwise."[47] Once a child has reached the age for compulsory education and is registered with a school in his or her area it is an offense for the parent to fail to have the child attend the school regularly; parents may be punished with a fine for failing to do so.[48] The duty for children to obtain an education thus falls both upon the parents, to ensure that they attend schools, and local education authorities, who are responsible for providing the schools.

Curriculum

The Secretary of State and LEAs have a duty to put in place, and follow, a curriculum that is balanced and broad and "promotes the spiritual, moral, cultural, mental and physical development of pupils at the school and of society and prepares pupils at the school for the opportunities, responsibilities and experiences of later life."[49] There is a national curriculum in place across England that consists of a foundation stage and then four key stages. During these stages, various arrangements are in place for assessing students and upon helping them achieve attainment targets. For the four key stages of education the core subjects include mathematics, English, science, design and technology, information and communication technology, physical education, history, geography, art and design, music, citizenship and a modern foreign language.[50]

Rights in Education

The right to an education is provided for in a number of international conventions to which the UK is a party, notably the Convention for the Protection of Human Rights and Fundamental Freedoms,[51] the European Convention on Human Rights and the Universal Declaration of Human Rights.[52] Further to this, the Education Act 1996 imposes a duty on the Secretary of State to "promote the education of the people of England."[53] When performing the duties under the various Education Acts, the Secretary of State must regard the general principle that pupils should be educated in accordance with the wishes of their parents "so far as that is compatible with the provision of efficient instructions and training and the avoidance of unreasonable public expenditure.[54] The Convention for the Protection of Human Rights and Fundamental Freedoms also provides for the principle that parents have the right to ensure that any education or training conforms with their own religious and philosophical beliefs; this principle, however, is only valid in England insofar as it is "compatible with the provision of efficient instruction and training, and the avoidance of unreasonable public expenditure."[55] These issues typically arise with regard to the provision of religious and/or sex education. The typical resolution of these issues is that parents request that their children are wholly or partly excused from these educational classes.[56]

Discrimination in its various forms (race,[57] gender,[58] disability,[59] and sexual orientation[60] or religion[61] in the higher and further education sectors) is prohibited when providing education in England and Wales. LEAs have a duty to identify children with special needs and to then make an assessment of what needs they have and then to make a statement of these special needs, to include details of the assessment and the special educational provisions that are to be made to meet these needs. The statement includes the type of school or institution the LEA considers to be appropriate for the child, or to specify the name of the mainstream public school that it considers appropriate for the child, and any special educational provisions that it considers necessary.[62] It is currently general policy to include special needs children into mainstream public schools unless this is incompatible with the wishes of the parents or would have a negative impact on the efficient education of other children.[63] If the statement of special needs names a public school, that child must be admitted to that school.[64]

Discipline

There is no longer a right for teachers or any member of staff to administer corporal punishment to pupils because it is considered that "it cannot be justified in any proceedings."[65] Members of staff of schools may use reasonable force to restrain pupils from committing an offense, causing personal injury or damage to property or prevent them from engaging in any highly disruptive behavior in school.[66] Discipline in schools in England is primarily achieved through after school detention, sanctioned under the common law, and typically requires parental consent or notice.[67] The ultimate sanction for repeated bad behavior is exclusion from the school, either on a temporary or permanent basis.

V. CHILD LABOR AND EXPLOITATION

There are extensive laws and regulations regarding child labor and exploitation in England and Wales. The main legislation restricting the use of children in employment is the Children and Young Persons Act 1933.[68] The term "child" in this context is defined as anyone of compulsory school age (up to age sixteen).[69] The general rules are that no child may be employed under the age of fifteen years, or fourteen years for light work;[70] be required to work during school hours; before 7 a.m. or after 7 p.m. on any day; or be required to work for more than two hours on any day they are required to attend school, for more than twelve hours in any week they are required to attend school; or for more than two hours on Sundays. For non-school days, children under the age of fifteen may work up to five hours a day on days that they are not required to attend school, not including Sundays, up to a maximum of twenty five hours per week. Those aged fifteen years or older may work up to eight hours per day on any day school attendance is not required, up to a maximum of thirty five hours per week, with the limit to working a maximum of two hours on a Sunday still applying. Anyone employing children over the age of fourteen must provide them with at least a one hour break after they have worked four or more hours.[71] It is an offense to employ a child in contravention of these laws, punishable by a fine. Additional provisions are applicable to children in the entertainment industry, which provides an exemption: that children can perform certain duties under a license.[72] Local authorities can also make by-laws to further restrict the hours or circumstances in which children may work.[73]

There are a number of laws that prohibit the use and exploitation of children in dangerous labor. The following examples are extracted from a House of Commons Library Standard note and include:

- Employment of Women, Children and Young Persons Act 1920, which prohibits the employment of children in any "industrial undertaking," including mines and quarries, manufacturing industry, construction, and the transport of passengers or goods by road, rail, or inland waterway;
- The Offices, Shops and Railway Premises Act 1963, which provides that no young person may clean machinery if to do so would expose him to risk of injury;
- The Betting, Gaming and Lotteries Act 1963, which prohibits the employment of persons under eighteen in effecting any betting transaction or in a licensed betting office;
- The Licensing Act 1964, which prohibits the employment of children in the bar of licensed premises;
- the Licensing (Occasional Permission) Act 1983, which prohibits any person under eighteen from selling or serving alcohol in premises authorized under the Act (paragraph 5(1) of the Schedule);
- The Merchant Shipping Act 1970, by virtue of which no person under minimum school leaving age may be employed on a ship registered in the UK, except as permitted by Regulations made under the Act; and
- The Manual Handling Operations Regulations 1992, which prohibit children from handling any heavy load which is likely to cause injury to them.
- The Prevention of Accidents to Children in Agriculture Regulations 1998 SI No.3262 prohibit the riding by a child on certain classes of vehicle or machine used in agricultural operations.[74]

The use of children in armed conflict is prohibited in England and Wales, and it is party to the Optional Protocol to the Convention on the Rights of the Child on the involvement of children in armed conflict.[75] The minimum age for joining the armed forces is sixteen years of age, and parental consent is required up until the prospective recruit reaches the age of eighteen.[76] In 2004 6,690 Members of the Armed forces were under the age of eighteen, representing 3.2 per cent of all Armed Forces' personnel.[77] Only those over the age of eighteen are deployed to operations, "in accordance with the UK position on the UN Convention on the Rights of the Child."[78]

VI. SALE AND TRAFFICKING OF CHILDREN

The prohibition of trafficking in children is addressed through a number of Acts of Parliament, notably the Immigration Act 1971 (the facilitation of illegal immigration);[79] the Asylum and Immigration (Treatment of Claimants) Act 2004,[80] (which introduced a new criminal offence of trafficking people into, within or out of the UK for the purposes of exploitation); the Children Act 1989;[81] the Children Act 2004[82] (child protection and care) and the Sexual Offences Act 2003.[83]

The Sexual Offences Act 2003 is currently the substantive piece of legislation regarding sexual offenses and introduced the specific offense of trafficking individuals into, within or out of the England and Wales for the purposes of sexual exploitation. The wording of the trafficking offence does not mirror that in the UN Protocol to prevent, suppress, and punish trafficking. During debates on the offense, Parliament noted that it was specifically not worded in this manner because Parliament "did not wish to limit the offences to those carried out by the use of threats, force, coercion, abduction, fraud, deception or abuse of power or vulnerability ... Its view was that where these abusive elements were present they could be charged in their own right."[84]

A person commits an offense of trafficking an individual for sexual exploitation under the Sexual Offences Act 2003 if he or she intentionally arranges or facilitates the arrival in, movement within or out of the UK, and intends to do an act, or believes that another person is likely to do an act, in respect to the person that he or she has trafficked in or out of England and Wales that, if performed, involves the commission of a "relevant offence."[85] The offense of trafficking covers situations where a person is brought through England and Wales as an interim destination and also covers situations where a person would be guilty of the offense, for example through arranging travel documents, even if the person being trafficked is ultimately not sexually exploited. The trafficking offenses all have extra-territorial application, making it possible to prosecute any British person that conducts the trafficking activity specified in the Act in any country in the world without the need for an equivalent offense in that country.[86] The maximum penalty for trafficking for the purposes of sexual exploitation is fourteen years imprisonment.

Trafficking to generally exploit people is also covered under the Asylum and Immigration (Treatment of Claimants, etc.) Act 2004. This Act provides that it is an offense for a person to arrange travel for someone into, within or out of the United Kingdom with the intention that he or she will exploit that person, or a belief that another person is likely to exploit them. A person is exploited if he or she is forced into labor or slavery; encouraged, required or expected to perform acts regarding the unlawful removal of human organs; has been subjected to force, threats, or deception designed to induce him or her to provide services of any kind or provide another person or enable another person to acquire benefits of any kind, is requested or induced to undertake any activity, having been chosen as the subject of the request or inducement on the grounds that he is young and an older person would be likely to refuse the request or resist the inducement.[87] These sections also apply to acts done outside England and Wales by British nationals, subjects, and citizens.[88] A person found guilty of an offense under this Act may be imprisoned for up to fourteen years.

The statutory framework for the basic protection of children once in England and Wales is provided for through the Children Act 1989 and the Children Act 2004. The Children Act 1989 places a duty on local authorities to prevent children in their area from suffering ill treatment or neglect by ensuring services are provided for them[89] and to investigate any situation where a child in their area is subject to an emergency protection order; is in police protection; or if there is reasonable cause to suspect that the child is suffering or likely to suffer from significant harm.[90] An example of services provided to children that have suffered from ill treatment or neglect is that of safe houses provided by West Sussex County Council, the local authority covering the area surrounding Gatwick Airport.[91]

The Children Acts provide Local Authorities with the power to apply to the court for an emergency protection order if there are reasonable grounds to believe that the child will suffer from significant harm if he or she is not removed to accommodation provided by the local authority; that the local authority are making enquiries that are being frustrated by access to the child being refused; or if inquiries are being made and frustrated through access to the child being unreasonably refused and there is reasonable cause to suspect that a child is suffering or likely to suffer significant harm.[92] Emergency protection orders can be granted by the courts for up to eight days and has the effect of giving the local authority the power to remove the child from the home or prevent the child from being removed from a hospital or state accommodation; it also gives the Local Authority limited parental responsibility for the child.[93]

VII. JUVENILE JUSTICE

A number of Acts, dating back to 1933, provide for the system of juvenile justice in England and Wales and attempt to ensure that a fair trial and fair treatment is given to children accused of crimes. The minimum age of criminal responsibility in England and Wales is currently ten years old.[94] Those below this age are considered *doli incapax* and thus incapable of forming criminal intent.[95]

Children arrested for crimes in England and Wales and held in custody must be separated from the adult population of the jail. Their guardians must be notified as soon as reasonably practicable and informed of the charges brought against the child and the child's place of detention.[96] During any court proceedings involving the child under the age of sixteen the law requires the attendance of the child's guardian during all proceedings, unless this is unreasonable in the circumstances of the case.[97] The general principle for children charged with crimes is that they should not be held in police custody but instead taken care of by social services in Local Authority accommodations. The principle is considered to be of such importance that police custody officers have a statutory duty to release juveniles to local authority accommodations unless they can certify that specific circumstances make it impracticable for this to occur, or for children aged twelve or over no secure accommodation is available, and no other local authority accommodation is adequate to protect the public from the serious harm posed by the child.[98]

The principal aim of the juvenile justice system is to "prevent offending by children and young people."[99] To achieve this aim, the juvenile justice system in England and Wales progresses through a series of steps.[100] The first two, which apply only to less serious crimes, aim at preventing the child from entering the juvenile justice system through a series of behavioral contracts and other methods designed to correct the child's behavior to prevent him or her from re-offending or committing a serious offense.[101] For example, a system of cautioning has been developed for young offenders through reprimands and warnings that are given to those who admit guilt to the police for their crimes and for whom there is sufficient evidence that any prosecution for the offence would be successful.[102] Upon receiving the reprimand or warning the young offender is then referred to the Youth Justice Board who arranges for the youth's participation in a rehabilitation programme.

For children to whom these preventive methods do not apply, for example, due to the seriousness of the offense, or who have exhausted them, the juvenile justice system then operates in the form of a Youth Court, which hears cases of ten to eighteen year olds.[103] This youth court was established to prevent children and young people from entering into contact or associating with adult suspects during any phase of a trial.[104] The public are excluded from these courts; further, reporting restrictions may be placed on what the media may publish from these proceedings. There are also laws that protect the anonymity of children appearing before the court.[105] The Youth Court is a specialized magistrates' court that is comprised of justices of the peace, with three normally present for each case.[106] The court has a range of different sentences for young offenders;[107] for example, supervision orders[108] that can have a variety of conditions attached to them or an Action Plan Order, an intensive, three month long community-based programme.[109] More serious custodial methods of punishment are detention and training orders.[110] These orders are normally given to children representing a "high level of risk [to the public], have a significant offending history or are persistent offenders and where no other sentence will manage their risks effectively."[111] They apply for a minimum period of four months to a maximum period of two years, with half of the sentence being served in custody and the remainder in the community supervised by a "youth offending" team.[112] Only those offenders over the age of fifteen may be sentenced to detention in a young offenders' institution, although this latter restriction does not apply to children aged ten and over convicted of murder.[113]

For very serious offenses, children are prosecuted in the Crown Court. A practice direction issued by the Lord Chief Justice of England and Wales in respect to Crown Court prosecutions of children requires that the "trial process should not itself expose the young defendant to avoidable intimidation, humiliation or distress. All possible steps should be taken to assist the young defendant to understand and participate in the proceedings. The ordinary trial process should so far as necessary be adapted to meet those ends."[114] The Children and Young Persons Act 1933 requires that the welfare of the defendant should be regarded during any criminal proceedings,[115] and the practice direction requires that breaks be frequently taken, that the formal court attire of robes and wigs not be worn, and that there be no recognizable police presence in court without good cause.[116] The Crown Court is the only court that is permitted to follow these rules for sentencing children between ten and eighteen years old that have committed an offense that is punishable by fourteen or more years' imprisonment for adult offenders, children that have committed murder, or certain sexual offenses, may be sentenced for up to the adult maximum for the same offense.[117] The young offenders are not placed in prisons alongside adults, but can be placed in secure training centers, secure children's homes, or young offenders' institutions.[118]

CONCLUSION

Overall, the legal regime applying to children's rights in England and Wales is voluminous and complex, with a large number of Acts providing varying rights for children. As an industrialized Western nation, children do have relatively extensive rights regarding both their protection in areas such as the criminal justice system and their entitlement regarding heath and education.

Prepared by Clare Feikert
Foreign Law Specialist
August 2007

End Notes

[1] PRINCIPLES OF MEDICAL LAW (Andrew Grubb and Judith Laing, eds., 2nd ed. 2004) 4.39. "The Crown as parens patriae is empowered and obliged 'to protect the person and property of ... those unable to look after themselves, including infants.' The Sovereign, as parens patriae, has a duty to protect those of his subjects who are unable to protect themselves, particularly children ... the powers of the Crown as parens patriae are exercised by the [courts]." 4.42.

[2] Children Act 1989 c. 41, § 3(1).

[3] The Convention on the Rights of the Child, with a Preamble and fifty-four articles, was adopted by the U.N. General Assembly on November 20, 1989, and entered into force on September 2, 1990. G.A. Res. 44/25, annex, 44 U.N. GAOR Supp. (No. 49) at 167, U.N. Doc. A/44/49 (1989); 28 I.L.M. 1448 (1989). For an online text, see the OHCHR Web site, http://www.ohchr.org/english/law/crc.htm (last visited July 23, 2007); it includes the 1995 amendment to article 43, paragraph 2 (G.A. Res. 50/155 (Dec. 21, 1995)), which entered into force on November 18, 2002. For the status of signatures, ratifications, and accessions, see the OHCHR Web site, http://www.ohchr.org/english/countries/ratification/11.htm (last visited July 27, 2007).

[4] The Optional protocol to the Convention on the Rights of the Child on the sale of children, child prostitution and child pornography comprises a preamble and seventeen articles. G.A. Res. A/RES/54/263 of 25 May 2000. It entered into force on January 18, 2002. For an online text, see the UNHCHR Web site, http://www.unhchr.ch/html/menu2/dopchild.htm (last visited July 23, 2007). For the status of ratifications and reservations to the STP, see the OHCHR Web site, http://www.ohchr.org/english/countries/ratification/11 c.htm (last updated July 13, 2007) (last visited July 24, 2007).

[5] The Child Soldiers Protocol, comprising a Preamble and thirteen articles, entered into force on February 12, 2002. G.A. Res. A/RES/54/263 of 25 May 2000. For an online text, see the UNHCHR Web site, http://www.unhchr.ch/html/menu2/6/protocolchild.htm (last visited July 23, 2007). For the status of ratifications and reservations to the Child Soldiers Protocol, see the OHCHR Web site, http://www.ohchr.org/english/countries/ratification/11_b.htm (updated as of July 13, 2007) (last visited July 23, 2007).

[6] The U.N. Declaration of the Rights of the Child comprises a Preamble and ten principles. G.A. Res. 1386 (XIV), 14 U.N. GAOR Supp. (No. 16) at 19, U.N. Doc. A/4354. For an online text of the Declaration, see the Office of the U.N. High Commissioner for Human Rights (UNHCHR) Web site, http://www.unhchr.ch /html/menu3/b/25.htm (last visited July 20, 2007) (unofficial source). A list of the Status of Ratification of the Principal International Human Rights Treaties is available on the same Web site, at http://www.unhchr.ch/pdf/ report.pdf (as of June 9, 2004) (last visited July 20, 2007).

[7] The European Convention on the Adoption of Children was opened for signature on April 24, 1967, and entered into force on April 26, 1968. C.E.T.S. No. 058. It comprises a Preamble and 28 articles. For an online text, see the COE Web site, http://conventions.coe.int/Treaty/en/Treaties/Html/058.htm (last visited July 27, 2007). Links to a chart of signatures and ratifications and other information are available via the same Web site, at http://conventions.coe.int/Treaty/Commun/QueVoulezVous.asp?NT=058&CL=ENG (last visited July 27, 2007).

[8] European Convention on the Legal Status of Children born out of Wedlock, opened for signature 10/15/1975, entry into force 8/11/1978, C.E.T.S. No. 85.

[9] Convention against Discrimination in Education, opened for signature 12/14/1960, entry into force 5/22/1962, 429 U.N.T.S. 93.

[10] The Convention for the Protection of Human Rights and Fundamental Freedoms, C.E.T.S. No. 005, with a Preamble and fifty-nine articles, was adopted on November 4, 1950, and entered into force on September 3, 1953. There have been eleven Protocols to the Convention, but as from November 1, 1998, Protocol 9 was repealed and Protocol 10 lost its purpose. For an online text as amended by Protocol 11 (E.T.S. No. 155, in force November 1, 1998), see the Council of Europe Web site, http://conventions.coe.int/Treaty /en/Treaties/Html/005.htm (last visited July 26, 2007). Other documents, such as the status of ratifications and an explanatory report, are also available through links provided on the same Web site, http://conventions. coe.int/Treaty/Commun/QueVoulezVous.asp?NT=005&CL=ENG (last visited July 26, 2007).

[11] The Hague Convention on the Civil Aspects of International Child Abduction, Hague No. 28, was adopted by the Hague Conference on Private International Law on October 25, 1980, and entered into force on December 1, 1983. T.I.A.S. No. 11,670, 1343 U.N.T.S. 89; 19 I.L.M. 1501 (1980).

[12] The Hague Convention on Jurisdiction, Applicable Law, Recognition, Enforcement and Co-operation in Respect of Parental Responsibility and Measures for the Protection of Children was adopted on October 19, 1996, and entered into force January 1, 2002. 35 I.L.M. 1391, 1396 (1996). It comprises a brief Preamble and 63 articles.

For an online text, see the Hague Conference on Private International Law (HCCH) Web site, http://hcch.e-vision.nl/index en.php?act=conventions.text&cid=70 (last visited July 27, 2007).

[13] The Hague Convention on the Protection of Children and Cooperation in Respect of Intercountry Adoption, comprising a Preamble and forty-eight articles, was concluded on May 29, 1993, and entered into force on May 1, 1995. 32 I.L.M. 1134 (1993). For an online text, see the HCCH Web site, http://www.hcch.net/index_en.php?act=conventions.text&cid=69 (last visited July 27, 2007).

[14] The European Convention on the Adoption of Children was opened for signature on April 24, 1967, and entered into force on April 26, 1968. C.E.T.S. No. 058. It comprises a Preamble and 28 articles. For an online text, see the COE Web site, http://conventions.coe.int/Treaty/en/Treaties/Html/058.htm (last visited July 27, 2007). Links to a chart of signatures and ratifications and other information are available via the same Web site, at http://conventions.coe.int/Treaty/Commun/QueVoulezVous.asp?NT=058&CL=ENG (last visited July 27, 2007).

[15] Convention on Consent to Marriage, Minimum Age for Marriage and Registration of Marriages, opened for signature 12/10/1962, entered into force 12/9/1964, 521 U.N.T.S. 231.

[16] The International Covenant on Civil and Political Rights, with a Preamble and 53 articles, was adopted by the U.N. General Assembly on December 16, 1966, and entered into force on March 23, 1976. G.A. Res. 2200A (XXI), 21 U.N. GAOR, 21st Sess. Supp. (No. 16) at 52, U.N. Doc. A/6316 (Dec. 16, 1966), 999 U.N.T.S. 171. For an online text, see the OHCHR Web site, http://www.ohchr.org/english/law/ccpr.htm (last visited July 26, 2007).

[17] Convention on the Elimination of All Forms of Discrimination Against Women comprising a Preamble and 30 articles, adopted by the U.N. General Assembly on December 18, 1979, and entered into force on September 3, 1981. G.A. Res. 34/180, 34 U.N. GAOR Supp. (No. 46) at 193, U.N. Doc. A/34/46.

[18] The European Convention on the Recognition and Enforcement of Decisions Concerning the Custody of Children, comprising a Preamble and 30 articles, was concluded in Luxembourg on May 20, 1980. E.T.S. No. 105. For an online text, see the Council of Europe Web site, http://conventions.coe.int/Treaty/EN/Treaties/Html/105.htm (last visited July 30, 2007). The UK included a reservation that is contained in the instrument of ratification, deposited on 21 April 1986 that "in accordance with the provisions of paragraph 1 of Article 17 of the Convention, the United Kingdom reserves the right to refuse recognition and enforcement of decisions relating to custody, in cases covered by Articles 8 and 9 or either of these Articles, on any of the grounds mentioned in Article 10."

[19] The Minimum Age Convention, comprising a Preamble and 18 articles, was adopted by the 58th Session of the General Conference of the International Labour Organisation on June 26, 1973 , and entered into force on June 19, 1976; I.L.O. No. 138. For an online text, see the Office of the U.N. High Commissioner of Human Rights (OHCHR) Web site, http://www.ohchr.org/english/law/ageconvention.htm (last visited July 25, 2007) (unofficial source).

[20] Convention concerning the Prohibition and Immediate Action for the Elimination of the Worst Forms of Child Labour, entry into force 11/19/2000, I.L.O. No. 182.

[21] The Universal Declaration of Human Rights, with a Preamble and 30 articles, was adopted by the U.N. General Assembly on December 10, 1948. G.A. Res. 217 A (III), U.N. Doc. A/810 at 71 (Dec. 10, 1948). For an online text, see the United Nations Web site, http://www.un.org/Overview/rights.html (unofficial source) (last visited July 24, 2007).

[22] The International Covenant on Economic, Social and Cultural Rights, with a Preamble and 31 articles, was adopted by the U.N. General Assembly on December 16, 1996, and entered into force on January 3, 1976. G.A. Res. 2200A (XXI), 21 U.N.GAOR, 21st Sess., Supp. (No. 16) at 49, U.N. Doc. A/6316 (Dec. 16, 1966), 993 U.N.T.S. 3. For an online text, see the OHCHR Web site, http://www.ohchr.org/english/law/cescr.htm (last visited July 23, 2007).

[23] National Health Service Act 1977, c. 49, §§ 1 and 3.

[24] THE DEPARTMENT OF HEALTH, THE NHS PLAN: A PLAN FOR INVESTMENT, A PLAN FOR REFORM, Cm. 4818-I, 1999 2000, http://www.dh.gov.uk/en/Publicationsandstatistics/ Publications/PublicationsPolicyAndGuidance/DH 4002960 and The Department of Health, Getting the right start: National Service Framework for Children, Young People and Maternity Services: Standard for hospital services, 2003, http://www.dh.gov.uk/en/Publicationsandstatistics/Publications/PublicationsPolicyAndGuidance/DH_4006182

[25] Department of Health, National Service Framework documents, June 2007, http://www.dh.gov.uk/en/Policyandguidance/Healthandsocialcaretopics/ChildrenServices/Childrenservicesinformation/DH_4089 111.

[26] National Statistics, Health Statistics Quarterly 34, Web Supplement: Death registrations in England and Wales: 2006, June 2007, at II, http://www.statistics.gov.uk/downloads/theme_health/Death_registration_2006.pdf.

[27] Children Act 1989 c. 41, §§ 2-3 and PRINCIPLES OF MEDICAL LAW (Andrew Grubb and Judith Laing, eds., 2nd ed. 2004) 4.49.

[28] Children Act 1989 c. 41, § 2 and PRINCIPLES OF MEDICAL LAW (Andrew Grubb and Judith Laing, eds., 2nd ed. 2004) 4.51.

[29] Family Law Reform Act 1969, c. 46, § 8(1) which provides "The consent of a minor who has attained the age of sixteen years to any surgical, medical or dental treatment which, in the absence of consent, would constitute a trespass to his person, shall be as effective as it would be if he were of full age; and where a minor has by virtue of this section given an effective consent to any treatment it shall not be necessary to obtain any consent for it from his parent or guardian."

[30] PRINCIPLES OF MEDICAL LAW, supra note 1, at 4.59.

[31] Gillick v West Norfolk and Wisbech Area Health Authority [1986] AC 112.

[32] In re R (A Minor) (Wardship: Consent to Treatment) [1992] Fam. 11 and PRINCIPLES OF MEDICAL LAW (Andrew Grubb and Judith Laing, eds., 2nd ed. 2004) 4.67.

[33] Williams v Eady (1893) 10 TLR 41 (CA).

[34] Education Act 1996, c. 56.

[35] Education Act 1997, c. 44.

[36] Education (Schools) Act 1997, c. 59.

[37] Special Educational Needs and Disability Rights Act 2001 c. 10.

[38] Further and Higher Education Act 1992 c. 13.

[39] Teaching and Higher Education Act 1998, c. 30.

[40] School Standards and Framework Act 1998 c. 31.

[41] Education Act 2002, c. 32.

[42] Education Act 2005, c. 18.

[43] Education Act 1996 c. 56, § 12.

[44] Education Act 1996 c. 56, and the Further and Higher Education Act 1992 c. 13.

[45] School Standards and Framework Act 1998 c. 30.

[46] Education Act 1996, c. 56, § 8(3)(a).

[47] HALSBURY'S LAWS OF ENGLAND (LORD MACKAY OF CLASHFERN, ed. 4th ed. Reissue 2006), Vol. 15(1) 15 and Education Act 1996, § 7.

[48] Education Act 1996, c. 56 § 444.

[49] HALSBURY'S LAWS OF ENGLAND (LORD MACKAY OF CLASHFERN, ed. 4th ed. Reissue 2006), Vol. 15(2) 913 and Education Act 2002, § 78.

[50] Education Act 2002 c. 32, § 84.

[51] The Convention for the Protection of Human Rights and Fundamental Freedoms (Rome, Nov. 4, 1950) TS 71 (1953), art. 28(1) provides that "state parties recognize the right of the child to education."

[52] The Universal Declaration of Human Rights, Art. 26(1) provides that "everyone has the right to education. Education shall be free, at least in the elementary and fundamental stages. Elementary education shall be compulsory."

[53] Education Act 1996 c. 56, § 10.

[54] HALSBURY'S LAWS OF ENGLAND (LORD MACKAY OF CLASHFERN, ed. 4th ed. Reissue 2006), Vol. 15(1) 13 and the Education Act 1996 c. 56, § 9.

[55] HALSBURY'S LAWS OF ENGLAND (LORD MACKAY OF CLASHFERN, ed. 4th ed. Reissue 2006), Vol. 15(1) 13.

[56] HALSBURY'S LAWS OF ENGLAND (LORD MACKAY OF CLASHFERN, ed. 4th ed. Reissue 2006), Vol. 15(1) 13.

[57] Race Relations Act 1976 c. 74.

[58] Sex Discrimination Act 1975 c. 65.

[59] Disability Discrimination Act 1995, c. 50.

[60] The Employment Equality (Sexual Orientation) Regulations 2003, SI 2003/1661.

[61] The Employment Equality (Religion or Belief) Regulations 2003, SI 2003/1660.

[62] Education Act 1996 c. 56, § 324.

[63] Education Act 1996 c. 56, § 316.

[64] Education Act 1996 c. 56, § 324.

[65] HALSBURY'S LAWS OF ENGLAND (LORD MACKAY OF CLASHFERN, ed. 4th ed. Reissue 2006), Vol. 15(1) 577 and Education Act 1996 c. 56, § 548.

[66] Education Act 1996, c. 56, § 550A.

[67] Cleary v Booth [1893] 1 QB 465 and Education Act 1996 c. 56, § 550B.

[68] Children and Young Persons Act 1933, 23 & 24 Geo. 5, c. 12.

[69] Education Act 1996 c. 56, § 558.

[70] This was previously thirteen years of age, but increased due to a European Union directive, implemented into the national law of England and Wales by the Children (Protection at Work) Regulations 1998, SI 1998/276.

[71] Children and Young Persons Act 1933 23 & 24 Geo. 5, c. 12, § 18.

[72] Children and Young Persons Act 1963 c. 37, and the Children (Performances) Regulations 1968 SI 1968/1728 (as amended).

[73] Children and Young Persons Act 1933 23 & 24 Geo. 5, c. 12, § 18.

[74] This list of acts and summaries are from House of Common's Library Standard Note, Employment of Children, SN SN/BT/653, 2003.

[75] The Child Soldiers Protocol, comprising a Preamble and thirteen articles, entered into force on February 12, 2002. G.A. Res. A/RES/54/263 of 25 May 2000. For an online text, see the UNHCHR Web site, http://www.unhchr.ch/html/menu2/6/protocolchild.htm (last visited July 23, 2007). For the status of ratifications and reservations to the Child Soldiers Protocol, see the OHCHR Web site, http://www.ohchr.org/english/countries/ratification/11_b.htm (updated as of July 13, 2007) (last visited July 23, 2007).

76 Army Act 1955 c. 18, § 2 and the Air Force Act 1955 c. 19, § 9. See also HOUSE OF COMMONS DEFENCE SELECT COMMITTEE, THIRD REPORT, 2004-5, HC 63-I, 69.

[77] House of Commons Defence Select Committee, Third Report, 2004-5, HC 63-I, 69.

[78] House of Commons Defence Select Committee, Third Report, 2004-5, HC 63-II.

[79] Immigration Act 1971, c. 77.

[80] Asylum and Immigration Act 2004, c. 19.

[81] Children Act 1989, c. 41.

[82] Children Act 2004, c. 31.

[83] Sexual Offences Act 2003, c. 42.

[84] House of Commons Research Paper, The Sexual Offences Bill, Bill 128, 2002-2003, 03/62, 2003, www.parliament.uk/commons/lib/research/rp2003/rp03-062.pdf referring to 189 HL Deb 13 May 2003 cc202-5.

[85] Sexual Offences Act 2003 c. 42, §§ 57-59. The 'relevant offences' are defined in section 60 of the Sexual Offences Act 2003. They are wide ranging and cover all forms of sexual offenses under the Sexual Offences Act 2003, from rape to causing or inciting prostitution, and also extend to taking or making indecent photographs of children that are offenses under the Protection of Children Act 1978. The purpose of having such a wide ranging definition is to: "offer greater protection against all forms of sexual trafficking, for example, for those who are trafficked in order to be sexually assaulted by others where there is no financial payment for the sexual services." Home Office Circular, Guidance on Part 1 of the Sexual Offences Act 2003, http://www.knowledgenetwork.gov.uk/HO/circular.nsf/1cc4f3413a62d1de80256c5b005101e4/F42DF595CC5A54DB80256E5F0 057517C/$file/final%20text.doc (last visited Aug. 7, 2007).

[86] Sexual Offences Act 2003 c. 42, §§ 57-59 and Home Office Circular, Guidance on Part 1 of the Sexual Offences Act 2003, 265, available at http://www.knowledgenetwork.gov.uk/HO/circular.nsf/1c c4f3413a62d1de80256c5b005101e4/F42DF595CC5A54DB80256E5F0 057517C/$file/final%20text.doc (last visited Aug. 7, 2007).

[87] Asylum and Immigration (Treatment of Claimants, etc.) Act 2004, c. 19, § 4(4).

[88] Id., § 5.

[89] Children Act 1989 c. 41, sch. 2, 4.

[90] Children Act 1989 c. 41, § 47.

[91] House of Commons Research Paper, The Sexual Offences Bill, Bill 128, 2002-2003, 03/62, 2003, available at www.parliament.uk/commons/lib/research/rp2003/rp03-062.pdf.

[92] Children Act 1989 c. 41, § 44.

[93] Id.

[94] Children and Young Persons Act 1933 23 & 24 Geo. 5, c. 12, § 60.

[95] LEGAL CONCEPTS OF CHILDHOOD, (Julia Fionda, ed., 2001) 85.

[96] Children and Young Persons Act 1933 23 & 24 Geo. 5, c. 12, § 34.

[97] Id.

[98] Police and Criminal Evidence Act 1984 c. 60, § 38(6).

[99] Crime and Disorder Act 1998, § 37.

[100] An overview of these steps is available online at Youth Justice Board for England and Wales, Youth Justice System, http://www.yjb.gov.uk/en-gb/yjs/TheSystem/ (last visited Aug. 2007).

[101] Id.

[102] Crime and Disorder Act 1998 c. 54, § 65.

[103] Criminal Justice Act 1991 c. 53, § 68.

[104] ANDREW BAINHAM, CHILDREN – THE MODERN LAW 494 (2nd ed. 1998).

[105] Children and Young Persons Act 1933 23 & 24 Geo. 5, c. 12, § 39 and the Youth Justice and Criminal Evidence Act 1999, c. 23, § 44.

[106] ANDREW BAINHAM, CHILDREN – THE MODERN LAW 494 (2nd ed. 1998).

[107] A brief overview of all methods – both sentence based and pre-court methods are summarized online at Youth Justice Board for England and Wales, Sentences, Orders and Agreements, http://www.yjb.gov.uk/en-gb/yjs/SentencesOrdersandAgreements (last visited Aug. 9, 2007).

[108] Powers of Criminal Courts (Sentencing) Act 2000, c. 6, §§ 64-67.

[109] Id., c. 6, §§ 69-72.

[110] Id., c. 6, §§ 100-107.

[111] Youth Justice Board for England and Wales, Detention and Training Order, http://www.yjb.gov.uk/en-gb/yjs/SentencesOrdersandAgreements/DTO (last visited Aug. 8, 2007).

[112] Id.

[113] Powers of Criminal Courts (Sentencing) Act 2000, c. 6, § 90.

[114] Practice Direction, Trial of Children and Young Persons in the Crown Court, Feb. 2000, 3, available at http://www.hmcourts-service.gov.uk/cms/926.htm.

[115] Children and Young Persons Act 1933 23 & 24 Geo. 5, c. 12, § 44.

[116] Practice Direction, Trial of Children and Young Persons in the Crown Court, Feb. 2000, 9-13, available at http://www.hmcourts-service.gov.uk/cms/926.htm.

[117] Powers of Criminal Court (Sentencing) Act 2000, c. 6 §§ 90- 91.

[118] Youth Justice Board for England and Wales, Custody, http://www.yjb.gov.uk/en-gb/yjs/Custody/ (last visited Aug. 8, 2007).

INDEX

F

G

H

I

J

K

L

U

V